"十二五"普通高等教育本科国家级规划教材

普通高等教育"十一五"国家级规划教材

北京高等教育精品教材
BEIJING GAODENG JIAOYU JINGPIN JIAOCAI

北京大学优秀教材

美英报刊文章阅读

（精选本）（第六版）

A QUALITY SELECTION OF ARTICLES FROM AMERICAN & BRITISH NEWSPAPERS & MAGAZINES

主　编　周学艺　赵　林
副主编　郭丽萍　刘满贵

编委　杨小凤　杨　博　陈文玉　丁剑仪
　　　张慧宇　刘雪燕　罗国华　韦毅民
　　　徐　威　叶慧瑛　左　进

北京大学出版社
PEKING UNIVERSITY PRESS

图书在版编目(CIP)数据

美英报刊文章阅读：精选本 / 周学艺，赵林主编 .6 版 . -- 北京：北京大学出版社，2024.8. --（大学美英报刊教材系列）. -- ISBN 978-7-301-35613-5

Ⅰ . H319.37

中国国家版本馆 CIP 数据核字第 2024GC4993 号

书　　名	美英报刊文章阅读（精选本）（第六版） MEI-YING BAOKAN WENZHANG YUEDU（JINGXUANBEN） （DI-LIU BAN）
著作责任者	周学艺　赵　林　主　编
责任编辑	李　颖
标准书号	ISBN 978-7-301-35613-5
出版发行	北京大学出版社
地　　址	北京市海淀区成府路 205 号　100871
网　　址	http://www.pup.cn　新浪微博：@北京大学出版社
电子邮箱	编辑部 pupwaiwen@pup.cn　　总编室 zpup@pup.cn
电　　话	邮购部 010-62752015　发行部 010-62750672　编辑部 010-62759634
印 刷 者	河北博文科技印务有限公司
经 销 者	新华书店
	650 毫米 ×980 毫米　16 开本　19.5 印张　495 千字 1994 年 12 月第 1 版　2001 年 10 月第 2 版 2007 年 1 月第 3 版　2007 年 7 月第 4 版　2013 年 12 月第 5 版 2024 年 8 月第 6 版　2024 年 8 月第 1 次印刷
定　　价	69.00 元

未经许可，不得以任何方式复制或抄袭本书之部分或全部内容。
版权所有，侵权必究
举报电话：010-62752024　电子邮箱：fd@pup.cn
图书如有印装质量问题，请与出版部联系，电话：010-62756370

前　言

《美英报刊文章阅读》(精选本)及其《学习辅导》首版于1994年,后又分别再版于2001年、2007年、2010年和2013年,深受高校学生和英语自修者欢迎,是同类教材中的佼佼者。2004年和2011年分别被评为**"北京高等教育精品教材"**,并获得**"第六届全国大学出版社优秀畅销书二等奖"**。2006年8月,周学艺先生主编的包括本书、《美英报刊文章选读》(上、下册)和《美英报刊导读》在内的**"大学英语报刊教材系列"**,被列为**"普通高等教育'十一五'国家级规划教材"**。

现在出版的《美英报刊文章阅读》(精选本)第六版,与前五版一样,是供大专院校英语和新闻专业及其他涉外专业三年级以上学生使用的教材,也可供考研者和具有相应程度从事外事、新闻编译等工作人员及英语爱好者自修之用。

《美英报刊文章阅读》(精选本)和《美英报刊文章选读》(上、下册)分别为不同英文水平的高年级学生而编写。"精选本"注释细,并配有《学习辅导》,学生更易读懂。"上、下册"课文多,题材更为多样广泛,学生和授课老师对课文有更多的选择余地。2009年10月又编著出版了《大学英语报刊文选》(非英语专业高年级用书)。以上三种教科书,尤其是本书,因配有"学习辅导",对大专、本科的自考生和考研生则更加具有参考价值。

报刊文选有其明显的时效性,第五版出版至今已有十余载,其间国际形势已发生了很大的变化,有些课文的内容已过时,为适应教学需要,特选编第六版。为方便自修者而编的"学习辅导",除了提供更多的生词解释、更详细的注释、问题参考答案和需要掌握的重点词语等内容外,第五版增加了 Summary, Background Information 和 Supplementary Reading,第六版予以保留。附录中还有"标题自我测试""外刊课考试说明""参考试题"等内容和读报重要参考资料。为了加深对词语和课文的理解能力,扩大与课文有关的词汇量和知识面,特选定此书的教材系列之一《美英报刊导读》(第二版)(下简称《导读》)作为学生进一步的助读和学习进修教材。年轻教员可将《导读》作为参考书,并且可视具体情况将《导读》内容充实到课堂教学中。

第六版全书共25课,更新了近三分之一课文,内容配合国策。

读报基本功

阅读美英报刊可以扩大视野,增长知识,学习现代英语,了解世界,获取信息。众所周知,报刊语言具有短、新、奇、活的特点,内容贴近当前实际,不但丰富有趣,且实用性强,所以人们喜欢看报。然而,学习任何知识都必须有基础,读外刊也不例外。我们认为,学生在中学和大学低年级的阶段首先要打好语言基础,到了大学高年级阶段,要读懂美英报刊,必须夯实两项基本功。

一、拓宽词义面和扩大词汇量

1. 拓宽常用词的词义面

新闻语言与我国学生在中学和大学低年级所学课文的规范语言不完全相同,他们所学大多是关于学习和人生哲理的一些故事,对报刊语言很陌生,词义面也窄,一见到 run, race, juice, measure, bill, Speaker, chemistry, establishment, community 等就可能只知道是"跑""竞赛""汁""措施""账单""发言人""化学""建立""社区"这些词的普通单一意义,而不知道从泛指到特指意义变了。如在时政文章中,这些词的意义变窄了,很可能分别为"竞选""竞选""神通""议案""法案""议长""关系""界、当权派或权势集团""共同体或社会"等词义。

英语词汇中的常用词绝大部分是多义词。1977 年 8 月 15 日,《泰晤士报》载文称,在现代报纸上,一个词有五六个意思是很平常的。这就增加了读报的难度。不过,此处所谓拓宽词义面,指初学者尤其要注意常见的多义词。不能一见到 culture, interest(s), resources, story 等就想当然认为只是"文化""利益""资源"和"故事"的意思。请看下列例句里的词义:

(1) Indeed, in many regions, "forestry" is synonymous with plantation **culture**. (在许多地区,所谓林业,事实上就是森林**栽培**的同义词。)

(2) Terrorists might hit American **interests** abroad. (VOA)
(恐怖分子可能会袭击在美国国外的美国**机构**。)

(3) Even as Harper was carrying out his espionage tasks, America's Polish mole was discussing the case with Harper's own Polish case officer. Later, he passed on the entire **story** to U. S. agents, including word that the Poles had received congratulations from Yuri Andropov, the late Soviet President and former KGB chief. (*U. S. News & World Report*)

(……后来，Harper 把全部**机密**都传递给了美国特工……)

书里结合课文,通过"语言解说"扩大读者词义面。例如用抽象意义的词来代表具体意义,从抽象到具体,词义有的好理解,有的艰涩难懂, presence 就是一个很好的例证(见第 16 课"语言解说")。对 establishment 等作了辨析和解说。此外,本书还指出报刊语言主要特点,其中包括修辞格中的借喻法、提喻法、隐语、委婉语等。这些都有助于扩大学生的词义面,提高他们对报刊语言的认识和理解。

2. 扩大词汇量

美英报刊题材广泛,内容丰富,包括政治、经济、外交、军事、法律、科技、社会、宗教、文教、旅游、时装、美容、广告、漫画等,真是上至天文下至地理,无所不包,堪称一部活的百科全书。大学生一、二年级所掌握的词汇量要读懂上述方面的文章根本不够应付,而且随着时代的快速变化,语言也与时俱进,新词如潮涌,新的表达法也不断产生。例如,围绕 2008 年美国大选,就创造出了"Bush fatigue"(因前总统小布什执政时不得人心而使民众及共和党人都对他极其厌烦)、ABB(Anybody But Bush)等。奥巴马当选前后,更多的词语杜撰出来,如 Generation O(bama)、Obamacan/Obamacon(原本支持共和党候选人的共和党人和保守派选民却把票投给了民主党自由派候选人奥巴马)、on-line Obama(靠网上筹款起家的奥氏)、Obamatum(奥氏竞选势不可挡)、New New Deal(奥政府为救市与 F. 罗斯福的"新政"既有相同也有不同的一面,故又加上一个 New 字)、smart power(美要将软硬实力结合起来运用的"巧实力")。而奥氏能上台执政归功于"It's the Economy, Stupid!"此处的 stupid 无贬义,只作"提醒"之用。

所谓新词,多数都是旧词扩展引申出新义,这是读报者的难题之一。如 hardware(计算机硬件)扩大引申为"军事武器或装备",现又引申为"法";而 software 引申为"武器研发计划",五角大楼行话喻战争中的"思想",还喻"创新"及与"法"相配合的"德"和"宗教"等。再如,launch window 这个宇航术语是 20 世纪 60 年代创造的词,window 指"brief period of time",即最佳或最有利的发射时机或时段。

本书尽可能通过比较法指出相同或类似概念的同义或同义现象的词,以及反义词,扩大学生的词汇量。如"Biden Inaugurated as the 46th President amid a Cascade of Crises"这一课的注释"administration"中与"government"作了比较,并说明两个词用法的差异。"Spies Among Us: Modern-Day Espionage"课文里的 Cold War (*cf.* cool/hot/shooting war)等。另外,还通过 presence, establishment, culture 和 generation 等"语言解说",扩大学生们的词义面和增强语言的认知和分析能力。又根据上下文,针

对在词典和网上都查不到的词义,如 illegals 等,也作了解释(见"间谍行话")。

又,本书除对"新闻写作"中"报刊语言主要特点"作了概括外,还尽可能结合课文内容加以说明。毋庸置疑,关于报刊语言特点,如爱造新词、常用委婉语、提喻法、借喻法、隐语、套语等特点,读报者是必须了解的。不然如见到本书第 14 课中出现的 entitlement(s) system 等表达方式就会感到茫然。

二、读报知识

我们认为,凡语言基本功已经过关者,读懂报刊的关键是必备各类用作参考和分析语言的文化知识。也就是说,与掌握语言一样,要读报入门,必须了解美英政府的组成、体制、党派、社会、科普、宗教等重要文化知识。学英语不能仅仅局限于语言本身,还要注意积累各方面的知识。尽管电脑可以帮忙,但代替不了自己的记忆。具有比较广泛的知识,才能收到更好的学习效果。否则,许多问题语焉不详,有的文章读不透,词语理解不深。如为什么美国的政治名言是"All politics is personal"(千选、万选,都是候选人本人在竞选),而英国竞选却主要靠政党(见《导读》第五章第二节"英美政治比较")? 为了说明知识的重要性,下面不妨再举四例:

1. 有的译者不了解美国民主党内自由派是主流,共和党内保守派占多数,将 Demopublican(由 Democrat 和 Republican 拼缀而成)译为美国历史上曾经出现过的"民主共和党人"。其实它现在的词义是"民主党内的保守派"。下面例句中的 Demopublican 指 2000 年美国大选中的民主党副总统候选人利伯曼(Joseph Lieberman),黑人民权运动领袖 Jackson 批评他身为民主党人,可"与共和党人的政见共同点多于民主党人",就是这个道理。

... Jesse Jackson did a number on Lieberman, accusing him of joining with Republicans to dismantle affirmative action programs. Jackson also drew a big laugh from the crowd when he branded Lieberman "a **Demopublican**" who had more in common with Republicans than Democrats. (*The Washington Post*)

(……杰克逊批评了利伯曼,指责他与共和党人一道取消了在就业和教育上照顾黑人和妇女的计划。杰克逊在谴责他是"**民主党内的保守分子**"时,又引起了听众一阵哄堂大笑。论政见,他与共和党人的共同之处要多于民主党人。)

2. 《国际先驱论坛报》在 2000 年 12 月 14 日发表的一篇题为"Decision: It's Bush"的文章中有这么一段:

Republicans narrowly retained control of the House in November. The new Senate will be split 50-50, and will include Mr. Lieberman. **But any ties will be broken by the new vice president, Mr. Cheney.**

（在十一月份大选后组成的新一届国会中，共和党仍勉强控制着众议院。在参议院，两党平分秋色，各占50席，而且民主党议员中还包括落选的民主党副总统候选人利伯曼。**然而，如果在表决中票数相等，出现相持不下的局面时，新任副总统切尼先生就会打破僵局，而有利于共和党。**）

此处，有的读者一定要问，为什么副总统能打破这种相持不下的局面？他不是参议员，有投票权吗？美国宪法规定，参议院议长（President of the Senate）一职由副总统兼任，在表决出现相持不下的局面时，他才有投票权。这样，问题就迎刃而解了。由此可见，这类问题光凭上下文是解决不了的，初学者必须逐渐积累和丰富读报所需的文化背景知识。

3. 1993年10月18日，克林顿任总统不久，《时代》周刊发表了一篇题为"It's All Foreign to Clinton"的文章，开头有这么一段：

Like most people, Bill Clinton is uncomfortable with what he doesn't know and avoids dealing with it. Fortunately for him, the nation he leads usually cares more about **Madonna** than **Mogadishu**; its turn inward following the Cold War's end coincides neatly with the President's passion for domestic affairs.

（像许多人一样，比尔·克林顿总统对不熟悉的事处理起来感到为难，所以总是避开。幸运的是，他所领导的国家通常关注**内政**胜过**外交**。随着冷战的结束，重点转向国内，正好与他热衷于内政巧合。）

有的学生曾问道："怎么将歌星与地名作比较呢？"还有的学生说："克林顿是不是对麦当娜感兴趣？真摸不着头脑。"众所周知，Madonna是美国曾放荡不羁的艳星，Mogadishu是索马里首都。克林顿上台时遇上索马里内战，美派兵干涉，结果吃了大亏。了解这一情况后，再联系此段谈到克林顿的"passion for domestic affairs"，经验老到的读者就能根据上下文定义此处的 Madonna 指的是 domestic affairs，而 Mogadishu 指 foreign affairs。记者在这里不过是玩了点文字游戏，因为这两个字都是"M"开头，押头韵（alliteration）。从此例可以看出，要学好美英报刊，还得了解"What's going on in the world"才行。

4. 1928年美国前总统胡佛在竞选总统时提出与家长式管理和国家社会主义相对立的一套经济政策主张，他说：

We are challenged with a peacetime choice between the American system of **rugged individualism** and a European philosophy of diametrically opposed doctrines—doctrines of paternalism and state socialism.

（形势要求我们在和平时期的两种做法之间做出选择，一种是美国对企业的**不干涉**做法，另一种是与美国截然对立的欧洲家长式管理和国家社会主义那一套。）

中西文化概念不同，理解有别。rugged individual 意为具有强烈个性的人，也指住在未开发边疆者。rugged individualism 指美国民族不受拘束、自由放任的特点，与我儒家文化截然不同。用于自由企业，则不容政府干预，让市场去调节。这就是所谓的"Government is best which governs least"（要想管得好，[政府对企业]就得插手少）。此处 rugged individualism 相当于 laissez-faire（[法语] the principle of allowing private business to develop without any state control）。不过，2008 年爆发了金融和经济危机后，美国前总统里根和英国前首相撒切尔夫人所热衷的这种放任自流、无政府监督的极端保守派经济政策已遭诟病。

课　　本

鉴于以上所谈的两项基本功，编者在选材时既注意趣味性，又首选具有新闻语言和文化知识两方面的文章。这样的选材原则，既基于第一主编多年的读报经历和体会，又符合掌握外语的规律。

美英各大报都在头版刊登国内外大事，人们看报也注重时文，学生在这方面知识却较贫乏，可多数外语专业毕业生将从事外事和教学工作。因此，第一主编从 1987 年至今所编写的教材课文内容，与其他同类教材的一个明显不同之处就是，不但顾及新闻的时效性，还尽量选一些新而信息量大和覆盖面广的文章，并不断地再版更新，这也是其他同类教材所不多见的。然而我们又不赞同盲目选材的做法，即一味追求材料新，今天选这篇，明天选那篇，忽视了学生最急需的是较系统的基本知识。课本，课本，一课之本，课本的优劣与学生能否通过一年半载的学习取得明显的进步关系重大。

课文不宜太浅，否则学生的学习目的会落空，教员也不能通过授课充实自己。记得 2002 年《21 世纪（英文）报》邀请两位美国新闻学教授和本书第一主编在黄山讲学时，他们中有一位谈到教学感受时说："In teaching newspapers, teachers learn more than students do."意近"教学相长"。

第六版仍保留了第五版中的若干课文。一是新闻有连续性。二是有的课文有值得学习或了解的语言或知识。三是有的文章所描写的有关国家的情况仍未过时。所以初学者切不可因其"旧"而忽视这些课文在打好基本功方面所起的作用。

为了夯实读报基本功,加深对课文的理解,编者结合课文所写的"语言解说""读报知识""学习方法"和"新闻写作"与注释和"前言"相辅相成,对学生具有指导性和启发性,能扩大他们的视野,有助于学习研究新闻语言。"语言解说"重点对媒体理解不当和学生易误解的如 presence, culture, establishment, administration 等加以指明。"读报知识"对美国总统选举、英国的议会、大选与全民公投等作了介绍。"学习方法"主要是读懂标题和名师指导词语学习和记忆法等。"新闻写作"指出了报刊若干写作法和语言主要特点。这并非要求学生立即习作,对其而言,要学好报刊,首先要读懂课文,而了解新闻写作特点又有益于读透文章。

众所周知,再新的课文也赶不上时事的发展,不久就会成为明日黄花。为此,在教学过程中如逢法国教师被杀、美国导弹袭击叙利亚或新冠疫情这样的大事,授课教师也可酌情选上一两篇作为补充,但不宜多,应坚持以课本为主,让学生打好读报基础。

教 和 学

根据编者的教学经验和我国多数学生的实际英文水平,对一般高校而言,本书的授课既不适合当做精读,也不宜做泛读。做精读会妨碍授课的进度,做泛读恐难度太大学生不易读懂。凡是到英美国家学习过的人都知道,他们在教学中很注重"量",课后教员所布置的课外读物和作业一大堆。我国外语教学往往过于注重"质"或"精"。本人主张走中间道路,即质和量并重。为此编者建议,每星期两课时教一篇课文外,根据不同学校学生的英语水平,本科生还要自修一篇。自修的课文应易于课堂上所授课文,授课老师和自修生可以根据不同情况,选择学习本教材中不同难度的课文。

教员授课时应以学生为中心,鼓励他们自己去探索和获取知识。上课时,教师可要求学生先回答 Pre-reading Questions,引导他们对课文的题材感兴趣,进入主题后,再学课文就较容易。同时,这还能促使他们预习和练习口语。接着再逐段或跳跃式选段对学生需要掌握的内容、新闻词语和背景知识进行阅读和问答—启发式讲解。如果备课充分,学生的英语水平又高,教员可采用美英教员教授母语的方法,抛开课本,以《导读》作参考,只讲有关课文的内容、重点词语、背景及写作手法等。这样,学生除预习外,课后还要结合教员在课堂上所讲的内容好好复习课文。这两种授课方式的好处是,学生通过自学和教师的启发性指导能举一反三,自己主动去掌握知识。与以教员为中心的灌输式教学法相比,学生更能巩固所学,发挥学习潜能。当然,这只是我们的实践和看法。我们相信,在调动学生主动学习的积极性方面还有更多、更好的教学法。

　　与中小学阶段不同的是,大学生一定要养成预习或自习的习惯,课前自己先看两遍。第一遍是粗读,快速浏览全文,结合标题,掌握本课的主要内容,并能回答课文前的 Pre-reading Questions。第二遍为细读,通过上下文猜测生词词义,掌握各段内容,并能基本回答习题的 Questions。

　　读者在学习了这套报刊文选后,借助《导读》*和《当代英汉美英报刊词典》,可以先看美英报纸上文字较浅显易懂的报道性文章,然后再看新闻周刊和社评体裁文章。这样,他们就能独自走上一条读懂报刊之路,这是我们编写此书的最终目的。(详见《导读》"读报经验教训谈")

　　此外,学生应在平时养成关心时事的习惯,关注国内外新闻,以便随时能学习和积累语言和读报知识。

　　众所周知,与以往相比,网络使更多人能读懂报刊,对学习起着不可或缺的作用。然而,凡事都有两面,我们不能由此而沉浸在网上阅读文章。需知,那只是 superficial reading,而在纸上能 deep reading,经过思考记忆,获得的知识才牢固。"数字阅读,人变浅薄。"这是以色列一项教学调研得出的结论。

　　全书课文均取材于美英报刊,编者相信,使用本书的读者和授课教师对其内容能够作出正确的判断,这是不言而喻的。

　　本书定会有错误或不妥之处,衷心希望读者不吝赐教。

赵　林
2021 年秋于嘉兴南湖
E-mail:363916021@qq.com
graceguo33@sina.com

---

* 《导读》指《美英报刊导读》(第二版)(周学艺编著,北京:北京大学出版社,2010 年出版)。

美英报刊的政治倾向性

美英等国报刊均非公办,不代表政府,一贯标榜"客观""公正","独立"于政府和政党,"不受约束",完全"自由办报",置身"意识形态之外"。是政府的监督员(watch dog),可批评政府各项政策,有乌鸦嘴之称,记者更戴上了无冕之王(uncrowned King)的桂冠。其实并非如此。

下面分别从立场、党派属性、惯用套路和用词四方面来看西方报刊的政治倾向性。

一、立场

事实上新闻业是有政治倾向的。例如1999年的科索沃战争,享有"舆论泰斗"美誉的《纽约时报》便渲染南斯拉夫在该省屠杀阿尔巴尼亚族,搞"种族灭绝",鼓动对南动武。《时代》周刊发表"Why He Blinked"(《他为何顶不下去了》)一文颠倒事实,对南领导人挖苦。70多天狂轰滥炸后,南总统米洛舍维奇接受了北约要求时,竟说是"他引发了这场空中打击战"(he [Milosevic] set off the air war)。只有《华盛顿邮报》对战争的合法性质疑。

1998年美国诬蔑美籍华裔科学家李文和(Wen Ho Lee)窃密。《纽约时报》曾发表长篇耸人听闻的报道,主张搞逼供,引用官员的话:"敲打头次数越多,他说的真话就越多。"后来只是轻描淡写承认报道失实。

纵观美英报刊和通讯社等媒体,应该说客观、公正的文章也是有的,但多数跟着本国利益或所支持的党派或政府的立场转。《纽约时报》的口号是"刊登一切适合刊登的新闻"(All the News That's Fit to Print),路透社的格言是"以维护新闻报道独立正直为己任"(to safeguard the independence and integrity of news service),其他报纸以此类推,全是鬼话。苏联解体后,一批知识分子移居美国,《纽约时报》为首的美国各大报竞相以头版头条大登特登这方面的消息。几个月后,他们中一些人发表声明,表示不习惯美国的就业和生活方式,决定返回俄罗斯。同样是这些报纸,有的不登,有的只在极不显眼的位置上刊登一则小消息,背后也是本国利益。这一点有的报刊说得很清楚,1997年11月《时代》周刊谈到中国由于经济的发展与影响力不断提高,美国无力阻止,建议政府竭力把中国往有利于美国利益的方向拉(We cannot prevent enhancement of

Chinese influence arising from its economic growth... though we should strive to channel it into directions that serve our national interest and peace of Asia),一语道破天机。

二、党派属性

美英报刊有的支持这个党或利益集团,有的支持那个党或利益集团,有的支持自由派,有的支持保守派。如《纽约时报》与美国东部自由派权势集团关系密切,2004年公开表态支持民主党总统候选人,对国际问题的报道和评论基本上反映了政府的外交政策和动向。《洛杉矶时报》代表西部利益集团的观点,支持西部政客入主白宫。《华盛顿邮报》在政治上较多支持民主党,在2000年美国大选中就公开支持民主党总统候选人。《读者文摘》反映中产阶级的观点,政治上代表保守派。《美国新闻与世界报道》在政治上支持共和党右翼。应该说,这些大报和著名的新闻周刊大多代表富人的利益。

美国民间一直流传着这样一种说法,即《纽约时报》是那些自认为应该统治美国的人看的报纸,《华尔街日报》是实际统治美国人看的报纸。无独有偶,据戴维斯(Ross Davis)所著《英国新闻界内幕》(*Inside Fleet Street*)一书说,英国报界也流传着这样的一首打油诗:

The Times is read by the people who run the country.

The Guardian is read by the people who like to run the country.

The Financial Times is read by the people who own the country.

The Daily Telegraphy is read by the people who remember the country as it used to be.(缅怀大英帝国者读《每日电讯报》。)

从这首诗里可以看出这些报纸的读者群体及其所代表的政治观点。

英国年鉴(*Britain* 1996)在介绍报纸(The Press)的政治倾向性时这样写道:

The press caters for a range of political views, interests and levels of education. Newspapers are almost always financially independent of any political party. Where they express pronounced views and show obvious political leanings in their editorial comments, these derive from proprietorial and other non-party influences.

Nevertheless, during General Election campaigns many newspapers recommend their readers to vote for a particular political party. Even newspapers which adopt strong political views in their editorial columns include feature and other types of articles by authors of different political persuasions.

(报纸迎合具有各种政治看法、兴趣和教育水平的读者,在经济上几乎与政党没有瓜葛。社评表达明确看法,具有明显政治倾向。可是,受到的影响只是它本身的,即使有外来影响,也与其他政党毫无牵连。话虽如此,大选期间,许多报纸都劝告读者将票投给某个特定政党。但这些报纸即使在社评栏中采取这种明显的政治观点,仍然刊登不同政治派别作者发表的包括特写和其他体裁的文章。)

年鉴在介绍期刊(The Periodical Press)时写道:

The leading journals of opinion include The *Economist*, an independent conservative publication covering a wide range of topics. *New Statesman and Society* reviews social issues, politics, literature and the arts from an independent socialist point of view, and the *Spectator* covers similar subjects from an independent conservative standpoint.

根据编者的研究,英国多数报刊如《泰晤士报》《经济学人》和《旁观者》支持保守党的政策或主张,而《卫报》和《新政治家》则支持工党。

三、惯用套路

中国发展经济叫"经济威胁",发展军力,又叫"军事扩张","意图不透明","威胁全球安全",误导舆论。中国在海外没有一兵一卒,却是威胁;美国四处驻军,经常动武,为何没有"美国威胁论"呢?美英媒体高喊"正义、自由、民主",花样翻新,骗了不少世人。

1. 直接灌输,巧妙暗示

顺应和利用受众的心理定势,根深蒂固的看法和观念,用大量信息进行直接灌输、辅以巧妙的背景和心理暗示,是西方媒体惯用套路。

2. 预定角色,刻意误导

2003年美国入侵伊拉克,借口摧毁核武器。美国媒体集体失声,无人责问布什政府证据是否确凿。记者在开战期间还与美军同吃同住(embedded reporters),成了掩饰真相、误导公众的"报喜鸟"了。对待闹西藏"独立",先设定达赖喇嘛是"西藏宗教领袖""人权卫士"和"人道传播者"。谁批他分裂国家,谁就被扣上"不人道""不维护人权""破坏宗教自由"等帽子。这就是西方媒体先划框框,定调子,按非黑即白的思维模式,把事件描绘成好莱坞电影式的善恶之争,引导受众得出一个结论:"中国不想让西藏人民享有宗教自由。"难道民主改革前的奴隶生活就是自由吗?

3. 媒体政府,高度默契

报道同一事件,出自西方媒体叫新闻,否则做叫宣传;同样是表达观点,西方媒体就一贯客观公正,别人讲出来就叫洗脑(brainwashing);别人采取同样行动,叫钳制新闻自由,发出不同声音,就不符合"普世价值"。2008年在达赖煽动下,藏独分子闹事行凶,西方政府和媒体密切配合,污蔑中国政府侵犯宗教自由,杀害教徒。德国一家报纸还用别国的照片栽赃中国军警镇压藏民。

4. 利用媒体,颠倒黑白

美国是世界上最强大的国家,军费开销最多,海外基地也最多,在世界各地逞狂。然而,在国际媒体中却没有构成"威胁",反而经常以"威胁受害者"的形象出现,大讲美国可能受到的各种威胁,如恐怖活动、生化袭击、来自伊朗的威胁等等。这与美国政府利用媒体梳妆打扮,息息相关。

美国主要借助媒体,控制全球话语权。据统计,全世界互联网网页的内容80%是用英文书写的。可见,在全球化时代,世界绝非平坦(flat),而是向讲英语的国家倾斜。美国"受害者"和"正义"形象就是这么来的。应该说,在争取受众意识、铺垫全球舆论方面确实达到了很高的专业水准,为他们在政治和外交空间争取到了相当大的回旋余地。之所以美国能成超级大国,媒体也功不可没。在美国,媒体对决策影响力除行政、立法和司法外处于第四位(fourth estate),所以舆论力量不可小觑。

四、用词

美国记者貌似用词十分考究,国内媒体常常在不知不觉中上当。外交部翻译室老翻译家程镇球先生指出:"美国媒体把表示支持本国或本国政府的热情叫做'patriotism'(爱国主义),把别人表示反对美国霸权主义的愤慨叫做'nationalism'(民族主义)。好像中国人没有'爱国主义',只有'民族主义',而'民族主义'离'排外主义'(anti-foreignism)和'仇外主义'(xenophobia)也就不远了。"此外,他们视中国发展为"威胁"(threat),本身则叫"研发"(development)。

不仅如此,美国媒体对不支持政府对外政策的民众也如此这般。例如2003年美国侵伊前夕,《今日美国报》说:"美国媒体一直不重视报道反战情绪。""一些媒体的工作就是使民众为即将到来的战争做好准备,以推销战争为己任。谁提出疑问就骂谁不爱国。"

对政治制度不同于西方的外国政府常用"Communist regime"(共产党政权),"totalitarian state"(极权国家),"rogue state"(流氓国家)等字眼。"regime","totalitarian"和"rogue"均为贬义词,对有的记者来说,"Communist"也是贬义词。媒体对民众一贯进行这样的洗脑。

西方记者和政客对苏联解体和东欧剧变欣喜若狂,渲染"共产主义垮台或崩溃了",请看下面的报道:

Once an important buffer between pro-Western Pakistan and the

Soviet Union, the country has lost much of its strategic importance since the **collapse of communism.** (*The Washington Post*)

美英报刊大力兜售西方价值观，还以"导师"自居，如《时代》周刊是这么写的：

Even before the official summit began, Clinton **tutored** China's President Jiang **on American values.**

这里把克林顿向江泽民主席介绍美国价值观说成是"tutor"（上课）了。

五、对我国媒体的影响

西方大国在很大程度上操纵着国际舆论的话语权。国内媒体有时很难摆脱影响。北约绕开安理会，轰炸南斯拉夫进行78天之久，明明是侵略（aggression），却称为"打击"（strike against Yugoslavia，不少美国报纸当时天天用来充当专栏标题），遗憾的是，国内报章杂志包括有的英语学习杂志也跟着这么说。人家把北约一方美化成"国际社会"或"世界各国人民"（international community），把迫降条件美化成"和平方案"（peace proposal），而我们有的英文报纸却照登不误。

六、擦亮眼睛，提高警惕

一般而言，美英报刊对内政常持怀疑和批评态度，与政府唱反调，但在外交上则坚决维护本国利益，或与政府立场一致，或小骂大帮忙。作为新闻媒体的重要组成部分，报刊想完全独立于政府也是不可能的。虽然它常标榜"新闻自由"，自诩"什么话都敢说"，"什么事都可报道"，其实自由是有限的，国家安全总是高于新闻自由。如2003年3月，美国以反恐的名义和伊拉克拥有对美国构成威胁的大规模杀伤性武器为借口，发动伊拉克战争以来，这种"新闻自由"一下子变得黯然失色，因为政府要求媒体在这个问题上都必须与其立场和观点保持一致。凡不听话者，轻则警告，重则勒令暂停营业甚至吊销执照。记者Peter Arnett还为此丢掉饭碗，不得不到英国去谋生。何况文章是人写的，西方记者的世界观和价值观与我们不同，当然看问题的方法和立场就与我们大相径庭，多数文章的观点是我们不能接受的。如《纽约时报》等主要报刊，一提到中国就在"人权、贸易逆差、军事威胁"等问题上大做文章。读书看报，我们不但要能读进去，还要能跳出来。阅历不深、常看这类报刊的年轻人要擦亮眼睛，提高警惕，千万别让他们潜移默化带偏了。我们对它们的文章一定要持分析、批判的态度，并使之为我所用。

了解以上情况，除有利于增强政治辨别能力，也有助于读者加深对文章内容的理解。

Contents

美英主要新闻报刊简介 ………………………………………… 1

Unit One
China Watch

Lesson 1

Text　With New Bank, China Shows U. S. It's Got Soft Power
　　　（亚投行显示中国软实力）
　　　(https://www.forbes.com) ………………………… 9
新闻写作　何谓 News ………………………………………… 18

Lesson 2

Text　China Opens Doors of State-run Companies to World's Top Talent
　　　（中国国企为世界高端人才敞开大门）
　　　(The Washington Post) ………………………………… 20
语言解说　Culture/Cultural …………………………………… 27

Lesson 3

Text　Tiger Mom … Meet Panda Dad
　　　（熊猫爸爸挑战虎妈育儿经）
　　　(The Wall Street Journal) ……………………………… 29
新闻写作　新闻体裁与报刊语言主要特点 …………………… 38

Unit Two
United States（Ⅰ）

Lesson 4

Text　Biden Inaugurated as the 46th President amid a Cascade of Crises
　　　（拜登当选美国总统，危机重重）
　　　(The New York Times) ………………………………… 41
读报知识　美国总统选举 ……………………………………… 56

Lesson 5

    Text   Five Myths About the American Dream

            （关于美国梦的五种误读）

            （*The Washington Post*）·· 58

    学习方法   读懂标题（Ⅰ）··· 65

Lesson 6

    Text   Debt Burden Alters Outlook for US Graduates

            （求学负债：美国毕业生前景堪忧）

            （*Financial Times*）·· 67

    学习方法   读懂标题（Ⅱ）··· 75

Unit Three
United States（Ⅱ）

Lesson 7

    Text   Is an Ivy League Diploma Worth It?

            （上常春藤名校，值吗？）

            （*The Wall Street Journal*）···································· 79

    读报知识   Ivy League，Seven Sisters & Russel Group ········· 85

Lesson 8

    Text   Pentagon Digs In on Cyberwar Front

            （五角大楼构筑网络战争攻防体系）

            （*The Wall Street Journal*）···································· 87

    读报知识   美英等国情治机构简介 ·································· 94

Lesson 9

    Text   Spies Among Us：Modern-day Espionage

            （间谍无处不在：现代谍报术）

            （*The Daily Beast*）··· 96

    语言解说   间谍行话 ··· 105

Unit Four
Britain

Lesson 10

    Text   Britain and the European Union：The Real Danger of Brexit

            （英国脱欧的现实危险）

    (*The Economist*) ·· 109
 读报知识 英国的议会、大选与全民公投 ···················· 116

Lesson 11
 Text Britain's Embattled Newspapers Are Leading the World in Innovation
    （英国报纸引领改革潮流）
    (*The Economist*) ·· 118
 新闻写作 导语（Lead）··· 125

Lesson 12
 Text Little Sympathy for Margaret Thatcher Among Former Opponents
    （铁娘子离世，反对派欢呼）
    (*The Guardian*) ·· 127
 读报知识 英国政党简介 ·· 135

Unit Five
World

Lesson 13
 Text Rethinking the Welfare State: Asia's Next Revolution
    （亚洲国家福利制度改革需慎行）
    (*The Economist*) ·· 137
 语言解说 委婉语 ·· 148

Lesson 14
 Text The Hopeful Continent: Africa Rising
    （充满希望的大陆：非洲正在崛起）
    (*The Economist*) ·· 150
 语言解说 Establishment ··· 157

Lesson 15
 Text US Launches First Direct Military Action Against Assad
    （美国导弹袭击叙利亚引争议）
    (*The Guardian*) ·· 159
 语言解说 Presence ·· 169

Unit Six
Society

Lesson 16

   Text   The Kids Who Might Save the Internet
          （少年侠客或将拯救英特网）
          （*The Christian Science Monitor*） ·················· 171

   语言解说   cyber 和 virtual ································ 182

Lesson 17

   Text   Does Online Dating Make It Harder to Find "the One"?
          （交友网站能找到意中人吗?）
          （*Time*） ·· 183

   语言解说   借喻词和提喻词(I) ······························ 191

Lesson 18

   Text   Yawns: A Generation of the Young, Rich and Frugal
          （年轻而富有,节俭而朴实）
          （The Associated Press） ······························· 194

   语言解说   Generation 何其多? ····························· 204

Lesson 19

   Text   Google's Zero-carbon Quest
          （谷歌的零碳计划）
          （*Fortune*） ··· 205

   新闻写作   报刊文体 ··· 217

Unit Seven
Business & Science

Lesson 20

   Text   Model Economics: The Beauty Business
          （模特经济学:美女产业）
          （*The Economist*） ·· 219

   新闻写作   报刊常用套语 ······································ 230

Lesson 21

   Text   "This Is Not the End": Experimental Therapy That Targets Genes Gives Cancer Patients Hope

（基因疗法给癌症患者带来希望）
　　　（*The Washington Post*）·················· 233
　语言解说　借喻词和提喻词(II)··············· 243

Lesson 22
　Text　Why Bilinguals Are Smarter?
　　　（掌握外语使你更聪明）
　　　（*The New York Times*）·················· 246
　广告与漫画　内容和语言特色················· 252

Unit Eight
Entertainment

Lesson 23
　Text　Bob Dylan:"The Homer of Our Time"
　　　（鲍勃·迪伦:"我们这个时代的荷马"）
　　　（*Los Angeles Times*）···················· 255
　语言解说　时髦词 Mogul, Mentor 和 Guru ········ 265

Lesson 24
　Text　He's Back All Right, Now with a Memoir
　　　（全面回忆:施瓦辛格王者归来）
　　　（*The New York Times*）·················· 267
　学习方法　名师指点词语记忆法··············· 277

Lesson 25
　Text　The Reality-television Business: Entertainers to the World
　　　（电视真人秀娱乐全球）
　　　（*The Economist*）······················ 280
　学习方法　词根的重要性····················· 288

美英主要新闻报刊简介

美国和英国的日报总数约两三千家,其中绝大多数是地方性报纸,全国性大报极少。美英各种期刊多达一万余种,其中多数是专业性和商务消费类刊物。下面分别简要介绍若干在美英国内外有影响的新闻报刊。

美 国 报 刊

美国报纸大体上可分为两种类型:通俗小报(tabloid)面向一般市民;大报(broadsheet)讲究质量,力求吸引知识界。小报为了迎合读者兴趣、追求轰动效应,对天灾人祸、罢工等新闻,挖空心思配上煽情的标题,对性、暴力、明星私生活则尽情渲染,配以大量图片,以招引读者,忽视了社会责任,结果降低了质量。发行量虽大,对重大问题却缺乏深远的影响力。严肃而高质量的大报,销量不及小报,影响力却大。

1. ***The New York Times*《纽约时报》**,1851 年创刊。曾属苏兹贝格(Sulzberger)家族所有。1969 年起,从家族企业变为股份公司,成为拥有多家美国报纸、杂志、电视台、广播电台和国外联合企业的集团。同《华盛顿邮报》和《洛杉矶时报》一起被列为美国最有影响的三家大报。它拥有一批名记者,有"美国第一大报"之说,也是获美国最高新闻奖"普利策奖"(the Pulitzer Prize)最多的一家美国报纸,订户遍及国内外。为了招徕更多的客户,2001 年发行网络版。2010 年开始探索线上订阅等经营模式。

《纽约时报》一贯标榜客观和公正,其报铭是,"刊登一切适合刊登的新闻"(All the News That's Fit to Print),但现在美国政府以爱国为名不让其自由行事。该报常用较大篇幅刊登政府重要文件和领导人讲话,不时发表一些批评政府政策的报道和评论,并在政府默许下披露一些内幕和机密。它与东部权势集团渊源较深,所报道和评述的国际新闻基本上反映美国政府的外交政策及其动向。它虽有"执美国舆论之牛耳"之说,然而这家有着 160 余年历史的报纸,2003 年却因报道两条假新闻出丑,信誉受损。后来又东山再起,2009 和 2010 年获多项普利策奖。2016、2017 年连续获得普利策国际报道奖,2018 年获普利策社论漫画奖。

其主要读者是美国政界、工商界和知识界等上层人士。2021 年日发行量约 34 万份,在美国日报排行榜上名列第三。

2. *The Washington Post*《华盛顿邮报》,1877年创刊。擅长报道美国政治动态,尤为注重报道美国国会消息,号称"国会议员和政府官员早餐桌上少不了的一份报纸"。与《纽约时报》一样,曾多次揭发政府丑闻。如导致尼克松下台的水门事件(Watergate)和副总统阿格纽(Spiro Agnew)丢官的索贿案。2013年,它又首先在美国刊登斯诺登(Edward Snowden)揭发情报机构的窃听事件。

该报原属格雷厄姆(Graham)家族所有,因在网络时代处境艰难,已于2013年8月卖给了亚马逊创始人贝索斯(Jeff Bezos),"华盛顿邮报公司"更名为"格雷厄姆控股公司"(Graham Holdings Company)。

邮报还出版小开张的全国性周末版(*The Washington Post National Weekly Edition*)。发行量名列第五。

3. *Los Angeles Times*《洛杉矶时报》,1881年创刊。号称美国最有影响的三大报之一,是西部老大。在20世纪50年代,曾因竭力支持尼克松竞选总统而引起美国政界重视,随后一跃成为全国有影响的大报。自由派色彩较浓。先前属洛克菲勒家族所有,后被芝加哥论坛报集团收购。该报销量排名第四。

4. *USA Today*《今日美国报》,由甘内特报业集团(Gannet Co., Inc)创办于1983年,是美国唯一的全国性日报,因为其他报纸都冠以New York,Washington和Los Angles等地方色彩的字眼。它利用通信卫星在全美各地同时印刷和发行,彩色技术的运用曾使美国其他报纸纷纷效仿。

该报报道翔实而不浮夸。原以国内新闻为主,较少刊载国际新闻,为迎合大众化趣味,一味模仿电视。为此而付出了巨大的经济代价,后来改变了这一倾向。在2009年,发行量退居第二。

5. *The Wall Street Journal*《华尔街日报》,创刊于1889年。社址在美国金融中心纽约市华尔街附近,几年前美籍澳大利亚媒体大亨默多克(Rupert Murdoch)买下该报及其母公司"道-琼斯公司"(Dow Jones & Company Inc.),以报道经济方面动态为主,是金融企业家必读的报纸。2009年,发行量夺回排名第一的位置。次年即叫板《纽约时报》。

"道-琼斯公司"与香港《南华早报》(*South China Morning Post*)、日本《经济新闻》和新加坡及马来西亚的《海峡时报》(*Straits Times*)合股,于1976年在香港出版《亚洲华尔街日报》(*The Wall Street Journal Asia*,曾用名 *The Asian Wall Street Journal*),行销亚洲各地。

美英主要新闻报刊简介

6. *International New York Times*《国际纽约时报》，2013 年 10 月 15 日由《国际先驱论坛报》(*International Herald Tribune*)改为现名,旨在提高《纽约时报》在全球的吸引力。早在 1963 年,由《华盛顿邮报》与《纽约时报》及原来的《纽约先驱论坛报》(*The New York Herald Tribune*)联手在巴黎出版,行销欧亚各地。后来由前两家合办,并发行亚洲版。2002 年变为《纽约时报》一家独办。主要读者群是在海外工作的美国人和讲英语的移民,影响力远大于发行量。

7. *The Christian Science Monitor*《基督教科学箴言报》，1908 年在美国波士顿创刊,由美国基督教教会创始人艾娣(Mary Eddy)(1821—1910)任社长。旨在抑制当时黄色报刊耸人听闻的新闻浪潮。历来少登犯罪及灾祸等消息,一贯拒绝刊登烟酒广告,以示忠于教义。以精心处理新闻报道、对国际问题分析透彻和具有独到之处而著称,以往常常入选美国十大名报。因资金不足,1989 年缩减版面,削减栏目,影响力大不如前。2009 年后仅出网络版。

8. *Time*《时代周刊》，1923 年创刊于纽约,由时代华纳出版公司(Time-Warner Inc.)出版(近年来时代已兼并 CNN 和 AOL[美国在线],后来又与 AOL 分离)。它是美国三大新闻周刊中最成功的一家,影响和发行量也最大。除发行国内版、军队版、大学生版外,还发行国外版。国外版又分欧洲版、亚洲版和拉丁美洲版。

《时代周刊》以报道精彩、及时,分析问题深刻和文字新颖取胜,自称是"现代英文的代表"。每期除综述一周国内外重大时事外,还对经济、科技、音乐、文教、宗教、艺术、人物、书刊、体育等方面的新闻精选整理,综合分析和评述,并配以插图和背景材料分类刊出,使之较一般报纸报道更具有深度,但又不是专业性杂志,旨在让没有时间天天读报的"忙人"了解世事。政治上较保守,倾向于共和党。

9. *Newsweek*《新闻周刊》，创刊于 1933 年,新闻周刊公司原属华盛顿邮报公司。2010 年 8 月,被美国一位亿万富翁买下,并从 2013 年开始只出电子版。同年 8 月又被 IBT 媒体集团收购,并于次年重启纸质版。在订阅等方面以《经济学家》为榜样,不再与原来的竞争对手《时代》周刊相似。

《新闻周刊》除了有名记者综述重大事件和报道、评论白宫新闻外,原来还聘请国外的名记者撰写专栏评论。

10. *U.S. News & World Report*《美国新闻与世界报道》，周刊,1948 年由 *The United States News*，*World Report* 和 *U.S. Weekly* 三家刊物合并而成。与《时代周刊》和《新闻周刊》并称为美国三大新闻周刊。

该刊着重登载美国政治、经济、军事和国防问题等综合性报道与评论。专题报道美国国内问题和对官方人物的访问是其一大特色。文字较上述两份周刊浅显易懂。

11. *Reader's Digest*《读者文摘》,创刊于 1922 年。号称资本主义世界发行量最大的月刊。用英、德、法、西、意、日、中、阿拉伯等 21 种语言在几十个国家和地区出版。2020 年总发行量为 302 万份,居美国各杂志之首。

该杂志原以摘取书刊的报道为主,现在文摘只占 60%,其余为本刊或特邀记者所写文章。编辑方针是"每月从一流杂志选出文章,去粗取精,力求紧凑,兴味永存"。每期内容广泛,从国内外政治、社会、科学到生活琐事,无所不包。体裁活泼,有小说、散文、日记、小品、游记等。另一特色是利用文末补白,插以警语、箴言、座右铭、笑话等。此外,为帮助读者扩大词汇量,还辟有"Word Power"栏,独具一格。

12. *Fortune* 前译《幸福》,现译《财富》杂志,创刊于 1930 年,由时代华纳公司在芝加哥出版。原为月刊,1978 年改为双周刊。以丰富专业知识为背景,对各行各业的经营,做深入研究报道,极具权威性。尤其是每年 5 月第一周刊登的美国企业 500 强排行榜(The Fortune 500)、8 月第二周刊登的外国企业 500 强排行榜(The Fortune 500 Outside the U.S.)、外国 50 家最大的银行排行榜(The Largest Banks Outside the U.S.)及全球 50 家最大的工业公司排行榜(The Largest Industrial Companies in the World)最具权威性。此外,有时还发表一些有分量的外交及军事方面的文章。

13. *Business Week*《商业周刊》,创刊于 1929 年。向全世界发行,每期约 95 万份。总部设在纽约,是美国著名财政企业杂志。国内版主要报道和评论美国的商业、经济、金融、贸易、企业经营和管理等方面,同时也报道一些世界经济和商业动态以及美国公司海外活动。1980 年创办国际版,栏目与国内版类似,以海外经济为主。

14. *Far Eastern Economic Review*《远东经济评论》,创办于 1946 年,周刊,在香港出版。1997 年香港回归祖国后,业主易人,由道-琼斯公司出版。主要报道和评论远东国家和地区的经济,但也发表政治、军事等方面文章。语言较《时代周刊》等浅显些。订户主要是该地区的公司,其次是投资和关注该地区的美欧公司。

英 国 报 刊

英国报刊发行与美国不尽相同,国内外财团控制的大报业集团的报纸占全英发行量的 90%,这些大集团以往又都集中在伦敦市中心的"舰队街"(Fleet Street)。因此,Fleet Street 原本常用来借喻伦敦或英国"报界"或"新闻界",但如今已风光不再。为了改善发行和促进海外销售,有的已迁往伦敦其他地区或外地城市,甚至到了海外,如《卫报》在德国发行国际版,《金融时报》直接在德国、美国和日本等国印刷发行。现在英国各报已纷纷缩小开张,但这与大报和小报无关,是两个概念。

英报按风格和内容分为 quality/popular/mid-market papers,"质量类(quality)"报纸是严肃的全国性日报,编辑水平高,读者对象是受过较高教育的上层和中产阶级人士。星期日各大报都单独出版,报名加上 Sunday,以示区别。*Daily Express*《每日快报》、*Daily Mail*《每日邮报》、*Daily Mirror*《每日镜报》、*Daily Star*《每日明星报》和 *The Sun*《太阳报》都是"通俗类(popular)"小报,消息不如 quality papers 那样严肃可靠,往往追求轰动效应。如《太阳报》就以登载英国王室成员和政界人士的桃色新闻和美女照片而"著称",发行量居首位,读者基本是工人阶级和中产阶级。"中间市场类(mid-market)"指介于这两者之间的报纸。下面介绍英国国内外有影响的几家质量类报刊和三份杂志。

1. The Times《泰晤士报》,创刊于 1785 年,是英国历史最悠久的报纸,也是西方最有影响的大报。读者为统治阶级、高级知识分子和工商、金融界人士。虽标榜"独立",其实政治观点中间偏右,支持保守党的政策或主张多些。英国有所谓"掌权者读《泰晤士报》"一说。该报的"读者来信"栏(Letters to the Editor)办得特别出色,许多知名人士在这个非正式论坛高谈阔论,对舆论有很大影响,大都代表当权派观点。

《泰晤士报》在世界各地派有记者,以较大篇幅报道和评论国际、国内重大新闻。过去曾由于内容过分严肃,不符合一般读者的趣味,因而发行量下降,利润锐减。1978 年底曾因劳资纠纷和经济问题停刊一年之久。1981 年,英国九大报业集团之一的国际新闻社(News International)老板、美籍澳大利亚媒体大王默多克从加拿大财阀汤姆森(Kenneth Thomson)手中买下该报。

《泰晤士报》有几种以周刊形式出版的副刊,其中《泰晤士报文学副刊》(*Times Literary Supplement*)被认为是英国最有影响的一家文学周刊,刊载的文章和书评具有权威性。

《泰晤士报》2019 年的月均用户数为 150 万人,在英国质量类报纸中排名第五。星期日无报,由《星期日泰晤士报》(*The Sunday Times*)补缺,俗称 "*The London Times*" 和 "*The Thunderer*"。在美国,该报又称 *The London Times* 或 *The Times of London*,以区别于 *The New York Times* 和 *Los Angles Times* 的简称 "*The Times*"。

2. *Financial Times*《金融时报》,1888 年创刊,是皮尔逊上市公司(Pearson plc)(培生集团)旗下一份国际性大报,也是世界上有代表性的一家金融商情报纸。在英国有"大老板们读《金融时报》"一说。各国政府、大企业家、银行和大学、研究机构均重视该报的报道与评论。政治上中间偏右。

《金融时报》着重报道财政、金融和工商等方面的消息、问题研究和动向。有时攻击英国政府的金融政策,因而往往影响官员的金融思想。它是英国每天提供伦敦股票市场的金融指数的唯一日报,因此闻名遐迩,在政治、文化等方面也发表文章与评论。重视国际消息,派驻海外的记者多,日发行量多年来一直称雄英国质量类报纸。

3. *The Guardian*《卫报》,创刊于 1821 年,原名《曼彻斯特卫报》(*The Manchester Guardian*)。20 世纪 50 年代末,迁至伦敦,去掉"Manchester"带地方色彩的字眼,同《泰晤士报》《每日电讯报》和《金融时报》构成英国质量类报纸的"四巨头"。英国有"有掌权欲者读《卫报》"一说。政治上中间偏左,倾向工党,主要读者群是中产阶级。

2013 年 6 月,美国前情报机构雇员斯诺登首先在中国香港将美国对全球的监控事件透露给《卫报》,该报登载后名声大振。

4. *The Daily Telegraph*《每日电讯报》,创刊于 1855 年,原为一家"通俗类(popular)"报纸,20 世纪 70 年代后期成为"质量类"报纸。在英国有"怀念昔日大英帝国时代者读《每日电讯报》"一说。该报常反映中间偏左的政治观点。

5. *The Independent*《独立报》,1986 年创办,是英国资历最浅的日报,属于 Tony O'Reilly 的 Independent News & Media 集团。与中间偏右的《泰晤士报》和中间偏左的《卫报》相比,《独立报》政治上较中立。

6. *The Economist*《经济学人》,创刊于 1843 年,是英国大型综合性周刊,与《金融时报》同属皮尔逊父子公司(S. Pearson & Son, Ltd),是《金融时报》报业集团的台柱,名气很大。每期一半篇幅刊载国际政治及时事文章,社论深受广泛重视。另一半专刊工商、金融、科学及书评。通常支持保守党观点,偶尔支持工党。

该刊撰稿不署名,不搞"文责自负",以示刊物对每篇文章负责。也不搞花哨的版面,以精彩的文章及准确的统计数字和图表来吸引高知读者,国际信誉卓著,是英国十大重要而畅销杂志中的佼佼者。

7. *The Spectator*《旁观者》,1828 年创刊,全国性周刊中历史最悠久的杂志,面向高级知识分子。公开支持保守党,反对工党的政策。对英国亲美疏欧的外交政策,常提出批评。在英国十大重要而畅销的杂志中名列第三。

8. *New Statesman*《新政治家》周刊,1913 年创办,公开支持、宣传工党的政策和主张,是其喉舌。

Unit One
China Watch

Lesson 1

课文导读

2016年1月16日,由中国倡议设立、包含有中、英、法、俄四大安理会常任理事国、15个G20国家在内的57个正式成员国参加的多边金融机构——亚洲基础设施投资银行(简称"亚投行")开始运营,标志着它作为一个多边开发银行的法人地位正式确立,以及中国在国际金融中发挥资本实力之尝试的成功。从此,作为世界第二大经济体的中国提高了在国际经济治理中的话语权,在国际金融规则制定方面获得了更大影响力,从而为本国及世界经济发展创造了更好的环境。

早在2015年3月23日,美国"福布斯"网站从中国展示软实力的角度报道了亚投行的筹建,指出亚投行的成立将是中国一种强大的软实力的体现,也是对美国金融霸主地位的挑战。美国势必会试图削弱和阻挠中国影响力的扩大和声望的提高,但美国也将为此付出地区性和全球性发展的代价。

Pre-reading Questions

1. How much do you know about Asian Infrastructure Investment Bank?
2. What is soft power in your mind?

Text

With New Bank, China Shows U.S. It's Got Soft Power[1]

1 The U.S. may have mastered the notion of soft power. But if there is one thing we can say about the world's No. 2 economy it is this: those guys in China sure know how to imitate.

2 China's proposed Asian Infrastructure Investment Bank (AIIB)[2] is soft power at its best. An idea once cast aside by the U.S., today even

the International Monetary Fund is getting in on China's latest big bank.[3]

3 IMF director Christine Lagarde[4] said there was "massive" room for IMF co-operation with the AIIB on infrastructure financing, the BBC reported this weekend.

4 The U.S. government won't want to be left out of this. It will probably lend support to the bank by sending experts and advisors to help inform governance structures and standards, say directors from the Center for Strategic & International Studies[5] in Washington. The U.S. can also work with European countries that have joined the bank in order to use their influence to ensure that the AIIB adheres to best practices, CSIS experts said last week.

5 AIIB is a multilateral development bank proposed by and majority controlled by China. It has a 36% stake in the governing structure of the bank as it is now. AIIB exists to finance the infrastructure needs in the Asia Pacific region and is different from China's latest development banking project, the so-called BRICS Bank[6]. The real name for that one is the New Development Bank (NDB), China created with Brazil, Russia, India and South Africa last summer. The BRICS bank is a dollar-denominated lending institution that will invest primarily in those five markets, but also in other countries of interest to its members.

6 This new bank is different. For those who love a good old fashion power struggle, the New Development Bank everyone thought was designed to replace the World Bank is sort of like a velociraptor. The AIIB is a T-Rex[7].

7 "China continues to aggressively position itself for a much more prominent role in the global financial system," says Jan Dehn, an economist with the Ashmore Group[8] in London. Ashmore loves China. It's one of the only foreign investment firms that has access to the local Chinese bond market, so it watches the country like a hawk. Or sticking with the dino-metaphors, a pterodactyl[9].

8 In the past few days, China has won notable support from Europe for the AIIB initiative, which together with the NDB directly challenges the influence of the Bretton Woods institutions[10]—the IMF and World Bank.

9 Over the years, the World Bank has been focused on improving the

lives of the poorest nations. It is not as interested in building mega dams in the Amazon that will help power industry.

10 "The single most important constraint to continued emerging market expansion is not external in nature—rather it is domestic in the shape of inadequate infrastructure," says Dehn. "The private sector in most emerging countries has expanded dramatically in recent decades, but the public sector's ability to expand infrastructure has not kept pace," he says, adding that "financial repression and regulatory measures" imposed by Western governments have largely made it impossible for institutional investors to channel sufficient funding into infrastructure.

11 It appears obvious that the greatest possible boost to global demand and therefore global growth would be unleashed by removing the supply constraints that are the cause of inadequate infrastructure in countries like China, a country that has spent hundreds of billions building entire cities and subway systems from scratch.

12 For AIIB member India, infrastructure is a necessity not only for business, but for basic needs like waste water treatment.

13 The World Bank's most recent and largest loan to India was a $500 million financing vehicle for small and mid-sized businesses. In 2014, however, the World Bank lent $107 million to build a highway in the state of Mizoram.

14 China wants more projects like that. The concern with U.S. and World Bank is that a World Bank loan won't just let heavy machinery saw down trees to build a highway. China might fund a project and not care that it goes through threatened bengal tiger habitats. The World Bank wouldn't fund that. There's just too many eyeballs on them. And the Bank has become more transparent over the years.

15 China has money to burn. It is becoming a source of capital in the region now. With AIIB, China can fund infrastructure in developing countries that will, in the future, be buying more made in China, or making Chinese branded products. China needs infrastructure it can rely on in Vietnam, Malaysia and even India. The new Indian government's "Make in India" policy is encouraging Chinese companies to set up manufacturing bases in northern India. These might be products that need to travel throughout India to get to customers, or fly to Singapore

to be shipped to consumers in Australia.

16　　AIIB would be a compliment to the two development banks already prominent in the region: the Asian Development Bank (ADB)[11] and of course the World Bank. The ADB invests the majority of its funds in infrastructure projects.

17　　The AIIB was first proposed by Chinese President Xi Jinping in October 2013 during an APEC[12] meeting in Indonesia. The bank was then established by a memorandum of understanding a year later, and was signed by 21 countries. The MOU specifies that it will have authorized capital of $100 billion, with initial subscribed capital of $50 billion. That makes it about the same size as the BRICS bank.

18　　Unlike the BRICS bank, AIIB has 32 members, including 6 non-regional members. Last week, the United Kingdom announced that it would join the AIIB. This announcement triggered similar statements by Germany, Luxembourg, France, and Italy. Australia, which first refused to join, hopped on board on Monday.

19　　The U.S. is on the back burner on this.[13]

20　　The National Security Council (NSC)[14] says, "We believe any new multilateral institution should incorporate the high standards of the World Bank and the regional development banks. Based on many discussions, we have concerns about whether the AIIB will meet these high standards, particularly related to governance, and environmental and social safeguards."

21　　The decision whether to join the AIIB is now partially being seen as a referendum on U.S. influence in Asia. Australia, the biggest Anglo-American outpost in the region, has voted in favor of China.[15]

22　　"Throughout history, great powers have acted in their own interests. The new great power is doing the same. Certainly neither the Americans, nor the British before them, acted otherwise,[16]" writes University of New South Wales[17] international law professor Ross Buckley in an op-ed posted on *The Sydney Morning Herald*'s[18] webpage today. "Given (that) these developments are inevitable, our participation in them becomes all the more important as it gives us an opportunity to influence and shape their future direction," Buckley states.

23　　Meanwhile, the perception of CSIS analysts is that the U.S. will fight expansion of Chinese influence and prestige. But, they warn, they will be seen doing so at the cost of regional and global development.

(From *https://www.forbes.com*, Mar 23, 2015)

New Words

Amazon /'æməzən/ *n.* the ~ 亚马逊河

Anglo-American /'æŋgləʊməˈrɪkən/ *adj.* of or relating to relations between England and the United States or their peoples

BBC *n.* British Broadcasting Corporation 英国广播公司

Bengal /beŋˈɡɔːl/ *n.* an area of southern Asia that includes Bangladesh and the Indian state of West Benga 孟加拉地区

bond /bɒnd/ *n.* an official document promising that a government or company will payback money that it has borrowed, often with interest 债券

channel /'tʃænl/ *v.* control and direct sth such as money towards a particular purpose 把〔钱、精力等〕导向〔特定目的〕;引导;把……用于

compliment /'kɒmplɪmənt, 'kɒmplɪment/ *n.* (= complement) sth added to complete or make perfect 补充

denominate /dɪˈnɒmɪneɪt/ *v.* to officially set the value of sth according to one system or type of money 以某种货币标价

dino-metaphors *n.* metaphors between dinosaurs species 不同类别的恐龙之间的比喻

economy /ɪˈkɒnəmi/ *n.* the system by which a country's money and goods are produced and used, or a country considered in this way 经济体

governance /'ɡʌvənəns/ *n.* the way in which a company or an organization is managed (公司、组织等的)管理方式;治理结构

habitat /'hæbɪtæt/ *n.* the natural home of a plant or animal 〔生态〕栖息地,产地

incorporate /ɪnˈkɔːpəreɪt/ *v.* to include sth as part of a group, system, plan etc.

infrastructure /'ɪnfrəstrʌktʃə(r)/ *n.* the basic systems and structures that a country or organization needs in order to work properly, for example roads, railways, banks etc 基础设施

initiative /ɪˈnɪʃətɪv/ *n.* an important new plan or process to achieve

particular aim or solve a particular problem 倡议，计划
mega /ˈmegə/ *a.* very big and impressive 宏大的
Mizoram *n.* （印度）米佐拉姆邦
memorandum /ˌmeməˈrændəm/ *n.* a written proposal or reminder 备忘录
monetary /ˈmʌnɪtri/ *a.* relating to or involving money 货币的
MOU *n.* memorandum of understanding 谅解备忘录
multilateral /ˌmʌltiˈlætərəl/ *a.* involving at least three different groups of people or nations 多边的；多国的
op-ed /ˌɒpˈed/ *n.* （abbreviation of）opposite the editorial page（报纸）专栏版，专栏文章
outpost /ˈaʊtpəʊst/ *n.* a military post stationed at a distance from the main body of troops 前哨
pterodactyl /ˌterəˈdæktɪl/ *n.* a dinosaur species 翼手龙
referendum /ˌrefəˈrendəm/ *n.* a direct vote by all the people to decide about sth on which there is strong disagreement, instead of the government making the decision 全民投票，公投
scratch /skrætʃ/ *n.* very beginning;（from ～）从零开始；白手起家
stake /steɪk/ *n.* share 股份
subscribe /səbˈskraɪb/ *v.* agree to buy or pay for shares 认购
transparent /træsˈpærənt/ *a.* easily seen through; easily understood or recognized 透明的；易懂的，显而易见的
T-Rex /tiː reks/ *n.* = tyrannosaurus (a dinosaur species, well-known as the "tyrant lizard" in the dinosaur family) 霸王龙；恐龙王
vehicle /ˈviːəkl/ *n.* a medium for (finance)（融资）平台
velociraptor /vəˈlɒsɪræptə(r)/ *n.* a dinosaur species 迅猛龙

Notes

1. soft power — a concept to describe the ability to attract and co-opt rather than by coercion (hard power), which is using force or giving money as a means of persuasion. Soft power is the ability to shape the preferences of others through appeal and attraction. A defining feature of soft power is that it is noncoercive; the currency of soft power is culture, political values, and foreign policies. 软实力

2. Asian Infrastructure Investment Bank (AIIB) — a multilateral development bank aiming to support the building of infrastructure in the Asia-Pacific region, proposed as an initiative by the government of

China. The bank currently has 61 member states while another 23 are prospective members for a total of 84 approved members. The bank started operation after the agreement entered into force on 25 December 2015. Major economies that are not members include Japan, Mexico, and the United States. The United Nations has addressed the launch of AIIB as having potential for "scaling up financing for sustainable development" for the concern of global economic governance. 亚洲基础设施投资银行(简称亚投行)

3. An idea once cast aside by the U. S. , today even the International Monetary Fund is getting in on China's latest big bank. — 美国曾表示对亚投行不感兴趣,然而,现在就连国际货币基金组织也想要与中国这家新设立的大银行进行合作。这里表现了美国对亚投行不屑一顾的态度。后文中"The U. S. government won't want to be left out of this"(Par. 4)和"The U. S. is on the back burner on this"(Par. 19)则表现了美国的不甘和不满。

    a. cast aside — to remove or get rid of sb or sth because you no longer need them 抛弃,废除
    b. get in on — to become involved in sth 参与;分享
    c. International Monetary Fund (IMF) — 国际货币基金组织

4. Christine Lagarde — (1956—) a French lawyer and politician who was the Managing Director (MD) of the International Monetary Fund (IMF) from July 2011 to July 2019. Lagarde was the first woman to become finance minister of a G8 economy and is the first woman to head the IMF. 克里斯蒂娜·拉加德,时任国际货币基金组织总裁。

5. the Center for Strategic & International Studies (CSIS) — An American think tank based in Washington, D. C. in the United States. The center conducts policy studies and strategic analyses of political, economic and security issues throughout the world, with a specific focus on issues concerning international relations, trade, technology, finance, energy and geostrategy. 美国战略与国际问题研究中心

6. BRICS Bank — the New Development Bank (NDB), a multilateral development bank established by BRICS States and headquartered in Shanghai, China. 金砖国家新开发银行(新开发银行)

    BRICS — the acronym for an association of five major emerging national economies: Brazil, Russia, India, China and South Africa. Originally the first four were grouped as "BRIC" (or "the BRICs"), before the induction of South Africa in 2010. The BRICS members are all leading developing or newly industrialized countries, but they are distinguished by their large, sometimes fast-growing economies and significant influence on regional affairs; all five are G-20 members. Since 2009, the BRICS nations have met annually at formal summits. China hosted the 9th BRICS summit in Xiamen in September, 2017. 金砖国家，或称金砖五国。

7. For those who love a good old fashion power struggle … replace the World Bank is sort of like a velociraptor. The AIIB is a T-Rex. — 用远古时代恐龙家族的权力争斗来比喻的话，意在取代世界银行的金砖银行是火鸡大小的迅猛龙，亚投行却是恐龙之王霸王龙。

velociraptor — one of the dinosaur genera most familiar to the general public due to its prominent role in the *Jurassic Park* motion picture series. In real life, however, it was roughly the size of a turkey, much smaller than the approximately 2m tall 80kg reptiles seen in the films. T-Rex is well-known as the "tyrant lizard", the king in the dinosaur family.（此处以比喻手法用为人熟悉的两种恐龙将 AIIB 和 NDB 相比较，形象地呈现出两家银行的体量。）

the World Bank — an international cooperative organization established in 1945 under the Bretton Woods Agreement to assist economic development, especially of backward nations, by the advance of loans guaranteed by member governments. It comprises two institutions: the International Bank for Reconstruction and Development (IBRD), and the International Development Association (IDA). 世界银行

8. the Ashmore Group — a large British investment manager dedicated to the emerging markets with $52.2 billion under management as at 31 December 2016. 英国安石集团

9. Or sticking with the dino-metaphors, a pterodactyl. — 或者继续用恐龙家族来做比喻，是会飞的翼手龙。

10. the Bretton Woods institution — 布雷顿森林体系（The International Monetary Fund (IMF) and the International Bank for Reconstruction and Development (IBRD), commonly known as the World Bank, were created in 1944 at a meeting of 44 nations (the Allies) at Bretton Woods, New Hampshire to rebuild devastated economies after the war and to promote economic stability and economic

development on a global scale. 1944年7月,44个国家的代表在美国新罕布什尔州布雷顿森林镇召开了著名的布雷顿森林会议,会议宣布成立国际复兴开发银行(世界银行前身)和国际货币基金组织(IMF)两大机构,确立了美元对国际货币体系的主导权,构建了战后国际货币体系的新秩序。)

11. the Asian Development Bank (ADB) — a regional development bank established on 19 December 1966, which is headquartered in Mandaluyong, Metro Manila, Philippines. The company also maintains 31 field offices around the world to promote social and economic development in Asia. From 31 members at its establishment, ADB now has 67 members, of which 48 are from within Asia and the Pacific and 19 outside. 亚洲开发银行

12. APEC — Asia Pacific Economic Cooperation 亚太经济合作组织

13. The U. S. is on the back burner on this. —这次美国靠边站了。

   put/leave sth on the back burner — to delay doing sth until a later time

14. The National Security Council (NSC)—(美国)国家安全委员会

15. The decision whether to join the AIIB is now…has voted in favor of China. — 现在,是否加入亚投行的决定被视为对美国在亚洲影响力的公投。作为英国和美国在该地区最大前哨的澳大利亚已经投出了支持中国的一票。

16. Throughout history, great powers … nor the British before them, acted otherwise. — 自古至今,大国都是本着自身利益行事的。无论是美国人还是其前辈英国人均无例外。新的大国也是如此。

17. University of New South Wales — (澳大利亚)新南威尔士大学

18. *The Sydney Morning Herald* —《悉尼先驱晨报》

Questions

1. What kind of bank is the Asian Infrastructure Investment Bank?
2. Who first proposed AIIB officially on behalf of China?
3. What is the difference between AIIB and NDB?
4. What is the attitude of the U. S. government towards the AIIB initiative?
5. What is the significance of AIIB according to the passage?

新闻写作

何谓 News

对新闻的定义众说纷纭，连英英词典的词源意义也只是用 probably 这样不确定词："Middle English *newes*, probably plural of *newe* (literally) that which is new, noun use of adjective; perhaps patterned on French *nouvelles*."(*World Book Dictionary*)这就是说，news 是 new 的复数。无论是报刊报道的新人、新事、新思想和新情况都突出一个"新"字，这是 news 的关键。否则，就不是新闻了。

一般而言，新闻（news）的定义有广义和狭义两种。广义的新闻泛指在媒体上出现的所有文章。狭义的新闻即"消息"，单指对最新发生的事件的客观报道，而不表达报道者的意见。世界各国对广义新闻的功能的解释各异，不存在被全球媒体普遍接受的定义或规定。尽管如此，其特性是共同的，即都是向公众报道新的事实，传递各种消息。这样，美英等国媒体就自我选择担任起提供信息、教育、改革、娱乐、激励等部分或所有角色。

美国报刊新闻尤其强调猎奇，将之奉为天条，正如俗话所说："狗咬人不是新闻，人咬狗才是新闻"(It is not news when a dog bites a man, but absolutely news when you find a man bites a dog)。为了加深对这句话的理解，不妨看看下面这幅美国政治讽刺漫画：

瞧，媒体是如何剧烈争抢这种庸俗的猎奇式"人咬狗"新闻的。
图中英文为"LOCAL NEWS"（当地新闻）

从西方新闻理论来看，表扬好人好事的正面新闻不是新闻，只有"坏"消息才是"好"新闻，是"乌鸦嘴"。如天灾人祸、社会丑恶现象、突发的悲剧性事件等，尤其战争是最典型的"坏"新闻。这样，我们在看西方媒体的报道，总是看到"好"的新闻少，"坏"的新闻多，包括对中国的报道也是负面内容多，正面内容少。新闻学的一个原则是："好事不出门，坏事传千里。"每天在媒体上所见所闻尽是"坏事"，不管是杀人放火，天灾人祸，无不即刻传播遐迩。在这种情况下，No news is good news. 得不到什么消息才是最好的消息。这与西方新闻的理念是分不开的。

还有人认为，所谓新闻，无非是天南海北之事，你看 NEWS 不就是 north, east, west 和 south 的首字母缩略词吗！此说是否有道理，也只能"见仁见智"了。（详见《导读》第一章第二节）

Lesson 2

课文导读

　　针对科研和技术人才缺口持续扩大的弊端,中国政府提出了人才优先发展的战略布局,旨在努力提升劳动人口的教育水平,发展创新经济,实现从"中国制造"型向"中国创造"型经济转变。"千人计划"就是一个人才发展项目,旨在吸纳外国专家和中国的海外学子来华工作,引导技术创新,以提升中国工业领域的竞争力。同样,中国为他们提供优厚的薪资待遇和永久居住签证。作者呼吁美国重视中国这一人才战略,但也客观地分析了中国现存的不尽如人意的科研环境以及引进人才战略面临的挑战。作者在提出质疑的同时,也引导我们思考一个问题:显然,单凭引进外智和吸引回国人员解决不了创新问题,那么中国创新的出路又在哪里?

Pre-reading Questions

1. How do you see the prospect of China's development?
2. What is mostly needed for China's innovation?

Text

China Opens Doors of State-run Companies[1] to World's Top Talent
By Vivek Wadhwa[2]

　　The top talent in countries around the world have a new suitor: the

Chinese government.

2   China has a severe shortage of skilled talent and, in a policy reversal[3], has decided to open its doors to talent from around the world. This could mean that the brilliant NASA[4] scientists the U. S. laid off, could find new employment — and a new home — in Shanghai or Beijing.

3   Chinese research labs have long had difficulty recruiting qualified workers to perform necessary research and development, and its corporations struggle to find competent managers. The situation will likely get worse as China's high-tech industries grow and it increases its national R&D[5] spending from the present 1.62 percent of GDP, according to the Chinese government, to the planned 2.5 percent by 2020. China's President Hu Jintao, in May 2010, declared talent development a national priority in order to fill the void. The goal is to dramatically increase the education level of China's workforce and to build an innovation economy[6].

4   China has launched several high-priority programs to encourage skilled Chinese to return home — all in an effort to meet the country's pressing talent demands. One of these programs is the "Thousand Foreign Talents Program[7]." The program's goal is to bring 2,000 experienced engineers, scientists, and other experts of Chinese origin back from the West. The government also announced that it aims to cultivate 100 "strategic entrepreneurs"[8] who can lead Chinese firms getting into the ranks of the world's top 500 countries.

5   Both efforts are running ahead of target according to Dr. Huiyao Wang[9], the Director General of the Center for China and Globalization[10] and an advisor to the Chinese government. China had recruited more than 1,500 "high quality talents," according to Wang, and 300 returnees had been enrolled in management training courses by August 2011. The courses were conducted by senior ministers. These individuals, while re-learning how to operate successfully within the Chinese system, are expected to serve as a critical catalyst in transforming China's innovation environment in ways that will enhance the country's competitive edge[11] across a range of key, strategic industries.

6   China is getting more ambitious, based on the initial recruitment successes of the returnee program.

7　　The Chinese government invited me to attend the International Conference on the "Exchange of Talent" held in Shenzhen on Nov. 5. Vice Premier, Zhang Dejiang launched China's "Thousand Foreign Talents Program," which, for the first time, opens China's doors to skilled foreigners to secure long-term employment in China. The Chinese government announced that it will allow foreign nationals to take senior roles in science and technology sectors and state-owned enterprises. They will also pay foreigners salaries equal to what they can earn at top paying jobs in America. And the government announced that it intends to offer permanent resident-type visas to foreign entrepreneurs.

8　　This announcement was front-page news in China, and its importance should not be underestimated in the U.S. where these developments were not widely covered. These programs, which were announced with amazing fanfare, represent a significant break from the traditional "use Chinese" policies and a greater openness to the outside world. Chinese governors and senior officials from across the country participated in the ceremonies, and the Chinese government claimed the conference had 100,000 attendees. The festivities that accompanied this were nothing short of dazzling, with cultural entertainers and acrobats brought in from all over China.

9　　Denis Fred Simon, author and Vice-Provost for International Affairs at the University of Oregon was one of the nine foreign experts at the Shenzhen conference. China, said Simon, sees talent as the next big global race for driving competitiveness and innovation. The country is determined to win this race if only to ensure it can complete the goal of transforming its economy. Wang also explained that the Chinese see this new talent pool as the key to moving from a "made in China" orientation to a "created in China" capability[12]. China's future growth, continued Wang, will rely more on the new talent strategy, even as its past successes were built mainly on its population dividend and investment.

10　　But sometimes things aren't as rosy as they seem.

11　　Some of the returnees have found themselves victims of discrimination and petty jealousy from those who stayed behind. Moreover, they have struggled to re-adapt to China's relationship-oriented culture[13], which stands in sharp contrast to the performance-oriented culture[14] of the West. Compared to the generally transparent set of rules and decision-making processes that are commonplace in U.S. and European research and university settings, returnees are frequently confounded by the "personalized" ways research proposals are evaluated and research grants are distributed. The reality is that despite the good intentions of the program, the Chinese research environment remains plagued by plagiarism, fraud, and other scandals.

12   There is an even greater challenge, however. Returnees are refusing to make full-time commitments to their new Chinese employers. Many have returned only sporadically, often not meeting the stated residency requirements of the Thousand Talents Program.

13   The best of the Chinese talent pool abroad has not yet chosen to return to China, especially in the science and technology fields, said Simon. Some who were considering returning home, he said, are still watching and waiting as their peers cope with the challenges of returning. Family considerations also pose an important barrier, said Simon, as many Chinese expatriates based overseas would prefer their children to complete their education abroad and not have to suffer through China's "examination hell" prior to college.

14   Discussions with Chinese government leaders in Shenzhen made it clear that Chinese leaders are not satisfied with the level of innovation in the country. I told them that I didn't believe that China could fix this problem merely through returnees. China would need to learn some of the techniques that Indian industry has employed to upgrade its workforce. China's most critical challenge will be to create a more conducive environment for entrepreneurship. Innovation requires risk-taking, breaking existing systems and challenging the norms. Within Hu Jintao's model of a "harmonious" society (what he calls "hexie shehui"), this presents some real challenges.

15   Until China allows and encourages more "out of the box[15]" thinking and behavior, it simply won't innovate, nor will it produce the types of breakthrough products top Chinese leaders wish to see coming out of China's research labs and key enterprises. (From *The Washington Post*, November 16, 2011)

New Words

acrobat /ˈækrəbæt/ *n.* one that performs gymnastic feats requiring skillful control of the body 杂技演员

attendee /ˌætenˈdiː/ *n.* a person who is present on a given occasion or at a given place 出席人

catalyst /ˈkætəlɪst/ *n.* sth that causes an important event to happen 催化剂；刺激因素

commonplace /ˈkɒmənpleɪs/ *adj.* ordinary; unremarkable 司空见惯的

conducive /kənˈdjuːsɪv/ *adj.* tending to promote or assist 有益的，有助于的

confound /kənˈfaʊnd/ *v.* to confuse and surprise by being unexpected 感到震惊

dazzling /ˈdæzlɪŋ/ *adj.* amazingly impressive 炫目的，非凡的

dividend /ˈdɪvɪdend/ *n.* a sum of money paid to shareholders of a corporation out of earnings; advantage 股息；利益；好处

enhance /ɪnˈhɑːns/ *v.* to increase or improve in value, quality, desirability or attractiveness 增强，使强化

entertainer /ˌentəˈteɪnə(r)/ *n.* one who tries to please or amuse 娱乐人士，使他人快活的人

entrepreneur /ˌɒntrəprəˈnɜː(r)/ *n.* one who organizes, manages, and assumes the risks of a business or enterprise 企业家

expatriate /ˌeksˈpætrɪət/ *n.* one who lives in a foreign land 身处异国他乡的人

fanfare /ˈfænfeə(r)/ *n.* a lot of publicity or advertising 炫耀，大张旗鼓的宣传

fraud /frɔːd/ *n.* deceit; trickery, or intentional deception 欺骗

norm /nɔːm/ *n.* a standard or model or pattern regarded as typical 规范

orientation /ˌɔːriənˈteɪʃn/ *n.* a usually general or lasting direction of thought, inclination, or interest 方向；定位

peer /pɪə(r)/ *n.* one that is of equal standing with another 同等的人，同龄人

petty /ˈpeti/ *adj.* marked by or reflective of narrow interests and sympathies; narrow-minded 小气的

plagiarism /ˈpleɪdʒərɪzəm/ *n.* an act or instance of plagiarizing 剽窃

plague /pleɪɡ/ *v.* to cause continual discomfort, suffering, or trouble to 使人痛苦，受罪

pool /puːl/ *n.* a supply of money, goods, workers or other resources, which is shared between and may be used by a number of people 共用的资源(钱、物品、人力等)

priority /praɪˈɒrəti/ *n.* sth that needs attention, consideration, service, etc., before others 优先考虑的事

Provost /ˈprɒvəʊst/ *n.* the head of certain colleges (某些学院的)院长

reversal /rɪˈvɜːsəl/ *n.* an act of changing from one state to the opposite state 逆转

recruit /rɪˈkruːt/ *v.* to fill up the number of (as an army) with new members 招募

returnee /rɪtəːˈniː/ *n.* a person who returns 海归,还乡者

rosy /ˈrəʊzi/ *adj.* characterized by or tending to promote optimism 乐观的

scandal /ˈskændl/ *n.* loss of or damage to reputation caused by actual or apparent violation of morality or propriety 丑闻 (*cf.* affair; -gate)

sector /ˈsektə(r)/ *n.* a part of a field of activity, esp. of business, trade, etc. (尤指商业、贸易等的)部门;界;领域,行业

sporadically /spəˈrædɪkli/ *adv.* appearing or happening at irregular intervals; occasionally 零星地,偶尔地

suitor /ˈsuːtə(r)/ *n.* one who courts a woman or seeks to marry her 追求女性欲与其结婚者

transparent /trænsˈpærənt/ *adj.* easily detected or seen through 透明的

vice-provost *n.* (大学)副校长

void /vɔɪd/ *n.* the empty area or space 空白

workforce /ˈwɜːkˌfɔːs/ *n.* the force of workers available 劳动力

Notes

1. state-run company — 国营企业。
2. Vivek Wadhwa — 美国杜克大学普拉特工程学院主任、哈佛大学法学院访问学者,商业创新领域的著名学者,曾经创立过两家科技公司,同时他还是美国商业周刊(*Business Week*)的专栏作家。
3. policy reversal — 政策转型 Here, it refers to a change of policy from encouraging Chinese students to study abroad to opening the door to talent from around the world.
4. NASA — *abbr.* National Aeronautics and Space Administration(美国国家航空和宇宙航行局。Started in 1958, it is the agency of the U.S. government that is responsible for the nation's civilian space

program and for aeronautics and aerospace research.）

5. R&D — *abbr*. research and development 研究与发展；研发
6. innovation economy — 创新经济，指以信息革命和经济全球化为背景，以知识和人才为依托，以创新为主要推动力，保持快速、健康发展的经济。
7. "Thousand Foreign Talents Program" — 海外高层次人才引进计划，简称"千人计划"。该计划主要是围绕国家发展战略目标，从 2008 年开始，在国家重点创新项目、学科、实验室以及中央企业和国有商业金融机构、以高新技术产业开发区为主的各类园区等，引进 2000 名左右人才并有重点地支持一批能够突破关键技术、发展高新产业、带动新兴学科的战略科学家和领军人才来华创新创业。
8. "strategic entrepreneurs" — 战略企业家。中国在 2010 年提出中央企业人才工作的重点是要培养 100 名左右战略企业家，即拥有大局观念和战略思维、忠实维护国有资产权益、引领企业做强做大的出资人代表队伍。
9. Dr. Huiyao Wang — 王辉耀博士，时任中国与全球化研究中心主任。
10. Center for China and Globalization—CCG，中国与全球化研究中心（全球化智库）an independent, non-profit think tank based in Beijing. CCG conducts research in a range of social science areas including world affairs, international talent issues, sustainable development, entrepreneurship and globalization. It was founded by a number of returned scholars from the west together with the Policy Advisory Committee(政策顾问委员会)of the China Western Returned Scholars Association（WRSA,欧美同学会）. Its aim is to utilise its "pool of first-class scholars, business leaders and experts in government, to address issues on how best to position China in a globalized world."
11. competitive edge — the strategic advantage one business entity has over its rival entities within its competitive industry. Achieving competitive advantage strengthens and positions a business better within the business environment. 竞争优势

    edge — advantage(新闻常用小词)
12. moving from a "made in China" orientation to a "created in China" capability — 从"中国制造"向"中国创造"能力的转型
13. relationship-oriented culture — 以人际关系或人情为主的现象、风气或环境。这样的氛围，一团和气，缺乏批评，难以创新。（见本课语言

解说 Culture/Cultural)
   -oriented — designed for, directed towards, motivated by, or concerned with(形容词性后缀)
14. performance-oriented culture — 以绩效为导向的气氛或氛围
15. out of the box (Par. 15) — remarkable or exceptional; extraordinary 出格的,摆脱常规的

Questions

1. What is the main reason for China to open its door to talents from other parts of the world?
2. What is the "Thousand Foreign Talents Program"?
3. So far, what has China been doing in welcoming the returnees?
4. What are the favorable conditions offered to attract those overseas talents?
5. What problems have some of the returnees found after coming back to China?
6. Why is there hesitation among those overseas Chinese?

语言解说

Culture/Cultural

现在不少人见到"culture"或"cultural"就不加思考地译为"文化(的)",什么企业文化、汽车文化、西瓜文化等,不一而足。本课的"culture of fear",是否也是"恐惧文化"? 这样的理解和翻译犹如一个小孩戴了一顶大人的帽子——不合适。"文化"涵盖的范围广,世界各国对其定义各异。所以此处只从具体例句的上下文加以商榷。

   1. Air Force whistle-blower Ompal Chauhan warned against "a type of cultural conditioning" in which a typical Pentagon manager "thinks more about his future employer than his current one. Loyalties become confused." (*U. S. News & World Report*)

   2. If the government sets the right climate, Thatcher believes, new business will flourish. But is modern-day Britain capable of creating the kind of enterprise culture Thatcher envisions? The plain truth is that Britain companies do not, for the most part, work as efficiently as their competitors. "Yes, we're creating new companies," says Stuart

Slatter, director of the Institute of Small Business Management of the London Business School, "but there is very little evidence that they will be a major source of new jobs." Slatter cites what amounts to a cultural handicap: "People lack the get-up-and-go to go out and succeed." (*Newsweek*)

例1中 a type of cultural conditioning 指五角大楼出现的"一股习以为常的损人利己的歪风",因为其管理军工企业的官员假公济私,满脑子想的是离任后到他所监管的企业谋个肥缺。

例2中 enterprise culture 在第一句已指明是"right climate",根据语境,意为"良好的企业环境"或"企业发展的良好氛围"。a cultural handicap 也在后面做了解释,即缺乏企业家那种奋斗创新的进取精神。

可见,以上两句中"cultural"和"culture"分别意味着"风气""环境"或"氛围""进取精神"。在本课出现的"relationship-oriented culture"和"performance-oriented culture",亦作"氛围"或"风气"讲为宜。(详见《导读》六章二节)

Lesson 3

课文导读

2011年,一位华裔美国妈妈出版了一本名为《虎妈战歌》的书(书名又译为:《我在美国做妈妈:耶鲁法学院教授的育儿经》)(Battle Hymn of the Tiger Mother),在中美两国引起了轰动,并引发了一场关于中美教育方式差异的大讨论。究竟什么才是教育孩子的终极目的?有人说她是尽心尽力的好妈妈,帮助孩子最大限度地发挥了潜能;也有人说她太过分了。这其中有一位自称是"熊猫爸爸"的美国父亲在《华尔街日报》上公开挑战"虎妈"的育儿方式。想到熊猫憨态可掬的外形就能够猜出几分,熊猫爸爸崇尚的是宽松的教育理念,并且怀着一份坚持到底的信心。到底他有什么勇气和理由向虎妈宣战?有着中国生活背景的他是否对于教育方式的差异有着更深刻的理解?

现在我国创造力虽然比不上美国,但也在不断进步。这是否都归结为中国的"死板"或应试教育?值得我们研讨。

Pre-reading Questions

1. How were you raised when you were young?
2. When you've skimmed the article, have you benefited from it or not?

Text

Tiger Mom[1] ... Meet Panda Dad[2]

By Alan Paul

1 I have watched the uproar over the Tiger Mom debate with growing annoyance that one simple question remains unasked: Where are the dads?

2 I am a father of three who has been on the frontline of parenting for years, thanks to my wife's demanding career and my own freelance lifestyle. I refuse to cede the entire discussion about proper child-rearing to mothers, Tiger or otherwise[3]. When my kids were 2, 4 and 7, our

family of five moved from suburban New Jersey to Beijing.

3   Our 3 1/2 years in China give me an unusual insight into what author Amy Chua claims is not only the best way of parenting but also the Chinese way.

4   During our first weeks in Beijing, we attended a talent show[4] at our children's British school and watched Chinese students ascend the stage and play Chopin etudes and Beethoven symphonies, while their Western counterparts ambled up and proudly played the ABCs under their flapping arms[5]. It was enough to make anyone pause and ponder the way we are raising our kids.

5   But time in China also taught me that while some here view a Chinese education as the gold standard, many there are questioning the system, noting that it stifles creativity and innovation, two things the nation sorely needs. Further, having seen it in action, I have a strong aversion to hard-driving "Tiger" parenting, certain that is not a superior method if your goals are my goals: to raise independent, competent, confident adults.

6   Call me the Panda Dad; I am happy to parent with cuddliness, but not afraid to show some claw.[6]

7   Though I have had primary child care duties since our eldest son was born 13 years ago, I too have always worked, sometimes juggling a variety of demanding deadlines with an increasingly complex family schedule[7]. As a result, controlled chaos reigns in our house — and it works for us, even if this has befuddled some friends and family members and sent weak-kneed babysitters scurrying for the door.

8   It has also been a plus for our children, giving them space to take on responsibilities, be independent and see their parents pursuing their own interests and careers while also being very involved in one another's lives. And it introduced them to a simple fact early: Life itself is controlled chaos and success depends on navigating it, rather than waiting for things to be perfect.

9   This is largely a male perspective. To make a sweeping generalization, moms tend to be more detail oriented, and order driven. Dads often care less about the mess, can live with a bit more chaos and more easily adopt a big picture view. If my wife and I swapped positions, life would certainly be more orderly. But she cedes to my style of parenting because I am in charge of the

day-to-day stuff. Her ability to do this is a key to us having a strong, thriving relationship; you can't backseat drive how your children are being raised[8].

10 This only works if you share the same basic values and the differences are small bore rather than big picture. She would not tolerate me calling the kids garbage or chaining them to a piano bench[9]; we would both view this as barbaric and counterproductive.

11 Kids raised in this fashion have more of an opportunity to develop their own personalities and interests. Our home is like a state university, where you can get a great education but you have to do your own legwork. A typical night: one kid has a big project due, another has a school play, the third has soccer practice; mom is working late because there is an international crisis brewing but she will barrel home to be sitting in the auditorium when the curtain rises[10]; and I am trying to help everyone while fielding calls on a story[11] I have to finish writing that night after the kids go to bed.

12 It's not the hyper-orderly household that Amy Chua portrays, but the kids are constantly learning to take responsibility for their own homework, play time and everything else. Doing so allows them to take genuine pride in their accomplishments. They need to succeed for their own benefit, not to prove that their parents are successful. It's sheer narcissism to believe that your child's every success and failure is a reflection of your worth[12]. Get over yourself[13].

13 Living in a Beijing housing compound, I watched Western and African kids running through the streets in roving packs of fun-seekers[14] while their Chinese friends looked dolefully out the window in the midst of long hours spent practicing violin, piano or character-writing. When they were done, they unwound by picking up video game consoles. It looked like a sad, lonesome way to grow up and nothing I would ever prescribe to my children. And of course it's not the only style of Chinese parenting. I saw plenty of kids smashing these same stereotypes.

14 It also seems insane to cast an eye around the upper-middle-class American milieu Ms. Chua is discussing and conclude that the problem is that our child-rearing is too laid back. The shallowness of this concept will be obvious to anyone who has ever stalked a suburban

soccer sideline or listened to New York parents prep their 18-month-old for nursery school interviews. God help us all if Ms. Chua's books convinces these same people that they simply have not been trying hard enough.

15 It's easy to understand a traditional Chinese drive for perfection in children: it is a huge nation with a long history of people thriving at the top and scraping by at the bottom without much in between. The appeal in contemporary America stems from a sense that our nation is becoming stratified in similar ways and is about to get steamrolled by China[15]. If you can't beat them, join them[16].

16 It's an understandable impulse but it's wrong. Forcing a child to constantly bend to your will can lead to docile mama's boys or girls seeking approval for everything they do — or lead to constant rebellion and head-butting. Banning playing and sleeping at friends' houses furthers a dangerous sense of isolation, denying them the ability to make the very social connections and interactions that they will need throughout life. These are the very skills that kids should be honing for success as a functioning adult, far more important than being able to play piano. Kids need more unstructured play[17], not less.

17 Aside from being a much cheaper option than babysitters, sleepovers also help children learn to sleep anywhere, in any bed, with any pillow. This is not an ability to be scoffed at. It is, in fact, one of three goals everyone should realistically set for raising their kids: get them to adulthood with no sleeping, eating or sexual hang-ups. Do that and you will have done your job, launching them off with the foundation needed to thrive.

18 Drop the hubris of thinking you can pick your children's friends, interests and musical passions. Instead, help them grow up to be highly functioning, non-neurotic contributors[18] with a strong sense of self. They will thank you.

19 And so will society. (From *The Wall Street Journal*, March 29, 2011)

New Words

amble /ˈæmbl/ *v.* walk slowly and in a relaxed manner 从容地走，漫步
ascend /əˈsend/ *v.* leads up to a higher position 上升；爬坡

aversion /əˈvɜːʒən, -ʃən/ *n.* a feeling of strong dislike or unwillingness 厌恶，反感

barbaric /bɑːˈbærɪk/ *adj.* extremely cruel or uncivilized 野蛮的；半开化的；粗俗的

barrel /ˈbærəl/ *v. infml* to move very quickly, esp. unsafely

befuddle /bɪˈfʌdl/ *v.* cause to be unable to think clearly 使迷快速移动不解

brew /bruː/ *v.* (esp. of sth bad) to be in preparation or ready to happen; develop 酝酿，孕育（尤指坏事）

cede /siːd/ *v.* give over 让给，放弃

compound /ˈkɒmpaʊnd/ *n.* an area enclosed by a wall, fence etc., containing a group of buildings（有围墙等的）场地（大院，楼群）

console /kənˈsəʊl/ *n.* a flat surface containing the controls for a machine, piece of electrical equipment, organ, etc.（机器、仪器等的）控制台，仪表盘

counterproductive /ˌkaʊntəprəˈdʌktɪv/ *adj.* achieving the opposite result from the one that you want to achieve 产生相反效果的；事与愿违的；适得其反的

cuddliness /ˈkʌdlɪnɪs/ *n.* state of being lovable, suitable for cuddling 可爱，值得拥抱

docile /ˈdəʊsaɪl/ *adj.* quiet and easily controlled, managed, or influenced 温顺的，驯良的

dolefully /ˈdəʊlfəlɪ/ *adv.* with sadness; in a sorrowful manner 寂寞地

demanding /dɪˈmɑːndɪŋ/ *a.* needing a lot of time, attention and effort 需要技能的，费力的

etude /eɪˈtjuːd/ *n.* a piece composed for the development of a specific point of technique 练习曲

flap /flæp/ *v.* to wave or move slowly up and down or backwards and forwards, usu. making a noise 摆动，拍动

freelance /ˈfriːlɑːns/ *n.* a writer or artist who sells services to different employers without a long-term contract with any of them 自由作家，自由记者

hang-up /ˈhæŋʌp/ *n.* difficulty, inhibition, obsession 困难，障碍

hard-driving *adj.* 要求过高的，过于苛责的

head-butt /ˈhedbʌt/ *v.* hit you with the top of their head 用头顶撞（某人的下巴或身体）；顶撞

hone /həʊn/ *v.* to yearn or pine 渴望；渴慕

hubris /ˈhjuːbrɪs/ *n.* overbearing pride or presumption 傲慢；狂妄自大

juggle /'dʒʌgl/ v. to give enough time or attention to your work and your family 尽力同时应付；尽量兼顾

legwork /'legwɜːk/ n. infml work that needs much walking about or tiring effort 跑腿活，跑外工作

milieu /miːˈljɜː/ n. (pl. milieus 或 milieux) the environmental condition 环境；周围

narcissism /'nɑːsɪsɪzəm/ n. an exceptional interest in and admiration for yourself 自我陶醉，自恋

navigate /'nævɪgeɪt/ v. to direct carefully and safely 驾驶

parent /'peərənt/ v. to act as a parent 抚育，养育

parenting /'peərəntɪŋ/ n. the activity of bringing up and looking after your child

plus /plʌs/ n. a welcome or favorable condition 有利的附加物，有利条件

roving /'rəʊvɪŋ/ a. (of groups of people) tending to travel and change settlements frequently （人群）流动的，徘徊的

scoff /skɒf/ v. infml to speak or act disrespectfully; laugh(at) 嘲弄，嘲笑

scrape /skreɪp/ v. to live, keep a business etc. with no more than the necessary money 勉强维持，艰难经营

scurry /'skʌri/ v. to move about or proceed hurriedly 急匆匆；赶忙

sheer /ʃɪə(r)/ adj. pure; unmixed with anything else; nothing but

sleepover /'sliːpəʊvə(r)/ n. an occasion of spending a night away from home or having a guest spend the night in your home (esp. as a party for children)（尤指小孩）在朋友家过夜的晚会

smash /smæʃ/ v. to defeat, destroy, or put an end to

sorely /'sɔːli, 'səʊr-/ adv. fml very much, greatly

stalk /stɔːk/ v. to hunt by following closely and quietly and staying hidden 潜步跟踪；潜进

steamroll /'stiːmrəʊl/ v. to crush or force using very great power or pressure 推进；压倒

stereotype /'steriətaɪp/ n. a fixed set of idea about what a particular type of person or thing is like, which is (wrongly) believed to be true in all cases 模式化的见解，老套，旧框框

stratify /'strætɪfaɪ/ v. usu. pass to arrage in separate levels or strata （一般用被动语态）使分层，使成层

stifle /'staɪfl/ v. to prevent from happening or developing 压制，阻止

symphony /'sɪmfəni/ n. 交响乐，交响曲

swap /swɒp/ v. to exchange or give (something) in exchange for

unwind /ˌʌnˈwaɪnd/ *v. infml* to stop being nervous; relax, esp. after a period of great effort and pressure 放松,松弛一下
uproar /ˈʌprɔː(r)/ *n.* loud confused noise from many sources 喧闹;吵闹
weak-kneed /ˈwiːkˌniːd/ *adj.* lacking strength of character or purpose 易屈服的;软弱的

Notes

1. Tiger Mom — Amy Chua(1962—), Yale law professor who raised her two daughters in Chinese parenting way. She got the name from her book *Battle Hymn of the Tiger Mother* published in 2011 in which Chua describes her efforts to give her children what she describes as a traditional, strict "Chinese" upbringing. Chua uses the term "Tiger Mother" to mean a mother who is a strict disciplinarian. Her article in the *Wall Street Journal* (WSJ) titled "Why Chinese Mothers Are Superior" on January 8, 2011 which is an excerpt from her book has generated widespread debate on what constitutes good parenting and Chua received ample criticism after the WSJ essay. (耶鲁大学华裔教授蔡美儿在《虎妈战歌》一书中描绘了自己教育两个女儿的严苛的中国方式,引爆了世界对东西方教育方式的大讨论。)

2. Panda Dad — The author calls himself Panda Dad as a scream of rage and frustration against the Tiger Mom hoopla (喧嚣). He weighs in on raising kids, unwilling to defer to the Tiger Mom way of child-rearing. This report as a Panda Dad manifesto for the WSJ quickly caught fire and caused a stir that led to him being interviewed on the NBC *Today* show.

3. I refuse to cede the entire discussion about proper child-rearing to mothers, Tiger or otherwise. — As for proper child-rearing, I don't want to just leave the discussion among mothers, no matter they are tiger mother or not. (就正确的育儿方式而言,我不能坐看只有妈妈参与的讨论,不管她们是不是虎妈。)

   cede to — to give to another person, esp. after losing a war 割让,放弃

4. talent show — an event where participants perform talents of singing, dancing, acrobatics, acting, drumming, martial arts, playing a unicorn instrument, or other activities to showcase skills, sometimes for a reward, trophy or prize. Many talent shows, like

school talent shows, are performances rather than contests, but some are actual contests, awarding prizes to their participants.

5. Chinese students ascend the stage ... under their flapping arms — Chinese students get on the stage playing difficult piece of music very skillfully, but their Western schoolmates walk leisurely up the stage and proudly play the simple song of ABCs with their arms waving up and down.

    a. Chopin — F. F. Chopin(1810—1849)was a Polish composer and virtuoso pianist. He is widely considered one of the greatest Romantic piano composers.（肖邦，波兰作曲家、钢琴家，19世纪欧洲浪漫主义音乐代表人物）

    b. Beethoven — Ludwig van Beethoven(1770—1827) was a German composer and pianist. A crucial figure in the transition between the Classical and Romantic eras in Western art music, he remains one of the most famous and influential of all composers.（贝多芬，德国作曲家、钢琴家、指挥家，维也纳古典乐派代表人物之一）

6. I am happy to parent with cuddliness, but not afraid to show some claw — I am happy to be a mild and amiable dad but I would show my authority and dignity if necessary.（我很满足于这种亲切可爱但有时也不怕显露威仪的父亲形象。）

7. juggling a variety of demanding deadlines with an increasingly complex family schedule — dealing with different writing tasks before the tight deadlines and at the same time arranging more complex family affairs.

8. you can't backseat drive how your children are being raised — you can't just give unwanted advice about how to raise your children; you have to take the responsibility and get involved in parenting on your own.

    backseat drive — to give unwanted advice to the driver about how to drive

9. calling the kids garbage or chaining them to a piano bench — calling the kids "garbage" or forcing them to practice piano for hours.（This is what the Tiger Mom did to her daughter.）

10. mom is working late because... when the curtain rises — No matter how busy mom is with her work related to the international crisis looming large, she will make time to attend in time the school play

performed by our kids. 作者的妻子也供职于擅长财经报道的《华尔街日报》，因此世界经济危机使得报道任务加重，工作繁忙。

11. while fielding calls on a story — while answering phone calls about a report
    field — to answer questions, telephone calls, etc. 回答，应对
12. It's sheer narcissism…a reflection of your worth. — If you believe your child's very success and failure is a sign of your worth, you are totally overestimating yourself.
13. Get over yourself — Make clear the fact; don't think so much of yourself.
14. … running through the streets in roving packs of fun-seekers … — running through the street wandering in crowds to seek fun. 走街串巷，自由地结伴玩耍
15. The appeal in contemporary America … get steamrolled by China. — 在当代美国出现这种呼声是源于这样一种感觉：我们的国家正在被按照类似的方式划分阶层，而且很快就要被中国所赶超。
    stem from — to exist or happen as a result of
16. If you can't beat/lick them, join them. — 赢不了，早入伙（以便从中获利）；胜不了，成朋友；败下阵，快归顺。这是吹得天花乱坠的商战策略，美国人的阿 Q 精神，政界、商界时髦语，倒不失为保住面子的好办法。此处的意思是，既然美国教育孩子的方法不如中国，就跟中国学好了。因为在一次世界中学生学习能力评估计划赛上，上海队名列第一，这震撼了美国。
17. unstructured play — play that is organized or regulated; free play
18. non-neurotic contributors — people who can contribute to the society without much anxiety or sensitivity

Questions

1. What role should a father play in child-rearing according to the author's experience?
2. What insight is given to the author by his several years in China?
3. Why does the author call himself Panda Dad?
4. How does the author think about order and chaos at home?
5. According to the article, is the American child-rearing too laid back?
6. What are the three final goals that everyone should realistically set for raising their kids in the author's view?

7. What is Mr. Alan Paul's attitude towards sleepovers?

新闻写作

新闻体裁与报刊语言主要特点

1. 新闻体裁

新闻体裁(forms of news writing)指报道形式,如何划分众说纷纭,不但中外不同,中国也不统一。例如中国有些学者主张分为以下五类:(1) 消息,包括动态、综合、经验、述评等四类消息。(2) 通讯,可分为人物、事件、概貌和工作等通讯及小故事五类。(3) 新闻特写,有人物、事件、旅行等特写及速写。(4) 调查报告。(5) 报告文学,一种介于新闻与文学之间的边缘体裁。有的主张分消息、特写、通讯、专访和述评五类。美英等国有人认为除消息报道体裁外,专稿、述评、采访、杂文、传记等都是特写体裁。然而,人们较多倾向于将它分为消息、特写和社评(社论和评论)三类。

消息(News)

消息报道分两类:一类是通讯社的电讯或报道,短小精悍,内容最真实,被称之为"纯硬性新闻"(pure hard news),有的报纸将之辟为"Brief(ly)"栏。另一类报刊的报道比通讯社的要详细得多,但有的由于夹杂着记者的推测和描绘,往往不如前者真实和经得起推敲。

特写(Feature)

新闻特写常指再现新闻事件、人物或场景的形象化报道,吸取了一般新闻报道和文艺作品的长处,其结构则取两者之长。消息在导语部分就往往把最重要、最新鲜、最吸引人的内容突出在最前面,而特写虽然也是一种新闻报道,但不少则常采取引人入胜的悬念式(suspended interest form)写作手法,逐渐娓娓道来。

社论和评论(Editorial & Commentary)

社论是一家报纸或杂志的编辑部发表的权威性评论,所代表的是编辑部的观点,是一家报纸的灵魂,要了解其对某事的倾向,需要从社论看起。它常以第三者口吻说话,或对人对事直接发表意见,表明立场、观点和倾向,或提出问题,或号召人们采取行动。评论是署名文章,往往在报道文章后就报道中提及的人和事发表评述,启示读者。这是社论和评论所不同的。社评类文章也报道事实,但以评论表明立场为最终目的,这与新闻报道只叙事而不评论大有区别。在文字上,报道类文章一般较简明,社论则较严肃正规,评论或言论(Opinion)则较活泼。评论可以嬉笑怒骂、讽刺影射,尤其常用借古讽今的手法。因此后两类文章较难读懂。读社论要了解有关人和事的背景,而读评论则还要有较深的语言功底和较广的知识,因为专栏作家在文章中常引经据典。

社论和评论往往都开门见山,在第一段点出论题,类似引子,引导读者往下读。接着就逐段逐点展开分析评说。末段则为结论。当然,有的写法并非如此,如将事实和结论都置于首段或前两段。这与特写采用的倒叙手法有别。

以上有关消息、特写和社评的写作手法和用语不同,《导读》均以文章为例进行解析。

2. 报刊语言主要特点

报刊语言的主要特点是简约、时尚、创新、引经据典、修辞色彩浓、(插)图文(章)并茂和程式化。这些特点与报刊体裁有关,报道性文章语言是非正式的,与公文体不同,也与高雅的文学语言有别,介于雅俗之间。本节所谈简约、创新等例子,是从语言运用的角度而言的,不是严格的语言学分析。省略、用缩略词、短字、句法上等的"简约",突出一个"短"字,其中有的用法与汉语很相似,尤其是名词代替形容词作定语用,这早在20世纪30年代就曾有学者指出过。所谓"时尚",主要指语言时尚,时髦词大量涌现,与创新有关。"创新"指报刊语言新、奇、活的特点,体现在新言新语层出不穷,旧词不断引申出新义,推陈出新,标新立异。语句、语法也在发展创新,只要读了《导读》"跟踪语言的变化和发展"这一节,就一目了然。"修辞色彩浓",主要指报刊常运用各种修辞手段,引经据典,成语典故多,用语新颖别致,形象生动。与文学语言相比,报刊语言在这些方面紧贴现实,更突出些。"图文并茂",主要指插图等与文章配合,交相辉映。文章里所插图表、漫画等加上简练的语言,形象生动、幽默等特点得到充分体现。程式化指读者能理解和明白的常用套语及新闻报道中固定的几种形式。应该说明的是,简约、时尚、创新和修辞色彩浓这四方面相互关联,创新是动力,而这些特点则正在推动当代英语向前发展。(详见《导读》四章二节)

Unit Two
United States (Ⅰ)

Lesson 4

课 文 导 读

  从 2017 年到 2020 年，特朗普总统以其特立独行之举在美国乃至全世界掀起了一场风暴，所过之处留下狼藉一片，美国社会矛盾更加尖锐，种族关系更加紧张，党派之争进一步加剧，社会体系进一步撕裂。此时，美国似乎需要一个能挽救其身份危机的新领袖。从 29 岁开始成为美国最年轻的参议员之一，并连续六次连任参议员，外交成就突出，三次竞选总统，担任奥巴马政府副总统八年，虽历尽人生磨难仍旧执着前行。这样的履历和实力让约瑟夫·拜登成功登上了总统宝座。然而拜登入主白宫之路并非坦途，不服输的特朗普依然在"垂死挣扎"。在经历了司法诉讼、重新计票、国会大厦骚乱等事件之后，拜登终于迎来了自己的就职典礼，不过这可能是几十年来最"寒酸"的就职典礼，也打破了 150 年来新旧交接的传统规则。如此冷清的场面似乎预示着拜登即使在解决了特朗普这个难题后，还将面临一连串的难题。拜登能否扭转乾坤，重拾美国的影响力，还需拭目以待。

  通过本课学习可以一窥美国政治和社会形态，了解总统大选和就职的基本知识。

Pre-reading Questions

1. Do you know anything about Joe Biden?
2. What do you know about the U.S presidential election?

Text

Biden Inaugurated as the 46th President amid a Cascade of Crises

Joseph Robinette Biden Jr. and Kamala Devi Harris took the oath of office at a Capitol[1] still reeling from the attack of a violent mob at a time when a deadly pandemic is still ravaging the country.

By Peter Baker

1   WASHINGTON—Joseph Robinette Biden Jr. was sworn in on Wednesday as the 46th president of the United States, assuming leadership of a country ravaged by disease, dislocation and division with a call to "end this uncivil war[2]" after four tumultuous years that tore at the fabric of American society.

2   Mr. Biden sought to immediately turn the corner on Donald J. Trump's polarizing presidency, inviting Republicans to join him in confronting the nation's dire economic, social and health crises even as he immediately began dismantling his predecessor's legacy with orders to halt construction of his border wall[3], lift his travel ban[4] and rejoin the Paris climate agreement[5].

3   With his hand on a five-inch-thick Bible that has been in his family for 128 years, Mr. Biden recited the 35-word oath administered by Chief Justice John G. Roberts Jr.[6] at 11:49 a.m., 11 minutes before the constitutionally prescribed noon hour. Vice President Kamala Devi Harris[7] was sworn in a few minutes earlier by Justice Sonia Sotomayor[8] using a Bible that once belonged to Thurgood Marshall[9], the civil rights icon and Supreme Court justice. Ms. Harris thus became the highest-ranking woman in the history of the United States and the first Black American and first person of South Asian descent to hold the second highest office.

4   The drama of the moment was underscored by the sight of Mr. Biden taking the oath on the same West Front of the Capitol[10] seized just two weeks ago by a marauding mob trying to block final ratification of Mr. Trump's election defeat. Without ever naming Mr. Trump, who left the White House early in the morning for Florida but still faces a Senate trial for provoking his supporters[11], Mr. Biden said that the

United States' democratic experiment itself had come under assault by extremism and lies but ultimately endured.

5 "Through a crucible for the ages, America has been tested anew and America has risen to the challenge," the president said in a 21-minute Inaugural Address[12] that blended soaring themes with folksy touches.

6 "The will of the people has been heard, and the will of the people has been heeded," he added. "We've learned again that democracy is precious. Democracy is fragile. And at this hour, my friends, democracy has prevailed."

7 Already abbreviated because of Mr. Trump's refusal to concede[13], the transition that ended Wednesday was like none before, not just from one party to another but from one reality to another. A president who came to Washington to blow up the system was replaced by one who is a lifelong creature of it. A president who seemed capable of almost anything at any moment was dislodged by one who fits comfortably in the conventions of modern politics.

8 Mr. Biden's broader message was conciliatory yet challenging, as he called on Americans to put aside their deep and dark divisions to come together to confront the coronavirus pandemic, economic troubles and the scourge of racism.

9 "We must end this uncivil war that pits red against blue[14], rural versus urban, conservative versus liberal," Mr. Biden said. "We can do this if we open our souls instead of hardening our hearts, if we show a little tolerance and humility, and if we're willing to stand in the other person's shoes, as my mom would say, just for a moment."

10 Mr. Biden used the word "unity" or "uniting" 11 times, saying that he knew it "can sound to some like a foolish fantasy" but insisting that Americans had emerged from previous moments of discord and could do so again.

11 "We can join forces, stop the shouting and lower the temperature," he said. "For without unity, there is no peace, only bitterness and fury. No progress, only exhausting outrage. No nation, only a state of chaos. This is our historic moment of crisis and challenge, and unity is the path forward."

12 A historic moment, but also a surreal one. Unlike most inaugurals

suffused with joy and a sense of new beginning, the nation's 59th inauguration on a chilly but sunny day served to illustrate America's troubles. Amid fear of further violence, Washington was transformed into an armed camp, with 25,000 National Guard troops[15] joining thousands of police officers in blocking off a wide section of downtown.

13 　　With the pandemic still raging and the death toll topping 400,000, Americans were told to stay away, leading to the eerie spectacle of a new president addressing a largely empty National Mall[16], filled not with people but with flags meant to represent the absent crowd. Mr. Biden and most of the participants wore masks through most of the activities.

Flags on the National Mall represent the crowds that could not attend the inauguration because of the pandemic. (Credit … Jason Andrew for The New York Times)

14 　　Many inaugural customs were scrapped because of the virus, including a lunch with congressional leaders in Statuary Hall[17], a full-scale parade down Pennsylvania Avenue[18] and the gala evening balls where the new president and his wife typically dance.

15 　　Instead, Mr. Biden reviewed military units[19] at the Capitol and later proceeded to the White House escorted by military marching bands

as well as drum lines from the University of Delaware and Howard University, the alma maters of the new president and vice president.

16 Mr. Biden and his wife, Jill Biden, his son Hunter Biden and his daughter Ashley Biden, as well as a passel of grandchildren and other relatives, emerged from the motorcade to walk the final blocks to the White House, but it was a gesture aimed more at cameras than the crowd because there were more police and National Guard troops than spectators.

17 In characteristic fashion, Mr. Trump defied custom by leaving Washington hours before the swearing-in, although Mike Pence[20], his vice president, did attend. In remarks to supporters before boarding Air Force One[21], Mr. Trump still could not bring himself to mention Mr. Biden's name but said, "I wish the new administration[22] great luck and great success." He did leave the traditional note for his successor, which Mr. Biden later called "a very generous letter."

18 Then, in a laying on of hands[23] of sorts by the world's most exclusive club[24] — a club that never accepted Mr. Trump, who likewise shunned them — three former presidents from both parties, Barack Obama, George W. Bush and Bill Clinton[25], joined Mr. Biden in placing a wreath at the Tomb of the Unknowns at Arlington National Cemetery[26]. (Jimmy Carter, at 96, was unable to attend, but spoke with Mr. Biden by phone on Tuesday night.)

19 If the pomp and circumstance were constrained by the challenges of the day, Mr. Biden's determination to get off to a fast start unraveling the Trump presidency was not. He signed 17 executive orders, memorandums and proclamations aimed at reversing major elements of the last administration, a significant repudiation of his predecessor and a more expansive set of Inauguration Day[27] actions than any in modern history.

20 Among other things, Mr. Biden issued a national mask mandate for federal workers and federal property, sought to extend an eviction pause and student loan relief, suspended construction of Mr. Trump's border wall, lifted the travel ban on certain predominantly Muslim countries, barred discrimination by the federal government based on sexual orientation or gender identity and imposed a moratorium on oil and natural gas leases in the Arctic National Wildlife Refuge[28].

21   Some of the orders were more symbolic than substantive, and enduring change will still require legislation. To that end, Mr. Biden unveiled an immigration overhaul? providing a path to citizenship for 11 million people living in the country illegally that will have to be approved by Congress in what is sure to be a contentious debate.

22   With Ms. Harris's inauguration and the swearing-in of two new senators later in the day, the Senate, evenly divided with 50 Democrats and 50 Republicans, flipped to the Democrats thanks to her tiebreaking vote as the chamber's president[29].

23   Mr. Biden was particularly determined to call out the forces of "political extremism, white supremacy[30], domestic terrorism," as he put it, implicitly faulting Mr. Trump's relentless bid to overturn the election with false accusations of widespread fraud — baseless claims that fueled the mob that ransacked the Capitol.

24   "Recent weeks and months have taught us a painful lesson," Mr. Biden said. "There is truth and there are lies, lies told for power and for profit, and each of us has a duty and a responsibility as citizens, as Americans and especially as leaders, leaders who have pledged to honor our Constitution and protect our nation, to defend the truth and defeat the lies."

25   In many respects, Mr. Biden could hardly be more of a contrast to the president he succeeded. A longtime senator, former vice president and consummate Washington insider, Mr. Biden prides himself on his experience working across the aisle[31] and hopes to forge a partnership with Senator Mitch McConnell[32] of Kentucky, the minority leader, and other Republicans.

26   At 78, Mr. Biden is the oldest president in American history — older on his first day in office than Ronald Reagan[33] was on his last — and even allies quietly acknowledge that he is no longer at his prime, meaning he will be constantly watched by friends and foes alike for signs of decline. But he overcame the doubts and the obstacles to claim the prize of his lifetime nearly [34] years after kicking off the first of his three presidential campaigns.

27   Mr. Biden arrived at the pinnacle of power with a tailwind of public support. Fifty-seven percent of Americans view him favorably, according to Gallup 34, a higher rating than Mr. Trump ever saw in

office. But in a measure of the impact of Mr. Trump's drumbeat of false accusations of election fraud, 32 percent? told CNN pollsters? that they did not believe Mr. Biden won the election legitimately.

28 　　Mr. Biden and Ms. Harris bring new diversity to the top echelon of government. Mr. Biden is only the second Catholic president after John F. Kennedy[35]. Ms. Harris, 56, a former senator and state attorney general from California, broke multiple gender and racial barriers in winning the vice presidency.

29 　　Performing at the Capitol ceremony were Lady Gaga, Jennifer Lopez and Garth Brooks[36], while a host of other famous entertainers participated in a virtual "Parade Across America" livestreamed[37] from 56 states and territories.

30 　　Instead of the formal dances, the new first and second couples were to take part in a 90-minute televised evening program called "Celebrating America" hosted by the actor Tom Hanks[38] and featuring stars like Kerry Washington, Bruce Springsteen, Eva Longoria, Lin-Manuel Miranda and Demi Lovato[39]. (From *The New York Times*, Jan. 20, 2021)

New Words

administer /əd'mɪnɪstə(r)/ *v.* to take responsibility for organizing and supervising a country, the law, or a test 监管(国家、法律、考试等); 执行

alma mater the school, college or university that you went to 母校

assume /ə'sjuːm/ *v. fml* to take or begin to have power or responsibility 承担(责任); 就(职); 取得(权力)

cascade /kæ'skeɪd/ *n.* a large amount (of sth)

concede /kən'siːd/ *v.* to admit that you have lost a game, an election, etc. 承认(比赛、选举等)失败

conciliatory /kən'sɪliətəri/ *adj.* having the intention or effect of making angry people calm 调解的; 抚慰的; 意在和解的

consummate /kən'sʌmət, 'kɒnsəmeɪt/ *adj.* extremely skilled; perfect 技艺高超的; 炉火纯青的

coronavirus /kə'rəʊnəvaɪrəs/ *n.* any of a group of RNA viruses that cause a variety of diseases in humans and other animals 冠状病毒, 日冕形病毒

crucible/ˈkruːsɪbl/ *n. fml* a place or situation in which people or ideas are tested severely, often creating sth new or exciting in the process 熔炉；严峻的考验；磨练

dire /ˈdaɪə(r)/ *adj. fml* extremely serious, bad or terrible 极其严重的；危急的

discord/ˈdɪskɔːd/ *n.* disagreement and argument between people 不和；纷争

dislocation/ˌdɪsləˈkeɪʃn/ *n.* disturbance from a proper, original, or usual place or state 混乱

dislodge/dɪsˈlɒdʒ/ *v.* to force sb to leave a place, position or job （把某人）驱逐出，赶出

dismantle /dɪsˈmæntl/ *v.* to end an organization or system gradually in an organized way （逐渐）废除，取消

drumbeat/ˈdrʌmbiːt/ *n.* a series of warnings or continuous pressure on sb to do sth （一系列的或持续的）警示；持续的压力

echelon/ˈeʃəlɒn/ *n.* a rank or position of authority in an organization or a society 职权的等级；阶层

eerie/ˈɪəri/ *adj.* strange, mysterious and frightening 怪异的；神秘的；恐怖的

emerge/iˈmɜːdʒ/ *v.* (~ from sth) to survive a difficult situation or experience （从困境或苦难经历中）幸存下来，摆脱出来

escort/ˈeskɔːt, ɪˈskɔːt/ *v.* to go with sb to protect or guard them or to show them the way 护卫；护送

eviction/ɪˈvɪkʃn/ *n.* the act or process of officially forcing sb to leave a house or piece of land 驱逐

expansive /ɪkˈspænsɪv/ *adj.* covering a large subject area, rather than trying to be exact and use few words 广泛的；全面的

fabric/ˈfæbrɪk/ *n. fml* the basic structure of a society, an organization, etc. that enables it to function successfully （社会、机构等的）结构

fault/fɔːlt/ *v.* to find reason(s) for criticizing sb/sth 批评

flip/flɪp/ *v.* to turn over into a different position with a sudden quick movement 快速翻转

folksy/ˈfəʊksi/ *adj.* simple, friendly and informal 淳朴友好自然的；朴实热情随意的

gala/ˈɡɑːlə/ *n.* a special public celebration, entertainment, performance, or festival. 庆典；盛会；演出

heed/hiːd/ *v.* to pay attention to sb's advice or warning and do what they suggest 注意；听从

icon /'aɪkɒn/ *n.* a famous person or thing that people admire and see as a symbol of a particular idea, way of life, etc. 崇拜对象；偶像

inaugural /ɪ'nɔːgjərəl/ *adj.* (of an official speech, meeting, etc.) first, and marking the beginning of sth important 就职的；开幕的；成立的；创始的 *n.* 就职演讲

inaugurate /ɪ'nɔːgjəreɪt/ *v.* to hold an official ceremony when someone starts doing an important job in government 开始，开创；举行就职典礼 **inauguration** *n.*

legacy /'legəsi/ *n.* a situation that exists now because of events, actions, etc. that took place in the past 遗产；遗留问题；后遗症

marauding /mə'rɔːdɪŋ/ *adj.* (of people or animals) going around a place in search of things to steal or people to attack（到处）抢劫的，劫掠的

moratorium /ˌmɒrə'tɔːriəm/ *n.* a temporary stopping of an activity, esp. by official agreement 暂停，中止（尤指经官方同意的）

motorcade /'məʊtəkeɪd/ *n.* a line of vehicles including one or more that famous or important people are travelling in（载着要人的）车队，汽车行列

outrage /'aʊtreɪdʒ/ *n.* an act or event that is violent, cruel or very wrong and that shocks people or makes them very angry 暴行；骇人听闻的事

overhaul /'əʊvəhɔː/ *n.* the act of examining carefully and making many changes in order to improve (a system or method) 改革；修订

pandemic /pæn'demɪk/ *n.* a disease that spreads over a whole country or the whole world（全国或全球性）流行病；大流行病

passel /pæsl/ *n. infml,* a large group of people or things of indeterminate number; a pack 一大批；一大群

pinnacle /'pɪnəkl/ *n.* the most important or successful part of sth 顶点；鼎盛时期

pollster /'pəʊlstə(r)/ *n.* a person or organization who asks large numbers of people questions to find out their opinions on particular subjects 民意调查员，民意测验专家

pomp /pɒmp/ *n.* the impressive clothes, decorations, music, etc. and traditional customs that are part of an official occasion or ceremony 排场；气派；盛况

prevail /prɪ'veɪl/ *v.* (of a proposal, principle, or opinion) to gain influence or is accepted, often after a struggle or argument; win 占上风；获胜

provoke /prəˈvəʊk/ *v.* to say or do sth that you know will annoy sb so that they react in an angry way 挑衅；激怒；刺激

ransack /ˈrænsæk/ *v.* to damage things in a building or make it very messy, often because they are looking for sth in a quick and careless way 洗劫

ratification /ˌrætɪfɪˈkeɪʃn/ *n.* the process of making a treaty or written agreement official by giving formal approval to it, usu. by signing it or voting for it 批准（条约或书面协议）

ravage /ˈrævɪdʒ/ *v.* to damage sth badly 毁坏；严重损害

reel /riːl/ *v.* (~ at/from/with sth) to feel very shocked or upset about sth 感到震惊；感到心烦意乱

repudiation /rɪˌpjuːdɪˈeɪʃən/ *n.* the act of refusing to accept or be associated with sth; the act of denying the truth or validity of sth 拒绝接受；否定，驳斥

reverse /rɪˈvɜːs/ *v.* to change sth completely so that it is the opposite of what it was before; to change a previous decision, law, etc. to the opposite one 彻底转变；撤销，废除（决定、法律等）

scourge /skɜːdʒ/ *n.* a person or thing that causes a lot of trouble or suffering to a group of people 祸害；祸根；灾难

scrap /skræp/ *v.* to cancel or get rid of sth that is no longer practical or useful 废弃；取消；抛弃；报废

shun /ʃʌn/ *v.* to deliberately avoid or keep away from sb/sth 有意回避

substantive /səbˈstæntɪv/ *adj. fml* dealing with real, important or serious matters 实质性的；本质上的；严肃认真的

suffuse /səˈfjuːz/ *v.* (be ~ d with) (of a book, movie, or piece of music) full of (a certain quality) 充满

tailwind /ˈteɪlwɪnd/ *n.* a wind that blows from behind a moving vehicle, a runner, etc., making it move faster 顺风

tumultuous /tjuːˈmʌltʃuəs/ *adj.* involving a lot of change and confusion and/or violence 动荡的；动乱的

uncivil /ʌnˈɪvl/ *adj. fml* not polite; lacking civility or good manners 无礼的；粗野的，不文明的

underscore /ˌʌndəˈskɔː(r), ˈʌndəskɔː(r)/ *v.* to draw attention to sth and emphasize its importance 突出显示；强调

unravel /ʌnˈrævl/ *v.* to make (a system, plan, relationship, etc.) start to fail or no longer stay together as a whole 解体；崩溃；瓦解

Notes

1. Capitol — the government building in Washington, D. C. where the U. S. Congress meets 美国国会大厦（常被用来喻指美国国会）
2. uncivil war — fight or conflict in a rude and discourteous way. Here Biden indicated the chaos and confusion brought by the Trump administration.
3. border wall—also known as Mexico-U. S. barrier. On Jan. 25, 2017, U. S. President Donald Trump signed an executive order for a wall to be built on the U. S.-Mexican border in a bid to stem illegal immigration. Although there was bitter fight over the wall funding, more than 450 miles of the border wall have been built by the end of 2020.
4. travel ban — in Jan. 2017, in the interest of national security, U. S. President Donald Trump imposed an entry ban on refugees and citizens from seven Muslim-majority countries including Iran, Iraq, Libya, Somalia, Sudan, Syria, and Yemen. He then announced the expansion of the travel ban on six more countries. The travel ban has met with strong opposition and mass protests both in the U. S. and around the world. On January 20, 2021, President Joe Biden issued a proclamation revoking the Trump travel bans. 旅行禁令，因为所涉国均为穆斯林为主要人口的国家，也称"穆斯林禁令"或"禁穆令"。
5. the Paris climate agreement — The Paris Agreement is a legally binding international treaty on climate change. It was adopted by 196 Parties at the 21th UN Climate Change Conference of the Parties (COP 21,第 21 届联合国气候变化大会) in Paris, on 12 December 2015 and entered into force on 4 November 2016. Its goal is to limit global warming to well below 2℃, preferably to 1.5℃, compared to preindustrial levels. Donald Trump announced in June 2017 that U. S. would withdraw from the Paris Agreement. And the U. S. formally left the Paris Agreement in Nov. 4, 2020, marking the only nation that abandoned this global agenda on combating climate change. On Jan. 20, 2021, hours after being sworn in as the new president, Joe Biden signed an executive order returning the U. S. to the Paris Agreement on climate change. 《巴黎气候协定》
6. John G. Roberts Jr. —（1955 —) the 17th chief justice of the U. S. since 2005. He is the youngest Chief Justice in 100 years. The

chief justice of the U.S. is the chief judge of the Supreme Court and the highest-ranking officer of the U.S. federal judiciary. 美国首席大法官是美国最高司法官员，主管美国最高法院，并在弹劾美国总统时主持参议院，同时还主持美国总统的宣誓仪式。

7. Kamala Devi Harris — (1964—) an American politician and attorney who served as Democratic Senator and Attorney General of California before becoming the 49th vice president of the U.S. 卡玛拉·哈里斯

8. Sonia Sotomayor —(1954—) an associate justice of the Supreme Court of the U,S. who has served since August 8, 2009. She is the third woman to hold the position. Sotomayor is the first woman of color, first Hispanic, and first Latina member of the Court. 美国最高法院共有9名大法官，由一名首席大法官和8名大法官组成，索托马约尔是美国历史上首位拉美裔最高法院大法官。

9. Thurgood Marshall — (1908 — 1993) an American lawyer and civil rights activist who served as Associate Justice of the Supreme Court from 1967 to 1991. He was best remembered for jurisprudence（法学）in the fields of civil rights and criminal procedure. Numerous memorials have been dedicated to Marshall after his death.

10. West Front of the Capitol — The east and west elevations of the Capitol building are formally referred to as "fronts", though only the east front was intended for the reception of visitors and dignitaries. 国会大厦西侧［从安德鲁·杰克逊（Andrew Jackson）至吉米·卡特（Jimmy Carter）总统，就职典礼主要在国会大厦的东门廊（East Portico）举行。自1981年罗纳德·里根（Ronald Reagan）总统举行就职典礼以来，仪式改在国会大厦的西侧举行。］

11. a Senate trial for provoking his supporters — on January 13, 2021, one week before his term expired, Donald Trump was impeached（弹劾）for the second time. Trump was alleged to have incited the January 6 attack of the U.S. Capitol, during which a mob of his supporters attempted to overturn his defeat in the 2020 presidential election by disrupting the joint session of Congress assembled to count electoral votes to formalize President-elect Joe Biden's victory. Five people died and more than 140 people were injured in the riot. The trial in the Senate started on February 9 and Trump was finally acquitted（宣告无罪）of the charges.

12. Inaugural Address — a speech given during the inauguration which informs the people of their intentions as a leader. Most U. S. Presidents use their Inaugural address to present their vision of America and to set forth their goals for the nation. 就职演说

13. Mr. Trump's refusal to concede — Usually, the loser of presidential elections concede victory to the winner by delivering a "concession speech" after the vote results are clear, when they publicly acknowledge that they've been defeated. However, Trump claimed electoral fraud and attempted to overturn the results.

14. pits red against blue — to test the strength of both parties in their fight against each other. (In the U. S., the two major political parties use the national colors as their symbols, i. e. red for Republican Party and blue for Democratic Party.)

15. National Guard troops — The U. S. National Guard is the primary reserve military force partly maintained by the states but also available for federal use if there is an emergency. 美国国民警卫队，简称联邦国民兵，是美国军队的重要后备力量，是接受联邦军费的有组织民兵部队。国民警卫队是美国武装力量整体的重要组成部分，也是隶属于各州政府的地方武装部队。

16. National Mall — a landscaped park in the middle of Washing D. C., stretching from the foot of the Capitol to the Potomac River. It is the premiere civic and symbolic space in the nation, often taken as the primary location for political demonstration, rallies, parades, and festivals. (美国)国家广场

17. Statuary Hall — The National Statuary Hall is a chamber in the U. S. Capitol devoted to sculptures of prominent Americans. The meeting place of the U. S. House of Representatives for nearly 50 years (1807—1857), the hall is also known as the Old Hall of the House. 国家雕塑厅；国会大厦雕像厅

18. Pennsylvania Avenue — a diagonal street in Washington D. C. that connects the White House and the Capitol and then crosses the city to Maryland. The section between the White House and Congress is called "America's Main Street." It is the location of official parades and processions, as well as protest marches. 宾夕法尼亚大道，亦称"美国大街"，是官方游行和民间抗议的地点，在美国政治文化中起着重要的作用。

19. reviewed military units — made an official inspection of a group of soldiers in a military show 阅兵
20. Mike Pence — Michael Richard Pence(1954—), the 48th vice president of the U. S. from 2017 to 2021. As a Republican, he served as the 50th governor of Indiana from 2013 to 2017. Despite Trump's urging to overturn the election results, Pence certified the Biden-Harris ticket as the winner of the election. (美国前任副总统)麦克·彭斯
21. Air Force One —the aircraft used to transport the U. S. president (美国现任总统乘坐的专机都被称为"空军一号",原为任何接载美国总统的空军飞机的航空无线电台呼号。)
22. administration — (in American English) the (period of) government, esp. of a particular president or ruling party 此词指"某一位总统或领袖领导下的政府",含有"临时"之意。此处的"the new administration"即新当选总统拜登领导的新一届政府。在本文第19段中还有"the last administration"指上一届特朗普领导的政府。还经常在此词前面加上总统的名字,例如现在的"the Biden Administration"。而"government"指国家的管理机构或体制(the governing body of a state or the system by which a state is governed),无论谁当政。本文第20段中的"the federal government"即指美国政府,不强调哪一届。
23. laying on of hands — (in Christian ordination, confirmation, faith healing, etc) the act of laying hands on a person's head to confer a spiritual blessing (基督教委任圣职礼、坚信礼或信心治疗时)按头礼
24. the world's most exclusive club — the world's most selective and privileged group, here refers to the group of American Presidents.
25. Barack Obama, George W. Bush and Bill Clinton — respectively served as the 44th (2009—2017), the 43rd (2001—2009) and the 42nd (1993—2001) president of the U. S. And Jimmy Carter served as the 39th president of the U. S. from 1977 to 1981.
26. Tomb of the Unknowns at Arlington National Cemetery — a monument dedicated to deceased U. S. service members whose remains have not been identified, located in Arlington National Cemetery in Virginia, across the Potomac River from Washington, D. C. 阿灵顿国家公墓无名战士纪念碑
27. Inauguration Day — The presidential inaugurations have happened

on Jan. 20 of the year following the November general election since 1937, when President Franklin Roosevelt took his second oath. (Before that time, inaugurations were celebrated on March 4.) If January 20 falls on a Sunday, celebrations are held on January 21.

28. Arctic National Wildlife Refuge — a national wildlife refuge in northeastern Alaska of the U.S. It is the largest national wildlife refuge in the country. The Trump administration approved leases in the pristine wilderness for oil and gas drilling program, but no major oil companies had bid for rights under the pressure from environmental advocates. President Biden suspended oil leases to block the drilling plans, fulfilling his promise to protect the refuge. 北极国家野生动物保护区

29. her tiebreaking vote as the chamber's president — The U.S. Constitution establishes the Vice President as president of the Senate, with the authority to cast a tie-breaking vote. The word "chamber" here is a replacement of "Senate".

A tie is a situation in a game or competition when two or more players have the same score. "To break the tie" means "to stop this situation." 美国副总统也以参议院议长的身份参与联邦立法机关的运作。大多数情况下副总统不会在参议院中投票，只在出现票数持平，需要打破僵局时才可以投下关键一票。

30. white supremacy — the belief that white people are superior to those of other races and thus should dominate them. The belief favors the maintenance and defense of white power and privilege. 白人至上主义

31. working across the aisle —在美国政治中，"跨过道"指不同党派（民主党和共和党）之间虽然存在意识形态分歧，但是在很多问题上可以达成一致，使国会立法获得通过。因此，"across the aisle"有"妥协"之意。

32. Mitch McConnell —（1942— ）an American Republican who has served since 1985 as a U.S. senator from Kentucky, and as Senate Minority Leader since 2021. He previously served as Senate Majority Leader from 2015 to 2021, and as Minority Leader from 2007 to 2015. 美国参议院政党领袖包括参议院多数党领袖与少数党领袖两人，由分属两党的参议员出任。他们分别承担两党在参议院的主要发言人职责，管理、组织参议院的立法与行政事务。少数党因为是在野党，往往会充当反对党的角色。

33. Ronald Reagan — (1911 — 2004) the 40th president of the U. S. from 1981 to 1989 and a highly influential voice of modern conservatism. Prior to his presidency, he was a Hollywood movie actor and union leader before serving as the 33rd governor of California from 1967 to 1975. He was 78 when he left office in 1989. 罗纳德·里根（文中说拜登就职的第一天比里根任总统的最后一天年龄还大。）
34. Gallup — Gallup, Inc. is an American analytics and advisory company based in Washington, D. C. Founded by George Gallup in 1935, the company is known for its public opinion polls conducted worldwide. In the U. S., presidential job approval ratings by Gallup is generally accepted by statisticians to gauge（判定）public support for the president of the United States during their term. 盖洛普咨询公司，以预测总统候选人及统计在任总统支持率的盖洛普民意调查而著称。
35. John F. Kennedy — (1917 — 1963) often referred to by his initials JFK, was the 35th president of the U. S. from 1961 until his assassination near the end of his third year in office. Kennedy ranks highly in polls of U. S. presidents with historians and the general public. He was the first Catholic elected president. 约翰·肯尼迪，
36. Lady Gaga, Jennifer Lopez and Garth Brooks — Lady Gaga（歌手、词曲作者、演员），詹妮弗·洛佩兹（歌手、演员、制片人）和加斯·布鲁克斯（乡村歌手）
37. livestreamed — broadcast on the internet while it is happening 对……进行网络直播
    stream — to play video or audio file on a computer while receiving it as a continuous stream, from the Internet for example, rather than having to wait until the whole of the material has been downloaded 用流式传输，流播（无须待整个文件下载到计算机便可播放互联网上的视频或音频文件）
38. Tom Hanks — (1956—) an American actor and filmmaker. Known for both his comedic and dramatic roles, he is one of the most popular and recognizable film stars worldwide. He won two consecutive Academy Awards for Best Actor for starring as a gay lawyer suffering from AIDS in *Philadelphia* (1993) and the title character in *Forrest Gump*（《阿甘正传》，1994）. Hanks has also

won 7 Primetime Emmy Awards（艾美奖）for his work as a producer of various limited series and television movies.
39. Kerry Washington, Bruce Springsteen, Eva Longoria, Lin-Manuel MiRanda And Demi Lovato —— 凯莉·华盛顿（演员）,布鲁斯·斯普林斯汀（摇滚歌手、词曲作家）,伊娃·朗格利亚（演员）,林曼努埃尔·米兰达（演员、作曲家、制作人）和黛米·洛瓦托（歌手、演员）

Questions

1. According to the report, under what circumstances did President Biden take office?
2. Did Mr. Trump attend Mr. Biden's inauguration?
3. What is the theme of President Biden's Inaugural Address?
4. Is the transition of presidency this time the same as the previous ones?
5. Why does the author say "Mr. Biden could hardly be more of a contrast to the president he succeeded"?
6. In what way have Mr. Biden and Ms. Harris brought new diversity to the top echelon of government?

读报知识

美国总统选举

总统选举（presidential election）也称大选（general elections）。美国宪法规定,参选总统必须是年满35岁、在美国出生的公民。选举在每隔四年的11月的第一个星期一后的星期二举行。候选人获胜后称为当选总统（President-elect）,在上届总统届满之年的1月20日午时宣誓就职。一届任期四年,因任期限制（term limits）,一任不得超过两届。

在大选的日子,愿意投票的合格选民把选票投给自己中意的总统候选人,这一选举方式被称为普选（popular election）,他们所投的票称为普选票或民选票（popular vote）。众所周知,美国大选是全民投票进行普选,但宪法规定,总统必须经各州选出的总统选举人（presidential electors）选举产生。这就是说,总统选举实际上实行间接选举,即所谓的"选举团"（Electoral College）制度。因为选举团成员是选民选出的,所以也具有直选的内涵。

选举团诞生于1787年美国宪法会议期间。宪法制定者们原本打算挑选出一群具有远见卓识的人组成选举团，聚到一起代表全体公民来选总统。但实际上，由于全国性的党派很快就控制了选举，选举团的代表只不过是名义上的，实际上代表的是选举他们当代表的那个党在该州的势力，他们投谁的票，是事先就定下来的。尽管与别国相比有些怪，美国还是保留了选举团制度。

选民在大选日投票中选出的是"选举人"[(presidential) electors]，而不是总统和副总统。选举结束后，哪个总统候选人在某一州得到的普选票最多，他就会得到该州的全部选举人票(electoral vote)，即这位总统候选人有权指定选举人代表该州参加选举总统的投票。这种"胜者全得"或"赢者通吃"(winner-take-all)的制度只有缅因州和内布拉斯加州例外。在这两个州，只有两张选举人票是通过全州普选产生，而其余（九分之五）的选举人票则是看州内各国会议员选区的选民投票结果分配的，哪个候选人在某区的选举获胜，他就将获得该选区的选举人票，而不是将全州的选票投给一个党的候选人。各州在国会里有多少国会议员，就有多少个选举人。尽管每个州的国会参议员的数量是相同的，都是两个，但众议员的数量则取决于各州在十年一度的人口普查中的人口数量，人口多的州在选举团中就有较多的代表。例如在 2020 年的大选时，加州有 55 个选举人，纽约州和得克萨斯州分别有 29 个和 38 个。在 50 个州中，阿拉斯加和特拉华等州，每州只有 3 个。因此，加州、纽约州和得州是总统候选人称为"必须取胜的州"(must-win states)。

各州的选举人于 12 月中旬在各州首府进行选举总统和副总统的投票，但最后的选举结果要到第二年 1 月初由国会正式公布。全美 50 个州加上哥伦比亚特区共有 538 张选举人票，当选总统者必须赢得半数以上即至少 270 张以上的选举人票。在 12 月选举人投票时，如果所有的总统候选人都未能获得过半数的选举人票，总统将由国会众议院选出。

正是由于选举团的存在，就可能导致某位候选人在普选中获胜，却把即将得到的总统宝座拱手让给对手的咄咄怪事。2000 年小布什最终赢得了佛罗里达州的 25 张选举人票，上面的悲剧就应验在民主党总统候选人 Al Gore 的身上。这种情况在美国早先已经发生过两次，分别是 1876 年与 1888 年。

General Election 的单复数视情况而定，如只指总统选举，单数即可。如包括国会和地方政府和议会等选举在内就用复数。所以报刊上有时用单数有时用复数就是这个道理。英国大选只指国会选举，所以只能用单数。

Lesson 5

课文导读

自 1620 年一群英国清教徒乘坐"五月花号"横穿大西洋来到马萨诸塞南部的科德角,希望建立一个自由、平等、没有宗教迫害的"天堂"起,"美国梦"已开始悄然萌芽:机会均等,自由民主,只要通过勤奋、坚忍、勇气和决心就能实现梦想,迈向繁荣。这些均在"五月花协议"中有所体现。随着时代的变化,而今的美国梦也在不断拓展,产生了新的诠释。发财致富,拥有不动产是否还是美国人一成不变的梦想?金融动荡,政治僵局是否熄灭了美国民众对美国梦的信心和热情?这个曾经自诩为自由、平等,努力奋斗就能收获幸福成功的美国梦正面临新一轮的种种困惑、误解及挑战。

Pre-reading Questions

1. What do you often associate the U. S. A with?
2. Do you think the American dream achievable?

Text

Five Myths About the American Dream
By Michael F. Ford

1. The American dream is about getting rich.

1   In a national survey of more than 1,300 adults that we completed in March, only 6 percent of Americans ranked "wealth" as their first or second definition of the American dream. 45 percent named "a good life for my family," while 34 percent put "financial security" — material comfort that is not necessarily synonymous with Bill Gates[1]-like riches — on top.

2   While money may certainly be part of a good life, the American dream isn't just about dollars and cents. 32 percent of our respondents

pointed to "freedom" as their dream; 29 percent to "opportunity"; and 21 percent to the "pursuit of happiness. " A fat bank account can be a means to these ends, but only a small minority believe that money is a worthy end in itself.

2. Homeownership is the American dream.

3   In June, a New York Times[2]-CBS News[3] poll found that almost 90 percent of Americans think that homeownership is an important part of the American dream. But only 7 percent of Americans we surveyed ranked homeownership as their first or second definition of the American dream. Why the discrepancy? Owning real estate is important to some Americans, but not as important — or as financially rewarding — as we're led to believe.

4   Federal support of homeownership greatly overvalues its meaning in American life. Through tax breaks[4] and guarantees, the government boosted homeownership to its peak in 2004, when 69 percent of American households owned homes. Subsidies for homeownership, including the mortgage interest deduction, reached $ 230 billion in 2009, according to the Congressional Budget Office[5]. Meanwhile, only $ 60 billion in taxbreaks and spending programs aided renters.

5   The result of this real estate spending spree? According to the Federal Reserve[6], American real estate lost more than $ 6 trillion in value, or almost 30 percent, between 2006 and 2010. One in five American homeowners is underwater, owing more on a mortgage than what the home is worth[7].

6   Those who profit most from homeownership are far and away the largest source of political campaign contributions[8]. Insurance companies, securities and investment firms, real estate interests, and commercial banks gave more than $ 100 million to federal candidates and parties in 2011, according to the Center for Responsive Politics[9]. The National Association of Realtors[10] alone gave more than $ 950,000 — more than Morgan Stanley[11], Citigroup[12] or Ernst & Young[13].

7   Homeownership is more important to special interests than it is to most Americans, who, according to our research, care more about "a good job," "the pursuit of happiness" and "freedom. "

3. The American dream is American.

8   The term "American dream" was coined in 1931 by James Truslow Adams[14] in his history "The Epic of America." In the midst of the Great Depression[15], Adams discovered the same counterintuitive optimism that we observe in today's Great Recession[16], and he dubbed it "the American dream" — "that dream of a land in which life should be better and richer and fuller for every man, with opportunity for each according to his ability or achievement."

9   However, the American dream pre-dated 1931. Starting in the 16th century, Western European settlers came to this land at great risk to build a better life. Today, this dream is sustained by immigrants from different parts of the world who still come here seeking to do the same thing.

10   Perceptions of the dream today are often more positive among those who are new to America. When asked to rate the condition of the American dream on a scale of one to 10, where 10 means the best possible condition and one means the worst, 42 percent of immigrants responded between six and 10. Only 31 percent of the general population answered in that range.

4. China threatens the American dream.

11   Our surveys revealed that 57 percent of Americans believe that "the world now looks to many different countries," not just ours, to "represent the future." When we asked participants which region or country is charting that future, more than half chose China. Nearly two-thirds of those surveyed mistakenly believe that the Chinese economy is already larger than the U.S. economy — it is actually one-third the size, with a population four times larger. China does own more than $1.1 trillion of U.S. debt, however; it is our largest creditor.

12   But the problem isn't just one nation. Japan holds almost $1 trillion of U.S. debt. Britain owns more than $400 billion. In 1970, less than 5 percent of U.S. debt was held by non-citizens. Today, almost half is. Neither China nor these other countries can be blamed for U.S. choices that have placed our financial future increasingly out of our hands.

13   Still, no matter how much we owe, the United States remains the world's land of opportunity. In fact, the largest international group coming to America to study is from China — 157,000 students in the 2010—2011 academic year. As recently reported in *The Washington Post*, the number of Chinese undergraduates at U.S. colleges increased 43 percent over the previous year.

5. Economic decline and political gridlock are killing the American dream.

14   Our research showed a stunning lack of confidence in U.S. institutions. 65 percent of those surveyed believe that America is in decline; 83 percent said they have less trust in "politics in general" than they did 10 or 15 years ago; 79 percent said they have less trust in big business and major corporations; 78 percent said they have less trust in government; 72 percent reported declining trust in the media. These recent figures are more startling when contrasted against Gallup polling from the 1970s, when as many as 70 percent of Americans had "trust and confidence" that the government could handle domestic problems.

15   Even so, 63 percent of Americans said they are confident that they will attain their American dream, regardless of what the nation's institutions do or don't do. While they may be worried about future generations, their dream today stands defiantly against the odds. (From *The Washington Post*, Jan 6, 2012)

New Words

chart /tʃɑːt/ *v.* to make a plan of what should be done to achieve a particular result 描绘

counterintuitive /ˌkaʊntərɪnˈtjuːɪtɪv/ *adj.* contrary to what intuition or common sense would indicate 违反直觉的

defiant /dɪˈfaɪənt/ *adj.* clearly refusing to do what someone tells you to do 挑战的 defiantly *adv.*

discrepancy /dɪsˈkrepənsi/ *n.* a difference between two amounts, details, reports etc. that should be the same 矛盾，差异

dub /dʌb/ *v.* to give sth or sb a name that describes them in some way 授予称号

gridlock /ˈɡrɪdlɒk/ *n.* a situation in which nothing can happen, usu.

because people disagree strongly 僵局

mortgage /'mɔːgɪdʒ/ *n.* a legal arrangement by which you borrow money from a bank or other financial organization in order to buy a house, and pay back the money over a period of years 抵押借款, 按揭

myth /mɪθ/ *n.* an idea or story that many people believe, but which is not true 传说, 神话

respondent /rɪ'spɒndənt/ *n.* someone who answers questions, esp. in a survey 回应者

spree /spriː/ *n.* a short period of time when you do a lot of one activity, esp. spending money or drinking alcohol 无节制的狂热行为

stunning /'stʌnɪŋ/ *adj.* very surprising or shocking 使人震惊的

subsidy /'sʌbsədɪ/ *n.* money that is paid by a government or organization to make prices lower, reduce the cost of producing goods etc. 补贴, 津贴

synonymous /sɪ'nɒnɪməs/ *adj.* a situation, quality, idea etc. that is synonymous with sth else is the same or nearly the same as another 同义的

underwater /ˌʌndə'wɔːtə(r)/ *adj.* (of a stock option or other asset) having a market value below its purchase value 价值缩水的, 资不抵债的

Notes

1. Bill Gates — (1955—) born in Seattle, former chief executive (CEO) and current chairman(董事长, 董事会主席)of Microsoft, the world's largest personal-computer software company, which he co-founded with Paul Allen. Gates is not only one of the best-known entrepreneurs of the PC revolution, in the later stages of his career, he also has pursued a number of philanthropic (慈善的)endeavors, donating large amounts of money to various charitable organizations and scientific research programs through the Bill & Melinda Gates Foundation(比尔及梅琳达·盖茨基金会).

2. *The New York Times* — a serious daily newspaper which is based in New York City. It is sold elsewhere in the US and in many other countries, and people in the US often just call it *"the Times"* 《纽约时报》

3. CBS News — the news tycoon corporation of American television and radio network CBS(Columbia Broadcasting System). CBS News' flagship program is the *CBS Evening News*(CBS 晚间新闻). Other

programs include a morning news show called, *CBS This Morning* (CBS 今晨), news magazine programs *CBS News Sunday Morning* (CBS 周日早间), *60 Minutes* (CBS 每周日晚 8 点一小时的专题报道栏目), *48 Hours* (CBS 电视台的犯罪纪实系列节目), and Sunday morning political affairs program *Face the Nation*. 美国哥伦比亚广播公司新闻频道

4. tax breaks — a special reduction in taxes（减税优惠,税额优惠）
5. Congressional Budget Office (CBO) — a federal agency within the legislative branch of the U. S. government that provides economic data to Congress. The CBO was created as a nonpartisan agency by the Congressional Budget and Impoundment Control Act of 1974, which was signed into law by President Richard Nixon on July 12, 1974. Official operations began on February 24, 1975. 国会预算局
6. The Federal Reserve — (＝The Federal Reserve System) the central banking system of the United States. It was created on December 23, 1913, largely in response to a series of financial panics, particularly a severe panic in 1907. 美国联邦储备系统
7. One in five American homeowners is underwater, owing more on a mortgage than what the home is worth. — One in five American homeowners is faced with assets shrinking, to such an extent that the mortgage loan they have to repay exceeds the real value of their property. 每 5 名美国房主就有一人资不抵债,也就是说他们要偿还的贷款超过他们住房本身的价值。

　　underwater — having a market value below its purchase value（美国房地产泡沫产生了一大批溺水房,即房屋所欠抵押贷款价值高于房屋价值,溺水房房主拥有的是负资产。这样的房子就像是沉在水底,等房价回升到贷款金额以上的价值时才算是浮出水面。于是很多房主就选择了放弃还贷,结果贷款银行收走房屋,房主失去住所。）
8. Those who profit most from homeownership are far and away the largest source of political campaign contributions. — Those organizations who have got the most interest from real estate mortgage donate the largest part of money for political election campaign. 获利最大的抵押贷款银行为政治竞选捐款最多。

　　far and away — by a great deal or amount; very much
9. the Center for Responsive Politics — a non-profit, nonpartisan research group based in Washington, D. C. that tracks the effects of money and

lobbying on elections and public policy. It maintains a public online database of its information. Their database OpenSecrets.org allows users to track federal campaign contributions and lobbying. 政治反应中心

10. The National Association of Realtors (NAR) — Headquartered in Chicago, whose members are known as Realtors. NAR is the largest trade association and one of the most powerful lobbying groups in North America with over 1.2 million members including NAR's institutes, societies, and councils, involved in all aspects of the residential and commercial real estate industries. NAR also functions as a self-regulatory organization for real estate brokerage. 美国房地产经纪人协会

11. Morgan Stanley — an American multinational financial services corporation headquartered in the Morgan Stanley Building, New York City. Morgan Stanley operates in 42 countries, and has more than 1300 offices and 60,000 employees. The main areas of business for the firm today are Global Wealth Management, Institutional Securities, and Investment Management. (摩根·士丹利投资公司)

12. Citigroup(or Citi) — an American multinational financial services corporation headquartered in Manhattan, New York City. Citigroup was formed from one of the world's largest mergers in history by combining the banking giant Citicorp and financial conglomerate(大型联合企业) Travelers Group in October 1998. It is currently the third largest bank holding company in the U.S. by assets. Citigroup has the world's largest financial services network, spanning 140 countries with approximately 16,000 offices worldwide. 花旗集团

13. Ernst & Young — one of the largest professional service firms in the world and one of the "Big Four" accounting firms, along with Deloitte, KPMG and PricewaterhouseCoopers (PwC). Ernst & Young is a global organization of member firms with 167,000 employees in more than 140 countries, headquartered in London, England. It was ranked by *Forbes* magazine as the eighth-largest private company in the U.S. in 2011. 安永会计师事务所

14. James Truslow Adams — (1878—1949), an American writer and historian, also the editor of a scholarly multi-volume *Dictionary of American History*. His *Epic of America* (《美国史诗》) was an

international bestseller.
15. Great Depression — It refers to the severe economic problems that followed the Wall Street Crash of 1929. In the early 1930s, many banks and businesses failed, and millions of people lost their jobs in the U.S. and in the UK and the rest of Europe. 大萧条时期
16. Great Recession — It refers to a major global recession characterized by various systemic imbalances and was sparked by the outbreak of the U.S. subprime mortgage(次级房贷)crisis and financial crisis of 2007—2008. 经济大衰退

Questions

1. What is the core of American dream?
2. Is the American dream American?
3. Do you believe that American dream reflects human nature and could be shared by other peoples?
4. Why isn't homeownership ranked first or second by most people in the American dream?
5. Do you think China is a threat to the American dream?
6. How do economic decline and political gridlock influence the American dream?

学习方法

读懂标题(Ⅰ)

报刊标题(Headline)常用的有主题、副题、插题、引题、提要题等几种形式,不过现在趋向于只采用主标题。一般说来,英美报刊标题,突出"点",一语中的;中文报刊标题照顾"面",面面俱到。两者各有千秋,区别较大。标题是新闻也是报刊的"眼睛"。应该生动、炯炯有神、引人入胜;反之,索然无味,无人愿看。它是新闻内容的高度概括,犹如提纲挈领,画龙点睛。

标题读不懂,就看副标题或提要。有一篇文章的标题是"The Greening of America"(1996/2/12 *U.S. News & World Report*)。乍一看,greening 费解,再读 subheadline 是"This year, candidates will spend more money than ever buying your votes"。这样就明白了,"greening"此处指"dollar or money"。这两个标题对了解下面课文内容起到了纲举目张的作用。读懂标题须掌握其主要特点;了解背景知识;具有文学功底。

一、标题特点

1. 缩略词

标题要简短而不得不使用缩略词(Abbreviations and Acronyms),汉语标题也有此特点。

(1) 机构。报刊中常用政治、军事、经济、文化、教育等重要机构的简称,如:
   a. **EU'S** Future: The Vision and the Slog
      EU = European Union(欧洲联盟)
   b. World Bank, **IMF**—Do They Help Or Hurt Third World
      IMF = International Monetary Fund
   c. **MIT**'s Leader Shape Program
      MIT = Massachusetts Institute of Technology(麻省理工学院)

为了快速读懂新闻标题,有必要熟悉一些重要国际组织(important international organizations)名称缩写如 G20,ASEAN(东盟)等。

(2) 除机构的首字母缩略词外,标题也常用其他形式的缩短词(shortened word),如:
   a. No Hope for 118 Crew of Russian **Sub**
      Sub = submarine
   b. University Entry Hard for Would-be **Vets**
      Vet = Veteran(退伍老兵)
   c. Put the **Sci** Back in **Sci-fi**
      sci = science; fi = fiction 必须注意,缩短词的拼法是固定的,不能随意乱造。

2. 短字

标题爱用常见的短字(short word),是报刊用语的一个特点。如:
   a. The **Gems** of War
      用"gems"不用"jewels"
   b. Dayton **Accord**, Reached
      用"accord"不用"agreements"
   c. Carter Man in China
      用"man"不用"representative"

读者一定见过这些词汇,但用在标题上,或许不一定知道其中如 man 和 accord 的意思。编者建议,初学者应该读记 Terry Fredrickson & Paul Wedel 合写的 *English by Newspaper* 和 Janice Abbott 写的 *Meet the Press* 这两本书里的 The Vocabulary of Headlines(报刊标题词汇一览)里的标题词汇,这对看懂标题和正文大有裨益。(详见《导读》四章一节)

Lesson 6

课文导读

　　这是一篇在若干调研报告基础上撰写的专题报道。2007—2008年的次贷危机引发了2008年10月的美国金融危机和全球危机及经济衰退或危机，对美国的经济造成了严重影响，就业机会减少，税收收入锐减，预算计划和项目不得不进行削减，教育预算当然也不能幸免。这样，政府给学生提供的资助和贷款势必减少。与此同时，学生面临两个问题：一是学费上涨，要想完成学业，中低收入家庭的学生不得不举债或兼职工作。二是莘莘学子在完成了学业，获得了学位后，能否苦尽甘来，找到工作，而该工作的薪酬是否与文凭相符，使他们能逐渐偿还助学贷款，开始自己职业生涯的春天？读完本文，便可见一斑。

　　现在我国的大学毕业生也面临着在大城市找工作的难题，只要拓展视野，到真正缺人才的西部和广大农村去，他们不是找不到用武之地，而是人才远远供不应求！这是与美国学生处境的不同之处。

Pre-reading Questions

1. Do you think college education can ensure one a bright future? Why or why not?
2. What are the factors that influence one's decision about choosing majors in college?

Text

Debt Burden Alters Outlook for US Graduates

By Shannon Bond and Jason Abbruzzese in New York and Robin Harding in Washington

1　　At universities across the US, the class of 2012[1] is celebrating the end of college. But, for the estimated 1.8m students receiving bachelor's degrees this spring, the financial crisis[2] that unfolded during their first year on campus in 2008 is still casting a long shadow over their futures.

2 Almost five years after the crisis began, the overall unemployment rate is still mired above 8 per cent while that for recent university graduates is stuck at 6.8 per cent.

3 For many young Americans, the promise of a degree has turned to disappointment as they find themselves struggling to find their first job, still burdened by student debt.

4 What is worse, studies show that graduating at a time of high unemployment can blight a young person's earning power for the rest of their career — and have an impact on the broader economy as well.

5 In a widely-cited paper, Lisa Kahn[3] of the Yale School of Management[4] looked at data from the early 1980s recession[5], and found a one-percentage-point increase in the unemployment rate for college graduates led to a 6—7 per cent drop in initial wages[6]. Even 15 years later, their wage loss was a statistically significant 2.5 per cent.

6 Seventeen-year-old Chelsea Katz, who plans to attend the University of Maryland[7] in the autumn, said she took into account the economy and possible debt when picking a school and choosing her degree.

7 "For a long time I have wanted to study business but definitely a major factor in that is the more promising outlook for a business major coming out of college," Ms. Katz said. "The idea of post-college debt definitely scares me but I try and focus on the present, not the future, while keeping in mind coming out of college with the minimum amount of debt possible."

8 A survey from Rutgers University[8] found two-thirds of graduates who finished college between 2006 and 2011 would have made different choices, such as majoring in another field, taking on more internships or part-time jobs, started looking for work sooner, choosing a different institution or even skipped higher education altogether.

9 "There's a lot of 'I wish I had known' thinking we see from the students encountering the harsh realities of the labour market," [9] said Carl Van Horn, director of Rutgers' Heldrich Center for Workforce Development[10], which conducted the study.

10 Half of the students surveyed were working full-time, with another 12 per cent working part-time and 20 per cent pursuing graduate or professional

degrees[11].

11   About a quarter of the employed graduates said their position was below their level of education, a quarter said they were earning less than they expected, and a quarter said they had to accept a job outside their field in order to find work.

12   The median starting salary for those who finished school between 2009 and 2011 fell to ＄27,000 from ＄30,000 in 2006 and 2007.

13   These conditions are squeezing young people's ability to repay the student loans that have become a standard part of higher education as soaring tuition fees outpace income growth[12].

14   In the past decade, published prices for tuition fees have risen 29 per cent at private schools and 72 per cent at public institutions, according to the College Board[13]. The public universities, once seen as a ticket to higher earnings for middle and low-income students, have been hard hit by deep cuts to state budgets that have transferred more of the cost burden on to students and their families[14].

15   "We as a nation have been disinvesting in postsecondary education," said Mark Kantrowitz, publisher of FinAid. org [15], a website on financial aid. "When grants don't keep pace with college costs, you have three main outcomes: students graduate with thousands of dollars of additional debt, students shift to lower cost schools, such as community colleges[16], which have a negative impact on graduation rates, or they just don't go to college."

16   As expenses have gone up and grants have gone down, students are left with one choice: borrowing more.

17   Two-thirds of students who graduated with a bachelor's degree in 2008 took on debt to finance their education, according to the Pew Research Center[17], compared with 59 per cent in 1996. The average amount of debt rose to ＄23,287 from ＄17,075 in the same period.

18   The US Senate[18] is wrangling over how to extend a modest subsidy for student loans that is due to expire at the end of June but, in a sign of growing political sensitivity over student debt, both Barack Obama[19] and his Republican challenger Mitt Romney[20] are calling for action.

19   In an address to graduates of New York's Barnard College[21] in May, Mr. Obama, a 1983 graduate, struck a sombre note[22]: "Just as you were starting out finding your way around this campus, an economic crisis struck that would claim more than 5m jobs before the

end of your freshman year... And you may be looking toward the future with that same sense of concern that my generation did when we were sitting where you are now."[23] (From *Financial Times*, June 1, 2012)

New Words

alter /'ɔːltə(r)/ v. to make or become different, but without changing into sth else

blight /blaɪt/ v. to have a deleterious effect on; ruin. 使产生恶果，毁坏

cast /kɑːst/ v. to turn or direct

disinvest /ˌdɪsɪn'vest/ v. take one's money out of a place or business in which one invested in 减资，投资缩减

expire /ɪk'spaɪə(r)/ v. (of sth which lasts for a period of time) to come to an end; run out

harsh /hɑːʃ/ adj. unpleasant or painful; severe

intern /'ɪntɜːn/ n. a person who has nearly finished professional training, esp. in medicine or teaching, and is gaining controlled practical experience, esp. in a hospital or classroom 实习医师；实习教师；实习生

median /'miːdiən/ adj. in or passing through the middle

mire /'maɪə(r)/ v. to cause (a person) to be caught up in difficulties 使……陷入困境

outlook /'aʊtlʊk/ n. future, probabilities

outpace /ˌaʊt'peɪs/ v. to perform a particular action faster or better than they can

promise /'prɒmɪs/ n. expectation or signs of future success, good results, etc.

promising /'prɒmɪsɪŋ/ adj. showing signs of likely future success; full of promise 有希望的，有前途的

recession /rɪ'seʃn/ n. a period of reduced trade and business activity

repay /rɪ'peɪ/ v. to return (what is owed) to (sb.); pay back 偿还，报答

scare /skeə(r)/ v. to cause sudden fear to; frighten

sensitivity /ˌsensə'tɪvəti/ n. the condition or quality of being strongly or easily influenced or changed by sth. 敏感

skip /skɪp/ v. to pass over or leave out; not do or deal with the next thing; fail to attend or take part in (an activity); intentionally miss 跳过，略过；故意错过

soar /sɔː(r)/ v. to rise rapidly or to a very high level

sombre /'sɒmbə(r)/ adj. sadly serious, grave, dark

squeeze /skwiːz/ *v.* to cause money difficulties to, esp. by means of tight controls or severe demands 给……造成财务困难

stuck /stʌk/ *adj.* fixed in a position; impossible to move

unfold /ʌnˈfəʊld/ *v.* to (cause to) become clear, more fully known, etc.

wrangle /ˈræŋɡl/ *v.* to argue, esp. angrily, noisily, and over a long period 争吵，争论

Notes

1. the class of 2012 — 美国指 2012 届毕业班，非 2012 级，而我国指的是 2012 年入学的新生。

2. the financial crisis — also known as the 2008 financial crisis. It is considered to be the worst financial crisis since the Great Depression of the 1930s, and resulted in the failure of key businesses, declines in consumer wealth, and a downturn in economic activity leading to the 2008—2012 global recession(世界经济衰退) and contributing to the European sovereign-debt crisis(欧洲主权债务危机). The financial crisis was triggered by the subprime crisis(次贷危机) which was caused by a complex interplay(相互作用或影响) of policies adopted by American government to encourage people to buy houses and provide easier access to loans for subprime borrowers(次级借款人). 金融危机由次贷危机(2007—2008)引起。见《导读》"经济用语"之详解。

3. Lisa Kahn — a labor economist with interests in organizations and education. From 2010 to 2011 she served on President Obama's Council of Economic Advisers(经济顾问委员会) as the senior economist for labor and education policy. She has examined the consequences of graduating from college in a bad economy, finding surprisingly long-lasting, negative wage effects.

4. the Yale School of Management — the graduate business school of Yale University 耶鲁管理学院

5. the 1980s recession — A recession in the United States from 1980 to 1982. The US entered a recession in January 1980 and returned to growth six months later. Although recovery took hold, the unemployment rate remained unchanged through the start of a second recession in July 1981. The downturn ended in November 1982. The principal cause of the 1980 recession included contractionary

monetary policy(紧缩货币政策) adopted by the Federal Reserve(美国联邦储备委员会) to combat double digit inflation and residual effects of the energy crisis(即 oil crisis。因阿拉伯国家和以色列打的"十月战争"而使中东国家对美国和其他西方国家进行石油禁运[Arab oil boycott]所致），and the second downturn was caused by the fact that manufacturing and construction failed to recover before more aggressive inflation reducing policy was adopted by the Federal Reserve in 1981.

6. a one-percentage-point increase…a 6—7 per cent drop in initial wages — the graduates' wages from their first job decreased by 6—7% once the unemployment rate increased by one percentage. 大学毕业生的失业率每增加一个百分点,他们的起薪就会减少 6—7%。

7. University of Maryland — a public(公立的) research university, located in the city of College Park in Prince George's County, Maryland. founded in 1856，the flagship institution(顶尖大学) of the University System of Maryland and the largest university in the state and in the Washington Metropolitan Area.

8. Rutgers University — a State(州立) University in of New Jersey, an American public research university and the largest institution for higher education in New Jersey. 罗格斯大学

9. There's a lot of 'I wish I had known' thinking the labour market. — From the students who are faced with severe realities of labour market，we find many of them feel regretful for their previous choice, and wish they would have made a different decision. I wish I had known 是虚拟语气。这里是说,美国大学生面对劳动力市场低迷,就业困难的严酷现实,就有了"我早知道就好了"这种想法。意指他们早知道会是现在的情况,他们当初会有不同的选择,可能选择不同的专业,不同的学校,甚至选择不接受高等教育等等。

10. Rutgers' Heldrich Center for Workforce Development — a research and policy organization，founded in 1997，dedicated to applying research to address the core challenges of New Jersey's and the nation's workforce. 罗格斯大学黑尔德里希人力发展中心

11. professional degree — A professional degree is an academic degree that prepares a person to practice a profession in a field like medicine，law，engineering，psychology，science，and others. Most jobs in these fields cannot be practiced without a first professional

degree. It can be awarded as undergraduate or graduate entry degrees. (Bachelors, Masters, or Doctorate). 专业学位，是相对于学术型学位而言的学位类型，培养目标侧重于适应特定行业和职业实际工作需要的人才。

12. These conditions are squeezing … as soaring tuition fees outpace income growth. — These conditions are making young people hard to pay back the student loans that have become very common in higher education because rising tuition fees surpass income growth.

13. the College Board — a not-for-profit membership association in the US, formed in 1900 as the College Entrance Examination Board (大学入学考试委员会), composed of more than 5,900 schools, colleges, universities and other educational organizations. It sells standardized tests used by academically oriented post-secondary education institutions to measure a student's ability.

14. The public universities … their families. — Government has cut the education budget greatly so the students and their families had to pay more. This hit hard the public universities which used to be seen as a guarantee to earn more money for students from middle and low-income families 大幅削减的州预算将更多的费用负担转移到了学生和学生家庭身上，给过去被视为来自中低收入家庭的学生们获得高薪工作的保障的公立大学造成了严重冲击。这里是指中低收入的学生原来青睐于公立大学，而随着学费更多被转嫁在学生身上，他们可能转而选择私立大学或社区大学等。

15. FinAid. org — a website that was established in the fall of 1994 as a public service, and provides a comprehensive source of student financial aid information, advice and tools on or off the web. Access to FinAid is free for all users and there is no charge to link to the site. 一个提供关于学生经济援助信息等全面信息来源的免费公共服务性网站

16. community colleges — sometimes called junior colleges, technical colleges, or city colleges. They are primarily two-year public institutions providing higher education and lower-level tertiary education, granting certificates, diplomas, and associate's degrees. Many also offer continuing and adult education. After graduating from a community college, some students transfer to a four-year liberal arts college or university for two to three years to

complete a bachelor's degree. 社区学院,两年制的专科学校,技术学院

17. the Pew Research Center — an American think tank(智库) organization based in Washington, D.C. that provides information on issues, attitudes and trends shaping the United States and the world. The Center and its projects receive funding from The Pew Charitable Trusts(皮尤慈善信托基金会).

18. US Senate — the upper house of the bicameral legislature(两院制立法机构之上院,虽不同于英国无权之贵族院,亦称之为上院) of the US, and together with the House of Representatives makes up the US Congress 美国参议院

19. Barack Obama — (1961—) the 44th US President(2009—2016), the first African American to hold the office.

20. Mitt Romney — (1947—) an American businessman, served as the 70th Governor of Massachusetts (2003 — 2007). the first Mormon(摩门教徒) to be a major and Republican party presidential nominee, but defeated by incumbent(在职的) Obama.

21. New York's Barnard College — a private women's liberal arts college founded in 1889 and a member of the Seven Sisters(七姐妹学院,此处省去了colleges。美国早期的七所女子文理学院联盟). It has been affiliated with Columbia University since 1900. 巴纳德学院

22. strike a sombre note — to express and communicate a serious and grave opinion

23. Just as you were starting out…when we were sitting where you are now. — Just as you began your college life and started to prepare for your future, an economic crisis attacked the US, which would lead to more than 5 million jobs lost before you finished your first-year study in the college…you may be feeling worried about your future just as my generation did as we were freshmen too when the early 1980's crisis struck. 这里的 economic crisis 就是指美国 2008 年爆发的金融危机而引发的经济危机。(见《导读》"经济用语")奥巴马在 1981 年至 1983 年期间就读于加利福尼亚州洛杉矶的西方学院[Occidental College],当时的美国经济也不景气。

Questions

1. Does the 2008 financial crisis influence the university graduates?
2. What can be learned from the result of Rutgers University's study?
3. Why does Chelsea Katz want to study business?
4. What conditions are squeezing American young people's ability to repay the student loans?
5. Why do American students have to borrow more money to finish their higher education?
6. Why do you think the authors cite Mr. Obama's speech in the last paragraph?

学习方法

读懂标题(Ⅱ)

3. 省略

(1) 标题往往只用实义词,略去虚词。省略最多的是冠词和动词"to be",其次是介词、连词、助动词和代词,有时连实义词甚至主句也省略掉。这是新闻多,节省版面的缘故,但以不影响理解为前提。例如:

a. Italian Ex-Mayor Murdered
   = (An) Italian Ex-mayor (Is) Murdered
b. Rail Chaos Getting Worse
   = (The) Rail Chaos (Is) Getting Worse
c. No Survivors in Gulf Air Crash
   = (There Are) No Survivors in (the) Gulf Air Crash
d. Alaskan Oil for Japan?
   = (Will There Be) Alaskan Oil for Japan?
e. Have Dollars, Will Sell
   = (If You) Have Dollars, (They) Will Sell
f. Ballots, Not Bullets
   = (The Algerians Want) Ballots, (Do) Not (Want) Bullets

(2) 并非所有的冠词都能省略。如:

a. West Point Makes a Comeback
   "西点军校东山再起"。"make a comeback"是成语,"a"不能省。
b. How America Sees the World
   "美国怎样看待世界?" "the World"冠词不能省,如省了,词义不同。

c. Killing in the Name of God

"邪教教主以上帝之名大开杀戒。""of God"作定语修饰"Name",所以这个"the"也不能省。还有因排行需要或从美观原则出发而保留冠词的。

(3) "and"常被逗号所取代。如:

a. Thailand, Malaysia Ink Sea Treaty

= Thailand (and) Malaysia Ink (a) Sea Treaty

b. Woman Kills Husband, Self

= (A) Woman Kills (Her) Husband (and) (Her)self

c. Volunteer, Terrorist Killed in an Ambush

= (A) Volunteer (and) (a) Terrorist (Are) Killed in an Ambush

(4) 动词"to be"有时由冒号取代,如:

a. Chinese Cooks: Masters at Turning a Turnip into a Flower

= Chinese Cooks (Are) Masters at Turning a Turnip into a Flower

b. Kaka: Brazil's Mr. Perfect

= Kaka(Is) Brazil's Mr. Perfect

(5) 动词"say, said"用冒号或引号代替。如:

Mao: We Should Support Third World Countries

= Mao (Says) (That) We Should Support (the) Third World Countries

(6) 以名词作定语组成的标题,既无动词,也无连词。如:

a. Channel Tunnel Halt

([英吉利海峡]隧道工程[暂]停[施]工)

b. Shotgun Death Riddle Drama

(枪杀事件,扑朔迷离)

c. Zoo Escape Drama

(动物园猛兽出逃,虚惊一场)

4. 时态

动词时态用法大大简化。如:

(1) 几乎都用一般现在时,这是标题的另一个重要特点。新闻所述的事件多半是刚刚发生、正在发生或将会发生,按英语语法规则应用动词的相应时态。但为了使读者感到是"新闻"而不是"旧闻",常用一般现在时来表示:

A. 过去发生的事,如:

a. 13 **Die** as crowded Van Crosses M4

b. Jeweler **Is** Slain

B. 正在发生之事,如:

Schools **Ask** Parents for Money Toward Books
(2) 用动词不定式表示将来时态,如:
Peking **to Fire** Test Rocket to South Pacific
(3) 过去分词表示被动语态:
A. 现在时态,如:
  a. U. S. Car Makers **Viewed** as Threat by Europeans
  b. Case **Probed**
B. 过去时态,如:
  Colombian **Sent** to U. S. for Drug Trial
C. 正在进行时态,如:
  Brazil Elite **Forced** to Make Loans
D. 现在完成时态,如:
  Petrol Bomb **Found** outside Cardiff Conservative Club

这些标题用动词不定式和过去分词所表示的时态与日常英语并无不同,只要语言基础打好了,一看就明白。动词现在式、不定式及过去分词在标题中所表示上述时态如何确定呢? 一是主要看导语(lead)。二是根据常识。如:

Brazil Elite **Forced** to Make Loans

RIO DE JANEIRO, May 6 (AP)—The economic elite of Brazil **is being forced** to lend money to the Treasury at 6-percent annual interest over two years...

(4) 应该说明,引语和设问式标题中,除现在时外,还可能有其他时态,如:
  a. "I **Was** Not His Mistress"
  b. Jones **Planned** to Kill Carter?
  c. "We **Won't** Quit"

这些时态的应用,主要是为了强调动作的时间性,否则会产生误解。

二、情况与知识

对初学者而言,要读懂标题,还必须具备各种文化知识,了解全球动态。否则,若不看消息体的导语和特写体的全文,单凭标题就望文生义,肯定会闹出笑话。见例句:

1. Bush's **Monica** Problem

乍一看,以为小布什总统也出现了克林顿与 Monica Lewinsky 那样的绯闻(Monicagate)。此标题是在揭发布逼几个联邦检察官(U. S. Attorney)辞职,任用亲信 Monica Goodling,由此揭开了他借反恐大搞窃听的内幕。

2. **Venus** Rising

Venus（Williams）是网坛美国黑人女明星，此处并非是"金星"。

三、具有文学功底

1. 引经据典型，或直接引用、套用、改用文学名著之名、《圣经》典故，或运用名言、谚语、习语等。如：

(1) A Farewell to Arms

苏联共产党总书记戈尔巴乔夫向时任美国总统里根建议彻底销毁核武，引用了海明威所著小说的书名《永别了，武器》。

(2) Liberty is the true mother of invention

强调自由对发明的重要性，套用谚语"Necessity is the mother of invention"（需要是发明之母）。

(3) Refugees in Dire Straits

"in dire straits"是习语，意思是"in a difficult or dangerous situation"。

2. 艺术加工型，运用各种修辞手段，如使用比喻、押韵、反语、夸张、双关语等手段以求得生动、形象、幽默、讽刺等效果。因此，读者往往难以一目了然，有的需读完全文才知道其主题思想。例如：

(1) Ballots，Not Bullets

"Ballots"和"Bullets"这两个发音近似的词具有某种语言上的效果。

(2) Soldiers Salary Soars

每个单词的第一个字母都是"S"，使用押头韵手法。

(3) Bovver Boy's Hover Ploy

这个标题的四个字为间隔押（尾）韵（alternate rhyme）。

(4) Thatcher's Style Wars

style wars 是 star wars 的谐音，为讽刺性俏皮语。

(5) African Statesman Still Sowing Seeds for Future

此标题中的"Sowing Seeds"是个双关语。

从以上两种类型的标题可以看出，标题体现编者和记者语言素养和文字技巧等综合水平，有的标题寥寥数字，有的拖沓冗长，有的平铺直叙，有的引经据典，有的极具艺术技巧，讲究修辞手段。日报天天出，不能过夜。期刊编者有时间推敲，标题比报纸精炼优美。（详见《导读》四章一节一、二、三和二节四）

Unit Three
United States(Ⅱ)

Lesson 7

课文导读

　　美国高中毕业生因为学费而对择校问题左右为难。据报道,在获得学士学位的毕业生中,有 2/3 的学生通过贷款支付高等教育费用,许多大学生毕业时已经负债累累。能进入常春藤名校,自然有利于求职及事业发展,许多研究显示,名校毕业生确实收入较高,申请就读名牌大学研究生的概率也较高。不过,常春藤名校学费昂贵,学生在读学士学位阶段较难获得助学金。目前就业市场情况不佳,不禁令人质疑,花高额学费上常春藤名校值得吗? 本文为我们讲述了几个大学生的真实故事,他们的选择看似"明智",却充满了无奈和迷茫:虽然公立学校学费低廉,但是学生们需要面对有限的选课条件、水平参差不齐的同学、薄弱的师资力量等问题,未来还要面临不能按时毕业、就业机会减少等风险。文章视角客观,多用引语;语言洗练,使用了很多动词词组和缩略语(如 land jobs, take on debt, med);文字生动,细致描绘了几个学生的心路历程。

Pre-reading Questions
1. How many Ivy League Universities do you know?
2. Which do you think is more important, the best college or the best major?

Text

Is an Ivy League[1] Diploma Worth It?
Fearing Massive Debt, More Students Are Choosing
to Enroll at Public Colleges Over Elite Universities.
By Melissa Korn

1 　　Daniel Schwartz could have attended an Ivy League school if he wanted to. He just doesn't see the value.

2 　　Mr. Schwartz, 18 years old, was accepted at Cornell University[2]

but enrolled instead at City University[2] of New York's Macaulay Honors College[3], which is free.

3   Mr. Schwartz says his family could have afforded Cornell's tuition, with help from scholarships and loans. But he wants to be a doctor and thinks medical school, which could easily cost upward of $45,000 a year for a private institution, is a more important investment. It wasn't "worth it to spend $50,000-plus a year for a bachelor's degree," he says.

4   As student-loan default rates climb and college graduates fail to land jobs, an increasing number of students are betting they can get just as far with a degree from a less-expensive school as they can with a diploma from an elite school — without having to take on debt.

5   More students are choosing lower-cost public colleges or commuting to schools from home to save on housing expenses. Twenty-two percent of students from families with annual household incomes above $100,000 attended public, two-year schools in the 2010—2011 academic year, up from 12% the previous year, according to a report from student-loan company Sallie Mae[4].

6   Such choices meant families across all income brackets[5] spent 9% less—an average of $21,889 in cash, loans, scholarships and other methods—on college in 2010—11 than in the previous year, according to the report. High-income families cut their college spending by 18%, to $25,760. The report, which is released annually, was based on a survey of about 1,600 students and parents.

7   The approach has risks. Top-tier colleges tend to attract recruiting visits from companies that have stopped visiting elsewhere. A diploma from an elite school can look better to many recruiters and graduate schools, as well. And overcrowding at state schools means students could be locked out of required courses and have difficulty completing their degrees in four years.

8   Mr. Schwartz started at the Macaulay Honors program at Queens College[6] this fall with "nagging" disappointment but has come to terms with his decision.

9   "I have to grow up. I have to incorporate what I want and what I can have," he says. "Even though people say money shouldn't be everything, in this situation, money was the most important thing."

10   He says he had grown enamored with the "prestige" of an Ivy League degree. His teachers cited the networking opportunities and

academic rigor. It didn't help that his father attended Princeton University and his uncle, Columbia University[7].

11   "I thought that the Ivy League title would really, really boost my chances of getting into a good med school[8]," Mr. Schwartz says. Now, he is aiming for top grades at Macaulay to remain competitive with Ivy League candidates.

12   There is little question that having a college degree gives candidates an edge in the job market. The unemployment rate for people with a bachelor's degree was 4.9% last month, compared with 10.5% for high-school graduates with no degree, according to the Bureau of Labor Statistics[9].

13   But a degree from a private college also is expensive and piles on debt. The average debt load for students who took out loans hit a record $27,200 for the class that graduated this year, says Mark Kantrowitz, publisher of student-aid websites Fastweb.com and FinAid.org. That comes as general per capita debt reached $47,260 in the second quarter, a figure that has been dropping in recent years, according to the Federal Reserve Bank of New York[10].

14   Jesse Yeh, a 20-year-old California resident, chose the University of California at Berkeley[11] over Stanford University[12]. Tuition at Berkeley, a state school, is about $14,460 for in-state students. At Stanford, it's $40,050.

15   Now he worries about graduating on time, having been locked out of some overcrowded courses, including Spanish and a public-policy elective. Berkeley says 71% of students who entered in 2006, the latest period available, graduated within four years. At Stanford, that number is closer to 80%.

16   Attending a private university still can pay off. Schools with large endowments have beefed up[13] their aid programs in recent years, which can make them less expensive than their public, cash-strapped counterparts. Brown University[14], for example, offers grants instead of loans for students whose families earn less than $100,000 a year. Harvard College[15] doesn't expect any contribution from families with annual incomes below $60,000.

17   But Carl Van Horn, director of the John J. Heldrich Center for Workforce Development at Rutgers University, says graduate outcomes often have more to do with major and how a student takes advantage of

networking and internship opportunities, than with school choice.

18   Natasha Pearson, 19, questions her decision to attend the City University of New York's Hunter College[16]. She says she turned down an offer from Boston College[17] after the school said her family would need to pitch in $30,000 annually.

19   She says there's a "wide variety" of academic ability among her Hunter classmates and that many of her courses are taught by graduate students, rather than by full professors.

20   "I can't help but wonder, had I gone to BC, where that could have taken me," she says. (From *The Wall Street Journal*, November 8, 2011)

New Words

beef /bi:f/ *v.* to make strong or stronger, improve
boost /bu:st/ *vt.* contribute to the progress or growth of
candidate /ˈkændɪdət/ *n.* a person who is being considered for a position 候选人
cash-strapped *adj.* not having enough money to buy or pay for the things they want or need 手头紧的；资金短缺的
diploma /dɪˈpləʊmə/ *n.* a document certifying the successful completion of a course of study 毕业文凭；学位证书
endowment /ɪnˈdaʊmənt/ *n.* a gift of money that is made to an institution or community in order to provide it with an annual income 资助；捐款
enamored /ɪˈnæməd/ *adj.* marked by foolish or unreasoning fondness 倾心的，迷恋的
grant /grɑ:nt/ *n.* an amount of money that a government or other institution gives to an individual or to an organization for a particular purpose such as education or home improvements 助学金，补助金
nagging /ˈnæɡɪŋ/ *adj.* continually complaining or faultfinding 唠叨的，挑剔的；使人不得安宁的
networking /ˈnetwɜ:kɪŋ/ *n.* social network 社会或人脉关系
pitch /pɪtʃ/ *vt.* to throw or toss something, such as a ball 投；扔
rigor /ˈrɪɡə/ *n.* excessive sternness 严格；严酷；严密
top-tier *adj.* of the highest degree, quality, or amount 顶级的；顶尖的

Notes

1. Ivy League — a group of eight universities in the north-eastern part of the US which have high academic and social status. The Ivy League is an athletic conference (体育赛事联盟) composed of sports teams from eight private institutions of higher education in the Northeastern US. The eight institutions are Brown University, Columbia University, Cornell University, Dartmouth College, Harvard University, Princeton University, the University of Pennsylvania, and Yale University. 常春藤联盟
2. Cornell University — located in Ithaca, New York, founded in 1865
3. City University of New York's Macaulay Honors College — 纽约市立大学麦考利荣誉学院

    City University of New York (abbr. CUNY) — public (公立的), located in all five New York City boroughs (行政区). Its administrative offices are in Yorkville in Manhattan.
4. Sallie Mae — or SLM Corporation, a publicly traded U.S. corporation whose operations are originating, servicing, and collecting on student loans. 萨利美(学生贷款)公司
5. across all income brackets — 包括所有收入阶层的家庭
6. Queens College — one of the senior colleges of the City University of New York 皇后区学院
7. It didn't help that his father attended Princeton University and his uncle, Columbia University. (Par. 10) — His father's and his uncle's diplomas at the two elite Universities did not influence his school-choosing decision. .

    a. Princeton University — private (私立的), located in Princeton, New Jersey, founded in 1746.

    b. Columbia University — private, located in New York City, founded in 1754.
8. med school — medical school, med = medical 报刊英语偏爱用那些短缩略的词,也称截短词,如:biz = business, sec = secretary, expo = exposition, vet = veteran 等。
9. the Bureau of Labor Statistics — a unit of the Department of Labor. It is the principal fact-finding agency for the U.S. government in the broad field of labor economics and statistics and serves as a principal agency of the U.S. Federal Statistical System. 美国劳工统计局

10. the Federal Reserve Bank of New York — the largest of the 12 Federal Reserve Banks of the United States. Working within the Federal Reserve System, the New York Federal Reserve Bank implements monetary policy, supervises and regulates financial institutions and helps maintain the nation's payment systems. 纽约联邦储备银行
11. the University of California at Berkeley — also referred to as UC Berkeley, public, located in Berkeley, California, established in 1868. 加州大学伯克利分校
12. Stanford University — founded in 1891. 斯坦福大学
13. beef up — to increase, strengthen, or improve 改善；提高；加强
14. Brown University — private, located in Providence, Rhode Island, founded in 1764.
15. Harvard College — one of two schools within Harvard University granting undergraduate degrees
16. the City University of New York's Hunter College — 纽约市立大学亨特学院
17. Boston College — a private Jesuit(教会的) university, located in the village of Chestnut Hill, Massachusetts, founded in 1863. 波士顿学院

Questions

1. Why did not Mr. Schartz enroll at Cornel University?
2. What was the general annual cost of top-tier colleges or Ivy League colleges such as Cornell university ?
3. What is the meaning of the phrase "land jobs" in the fourth paragraph?
4. What is the reason for those students at state schools who are locked out of required courses and have difficulty completing their degrees in four years?

> 读报知识

Ivy League, Seven Sisters & Russel Group

The Ivy League　常春藤联合会

美国东部八所名牌大学。原为这些大学体育联合组织的名称。它们以历史悠久、教学和研究成果卓著而享有社会声誉，因砖楼墙上有常春藤蔓延而得名。这些学校是：在罗得岛州的布朗大学(Brown University)、在纽约市的哥伦比亚大学(Columbia University)、在纽约州的康奈尔大学(Cornell University)、在新罕布什尔州的达特茅斯学院(Dartmouth College)、在马萨诸塞州的哈佛大学(Harvard University)、在宾夕法尼亚州的宾夕法尼亚大学(University of Pennsylvania)、在新泽西州的普林斯顿大学(Princeton University)和在康涅狄格州的耶鲁大学(Yale University)。这些学校大多建于18世纪，哈佛最早，建于1636年。

The Seven Sisters　七姐妹女子学院

美国七所最著名的女子学院及其组成的联合会，原名七学院联合会(the Seven Colleges Conference)，1915年由马萨诸塞州的霍利奥克山(Mount Holyoke)、史密斯(Smith)、韦尔斯利(Wellesley)和纽约州的瓦萨(Vassar)等四所学院组成，后又有纽约市的巴纳德(Barnard)、宾夕法尼亚州的布林马尔(Bryn Mawr)和马萨诸塞州的拉德克利夫(Radcliffe)等三所学院加入。作为联合会成员，七所学院的校长及其他领导人经常商讨共同的教学目标与问题，制定互利的招生政策。这些学校教学标准较高，相当于常春藤联合会(the Ivy League)大学。七所学校均建于19世纪。瓦萨学院现也招收男生。

The Russel Group　罗素大学集团

1994年成立，现有24所英国最卓越的公立研究性大学，其中以金三角各校　Oxford/Cambridge/London Universnty(牛津、剑桥和伦敦大学)为代表。该联盟被誉称为英国的常春藤联合会。

Lesson 8

课文导读

提到现代战争,大多数人脑海里浮现的是美国电影中展现的航母战斗群、核潜艇、隐形飞机、导弹等先进武器,以及美国在20世纪末、21世纪初主导的科索沃、阿富汗、伊拉克、利比亚等战争。我们不禁要问:未来的战争会是什么样的呢?它将向何方向演变?

美国成天叫嚷遭到中国网络攻击。然而,天有不测风云,它却被一无名小将打败了。据前CIA和NSA雇员斯诺登(Edward Snowden)披露,NSA对全球电话和网络通信实行监听和攻击,甚至连美国公民、在美外国人和机构也不放过。此事使美国颜面尽失。不断指责他国对其进行网络攻击,到头来它才是最大始作俑者,可见其多么虚伪。Edward揭密的同时生出两个新词:PRISM(personal record information system for management)scandal,(棱镜门丑闻)和surveillancegate。

随着信息技术的大量应用和普及,我们社会生活的各个方面越来越离不开网络,网络信息已成为保持社会正常运行的神经中枢。信息时代,一旦网络系统遭到破坏,社会就会陷入全面瘫痪。然而,网络信息安全面临的威胁已不是理论上的想象和推测,而是每天都在人们身边发生的事实。近年来,网络攻击和入侵事件从数量规模到危害程度不断升级,已对国家安全构成严重危害。美国不断装扮成网络领域的受害者,借此,它大力招募网络高手,建立培训学校和网战司令部,欲成为军力更加无敌的超级大国。

通过本文的学习,我们深刻体会到网络战争的时代已经来临,网络空间已成为继陆地、海洋、空中和太空之后的第五维作战空间。为我国安全计,人们必须提高警惕。

Pre-reading Questions

1. Do you know anything about cyberwar?
2. What is your view of cyberwar in the future?

Text

Pentagon Digs In on Cyberwar Front[1]
Elite School Run by Air Force Trains Officers to Hunt
Down Hackers and Launch Electronic Attacks
By Julian E. Barnes

1   The U. S. military is accelerating its cyberwarfare training programs in an aggressive expansion of its preparations for conflict on an emerging battlefield.

2   The renewed emphasis on building up cyberwarfare capabilities comes even as other defense programs have been trimmed. Along with unmanned aircraft[2] and special operations, cyberwarfare is among the newer, more high-tech and often more secretive capabilities favored by the Pentagon's current leadership.

3   In June, the U. S. Air Force's elite Weapons School[3]— the Air Force version of the Navy's famed "Top Gun" program[4]— graduated its first class of six airmen trained to fight in cyberspace. The new course, at Nellis Air Force Base in Nevada[5], trains airmen working at computer terminals how to hunt down electronic intruders, defend networks and launch cyberattacks.

4   "While cyber[6] may not look or smell exactly like a fighter aircraft or a bomber aircraft, the relevancy in any potential conflict in 2012 is the same," said Air Force Col.[7] Robert Garland, commandant of the Weapons School. "We have to be able to succeed against an enemy that wants to attack us in any way."

5   The training effort comes amid a push by the Obama administration to rapidly deploy offensive and defensive techniques across the government, including at the Central Intelligence Agency[8], other intelligence agencies and the Department of Homeland Security[9].

6   Cyberwarfare techniques have been deployed in an apparent U. S. and Israeli campaign to undermine Iran's nuclear program[10], elements of which were reported last month by the *New York Times*. The U. S. also contemplated using cyberweapons to incapacitate Libyan air defenses in 2011, before the start of U. S. airstrikes.

7   The military's cyber buildup began in 2008, leading to creation of a formal "U. S. Cyber Command[11]." The command marshals computer-

warfare capabilities from across the military and integrates them with expertise at the National Security Agency[12]. Some of the defenses could someday be extended to the private sector.

8   Overall the Air Force spends about $4 billion a year on its cyber programs, though the training initiatives are a fraction of that cost.

9   Other military services also are taking steps to strengthen cyberwarfare capabilities and training. The Navy is revamping courses for 24,000 people trained each year at the Center for Information Dominance[13] each year.

10   "It is that full span, from peace time to war and everything in between," said Capt. Susan Cerovsky, commander of the Center for Information Dominance.

11   James Cartwright, a retired Marine general and former vice chairman of the U. S. Joint Chiefs of Staff[14], argues the new emphasis on cyber training is critical. But he said the military should do a better job publicizing that it is working to hone all of its cyber capabilities — both defensive and offensive.

12   "For cyber deterrence to work, you have to believe a few things: One, that we have the intent; two, that we have the capability; and three, that we practice — and people know that we practice," Gen. Cartwright said.

13   The full range of U. S. cyberweapons is a closely guarded secret. U. S. officials have said the military is developing weapons aimed at cutting off power to precise, limited locations.

14   "Our curriculum is based on attack, exploit and defense of the cyber domain," said Lt. Col. Bob Reeves, who oversees the cyber course as commander of the 328th Weapons Squadron[15].

15   The U. S. also has acknowledged it has cyberweapons that could help suppress enemy air and sea defenses. Israel used cyber techniques to hide its aircraft in a 2007 attack on a Syrian nuclear facility, according to current and former officials.

16   Such methods are taught at Weapons School, officials acknowledge. The course focuses on combining cyber power with more traditional combat, said Lt. Col. Reeves. That includes "affecting an adversary's computer system in a way that allows us to fly in an airstrike more effectively, with less resistance," he said.

17   Lt. Col. Steven Lindquist, one of the inaugural students, said the

course asks officers to study how an attacker could launch a cyberattack against an Air Force command center or an individual airplane, and to construct defenses. An Air Force "aggressor" team at Nellis then tests the defenses.

18   "The Air Force aggressor acts as a hacker coming against us and we see how our defensive plan measured up," said Lt. Col. Lindquist.

19   The Air Force Weapons School provides advanced training for a handful of elite officers each year in traditional skills, like teaching aerial combat, reconnaissance and bombing, and also for the growing ranks of drone pilots. Adding the cyberwarfare course to the most elite school, officials say, is important to changing the mindset of the military, where many still regard radios, telephones and computers as communications tools — not targets and weapons.

20   "We know this is a contested domain," said Lt. Col. Timothy Franz, staff director for the Air Force Office of Cyberspace Operations[16]. "There are people out there trying to get into your telephones and networks for military purposes[17], and we recognize that having similar capabilities is imperative for the future fight." (From *The Wall Street Journal*, July 9, 2012)

New Words

adversary /ˈædvəsəri/ *n.* a country or person you are fighting or competing against 敌手；对手

aerial /ˈeəriəl/ *n.* (of an attack, etc.) from an aeroplane

aggressor /əˈgresə(r)/ *n.* a person or country that starts a fight or war with another person or country

buildup /ˈbɪldʌp/ *n.* a building up, as of military forces; increase in amount or number; a   process of growth; strengthening; development 集结；累积；形成

commandant /ˈkɒməndænt/ *n.* the army officer in charge of a place or group of people 司令官；〈美〉(陆军军官学校的)校长

contemplate /ˈkɒntəmpleɪt/ *v.* to think about sth. that you might do in the future 企图，打算

cyber- *prefix* relating to computers, esp. to messages and information on the Internet 计算机(网络)的，信息技术的

cyberattack/ˈsaɪbəəˈtæk/*n.* illegally getting access to others' computer system in order to obtain secret information or cause damage by means of email and other tools of the Internet 网络攻击

cyberwarfare /'saɪbə'wɔːfɛə/ *n.* politically motivated hacking to conduct sabotage and espionage 网络战

cyberspace /'saɪbəspeɪs/ *n.* all of the data stored in a large computer or network represented as a three-dimensional model through which a virtual-reality user can move 网络空间

deploy /dɪ'plɔɪ/ *v. fml* to use sth. for a particular purpose, esp. ideas, arguments etc. 采用;部署

deterrence /dɪ'terəns/ *n.* the prevention of sth, esp. war or crime, by having sth. such as weapons or punishment to use as a threat 威慑,阻吓

domain /dəʊ'meɪn/ *n.* an area of activity, interest, or knowledge; realm 领域,……界

drone /drəʊn/ *n.* an aircraft that does not have a pilot, but is operated by remolde control 无人机

fraction /'frækʃn/ *n.* a very small amount of sth

hacker /'hækə(r)/ *n.* sb who secretly uses or changes the information in other people's computer systems

hone /həʊn/ *v.* to improve your skill at doing sth, esp. when you are already very good at it 磨炼(技能)

imperative /ɪm'perətɪv/ *adj.* extremely important and needing to be done or dealt with immediately

inaugural /ɪ'nɔːgjərəl/ *adj.* marking the beginning of a new venture, series, etc. 开始的,揭幕的

incapacitate /ˌɪnkə'pæsɪteɪt/ *v.* to stop a system, piece of equipment etc. from working properly

intruder /ɪn'truːdə(r)/ *n.* sb. who illegally enters a building or area, usu. in order to steal sth 入侵者

Iran /ɪ'rɑːn/ *n.* a country in southwest Asia, between Iraq and Afghanistan 伊朗

Israeli /ɪz'reɪlɪ/ *adj.* relating to Israel or its people 以色列的

Libyan /'lɪbɪən/ *adj.* relating to Libya or its people 黎巴嫩的

marshal /'mɑːʃl/ *v.* to organize all the people or things that you need in order to be ready for a battle, election etc. 整理,排列,集结

mindset /'maɪndset/ *n.* one's general attitude, and the way in which they think about things and make decisions 思维模式

Nevada /ne'vɑːdə/ *n.* a state in the western U.S, between California and Utah. Nevada is mostly desert, and it is the driest part of the U.S. 内华达州

oversee /ˌəʊvəˈsiː/ *v.* to be in charge of a group of workers and check that a piece of work is done satisfactorily 监督；监管

reconnaissance /rɪˈkɒnɪsns/ *n.* the military activity of sending soldiers and aircrafts, or by the use of satellites, to find out about the enemy's forces 侦察

relevancy /ˈreləvənsiː/ *n.* the condition of being connected with the matter at hand; the state of having practical value or importance

revamp /ˌriːˈvæmp/ *v.* *infml* to change sth in order to improve it and make it seem more modern 改进，更新

secretive /ˈsiːkrətɪv/ *adj.* liking to keep one's thoughts, intentions, or actions hidden from other people

squadron /ˈskwɒdrən/ *n.* a military force consisting of a group of aircraft or ships 中队

trim /trɪm/ *v.* to reduce a number, amount, or the size of sth.

Notes

1. Pentagon Digs In on Cyberwar Front — 五角大楼决心在网络战领域发力

    a. Pentagon — the headquarters of the U. S. Department of Defense. The Pentagon is often used metonymically to refer to the U. S. Department of Defense rather than the building itself. 五角大楼，借指美国国防部

    b. dig in — to go resolutely to work

2. unmanned aircraft — commonly known as a drone, is an aircraft without a human pilot on board. Its flight is controlled either autonomously by computers in the vehicle, or under the remote control of a pilot on the ground or in another vehicle.

3. the U. S. Air Force's elite Weapons School — a unit of the U. S. Air Force, assigned to the 57th Wing（第57联队）. It is stationed at Nellis Air Force Base, Nevada. Its mission is to teach graduate-level instructor courses, which provide advanced training in weapons and tactics employment to officers of the combat air forces. 美国空军军械学院

4. "Top Gun" program — The U. S. Navy Strike Fighter Tactics Instructor program, more popularly known as TOPGUN. 美国海军战斗机武器学校培训课程。TOPGUN 其实是一个空战训练课程的代号, 它开创了假想敌训练模式的先河, 目的是为了训练"海军飞行员毕

业后的空中格斗技能"。好莱坞曾以此为背景，拍摄《壮志凌云》，其英文原名就是 TOPGUN。

5. Nellis Air Force Base in Nevada — a U. S. Air Force Base, located NE of Las Vegas, Nevada. 内利斯空军基地

6. cyber — Here it is short for "cyberwar." ("cyber"并不是一个独立的单词，常用以构成复合词成分。本课中除 cyberwar 以外，还出现了 cyberspace, cyberattack, cyberweapon, 另外还有 cyber capabilities, cyber domain, cyber power, cyber program 等。在后面四例中，都以独立的单词形式出现，这反映了它正在从构词成分演化成词的过程。)

7. Col. — abbr. Colonel（上校）。本课还出现了"Capt.（Captain 上尉）","Gen.（General 上将）","Lt. Col.（Lieutenant Colonel 中校）"等军衔的缩写形式。

8. the Central Intelligence Agency — CIA, the department of the US government that collects information about other countries, esp. secretly. （美国）中央情报局

9. the Department of Homeland Security — a cabinet department of the U. S. federal government, created in response to the September 11 attacks, and with the primary responsibilities of protecting the U. S. and U. S. territories from and responding to terrorist attacks, manmade accidents, and natural disasters. （美国）国土安全部

10. Iran's nuclear program — launched in the 1950s with the help of the U. S. as part of the Atoms for Peace program. The participation of the U. S. and Western European governments in Iran's nuclear program continued until the 1979 Iranian Revolution that toppled the Shah of Iran（伊朗国王）. Later, the West has to destroy the program. The US and Israil used stuxnet(震网病毒)to undermine it in 2011.

11. U. S. Cyber Command — an armed forces sub-unified command subordinate to U. S. Strategic Command. It centralizes command of cyberspace operations, organizes existing cyber resources and synchronizes（使同步）defense of U. S. military networks. 美国网战司令部

12. the National Security Agency — NSA, an intelligence agency of the U. S. Department of Defense responsible for the collection and analysis of foreign communications and foreign signals intelligence, as well as protecting U. S. government communications and

information systems, which involves information security and cryptanalysis（密码分析）. Former CIA website blower（揭密者）Edward Snowden, the former NSA contract employee provided the Guardian in July 2013 with top-secret NSA documents leading to revelations about US global surveillance on phone and internet communications.（美国）国家安全局

13. the Center for Information Dominance — a branch of the U. S. Navy. Its mission is to deliver full spectrum Cyber Information Warfare, and Intelligence Training to achieve decision superiority.（美国海军）信息控制中心
14. the U. S. Joint Chiefs of Staff — a body of senior uniformed leaders in the U. S. Department of Defense who advise the Secretary of Defense, the Homeland Security Council, the National Security Council and the President on military matters. 美国参谋长联席会议，其主席为军中最高首长。
15. the 328th Weapons Squadron — a USAF Weapons School training unit located at Nellis Air Force Base, Nevada. 美国空军第328武器中队
16. Cyberspace Operations — The term has been proposed to mean the employment of cyber capabilities where the primary purpose is to achieve military objectives or effects in or through cyberspace. Such operations include computer network operations and activities to operate and defend the Global Information Grid. 网络空间战，即通过网络或在网络内部，以达成军事目的或影响为主要目标而对网络功能的运用。这样的作战是指为了操控和防护全球信息网格所进行的计算机网络作战和行动。
17. There are people … for military purposes. — 这是美国最典型的贼喊捉贼伎俩。

Questions

1. Why does the Pentagon show much interest in cyberwarfare?
2. What is the Air Force version of the Navy's "Top Gun" program mainly about?
3. How does the U. S. Cyber Command deal with the cyber world?
4. Why does the Air Force set up the "aggressor" team?
5. Why is it important to add the cyberwarfare course to the most elite school?

> 读报知识

美英等国情治机构简介

国家安全为头等大事,称为 high foreign policy,经济援助政策则为 low foreign policy。美英等国情报和治安机构常见诸报端,有的一般词典中查不到,行话更费解。为此,特在此先将机构简介如下:

1. 美国

美国主要有 16 个情治机构,下面将常见诸报端的几个简介如下:

FBI(Federal Bureau of Investigation) 联邦调查局成立于 1908 年,是负责国内治安和反间反颠覆活动的政府机构,属司法部管辖。

CIA(Central Intelligence Agency) 中央情报局是 1947 年建立的独立机构,从事美国以外的情报与反情报活动,搜集有关国家安全情报。总部设在弗吉尼亚州兰利(Langley,Langley 可指代 CIA)。

中情局控制的情报机构,据称由于在"9·11"事件和伊拉克战争中情报工作失误,地位已大大削弱。原来负责向总统汇报工作,此任务现已划归国家情报总监(DNI,Director of National Intelligence)。

Defense Intelligence Agency(DIA) 国防情报局是总局,听取国防部所属情报机构汇报。

National Security Agency/No such Agency(NSA) 国家安全局是国防部情报机构,保护本国通信安全和通过截收、破译、监听来搜集国内外通信情报的机构,成立于 1952 年。又名 Central Security Service,属绝密单位,已有 50 多年历史,美国政府一直讳莫如深,总说"No Such Agency"(没有这个部门),缩写与国家安全局一样。媒体讽刺说,美国国家安全局的英文名字不是"National Security Agency",而是"No Such Agency"。直到 20 世纪 70 年代初,美国政府才肯认账。

National Counterterrorism Center(NCC) 国家反恐中心,是为防止"9·11"事件重演于 2005 年成立。

Terrorist Threat Integration Center(TTIC) 防止恐怖威胁综合中心,由国土安全部、国家反恐中心、国防部和其他有关机构的成员组成,旨在防止恐怖分子袭击美国机构。

United States Secret Service 特工处,常简称 Secret Service,原隶属于美国财政部,2002 年国土安全部(Department of Homeland Security)成立后,划归新部管辖。原从事查抄伪币等经济事务,现专司保卫总统和其他高官、来访领导人的人身安全。

2. 英国

英国主要有三大情报机构,因为 GCHQ 太机密,常见报的是 MI5 和 MI6。

MI5 (Military Intelligence, Section Five) 军(事)情(报)五处是沿用战时旧称,并非军方情报部门,事实上是英国两个情报局之一,正式名称为 the Intelligence Service(安全局),相当于美国 FBI,负责国内安全及国内反间活动。

MI6 (Military Intelligence, Section 6) 军(事)情(报)六处也是沿用战时旧称,正式名称为 the Secret Intelligence Service(SIS)(情报局),职能相当于美国 CIA。

GCHQ (Government Communications Headquarters) 政府电信总局是英国从事保障电信安全、搜集外国通讯情报、破译密码等任务的政府机构,职能相当于美国的 NSA。据揭露,美英对伊战前夕,曾窃听联合国秘书长科菲·安南(Kofi Annan)的谈话。

3. 苏联

提到情报机构或斗争,至今这两个机构常映入读者的眼帘:**KGB** (Komitet Gosudarstvennoi Bezopastnosti) 克格勃(1954－1991),起美国 CIA 负责对外情报活动及 FBI 负责对内的反间和维持治安的双重作用的苏联政府机构(英译 Committee/Commission for/of State Security[国家安全委员会]);**GRU** 格鲁乌即苏联军队总参谋部情报总局(英译 Chief Directorate of Intelligence of the General Staff)

4. 俄罗斯

Federal Security Service/Federal Service of Security(FSS) 联邦安全局系由联邦反间谍局改组而成,前身是 KGB。1995 年,叶利钦总统将原联邦反间局改组为联邦安全局,强化其内外职能,不仅反间,还刑侦,恢复了因改组剥夺掉的一系列特权,拥有预审权、侦讯室及特种部队。

5. 法国

DGSE(Direction Generale de la Securite Exterieure) 对外安全总局

6. 以色列

Mossad 摩萨德,以色列情报和特务局(英译 the Institution for Intelligence and Special Duties),负责对外的情报机构,创建于 1951 年。Al 意为至高无上,是 Mossad 的化名(Al 为希伯来文,等于英文 above)。

Shin Bet/Beth 辛贝特:以色列"国家安全总局",负责对内的安全机构。(详见《导读》五章四节)

Lesson 9

课文导读

2010年6月28日,美国情报部门和司法部门逮捕了10名在美国为俄罗斯搜集情报的秘密特工。这些"俄罗斯对外情报局秘密特工"被指在美国多年"深度潜伏",借助高技术暗中联络,采取多种手段向美国政府决策层渗透,搜集核武器、美国对俄政策等情报。该消息一传出立刻引发世界各大媒体的广泛关注。7月8日,这10名被告在纽约一家法庭认罪,被判驱逐出境。作为交换条件,俄罗斯同意释放4名被控与西方情报机构有接触的在押人员。7月10日,美俄在维也纳机场交换间谍。至此,这起美俄落网特工交换事件尘埃落定。这起引人注目的间谍案处理得如此默契,说明双方政府对情报工作都心照不宣。冷战时代,美国和苏联曾在柏林多次进行过spy swap,故这并非鲜为人知。

通过此课,我们可以了解不同层面和地域当代情报活动的特点,熟悉英美情报机构,并学习到和情报工作相关的词汇和行话。

Pre-reading Questions

1. What do you know about CIA?
2. Do you think James Bond and Jason Bourne are typical spies in modern espionage? Why?

Text

Spies Among Us: Modern-day Espionage

Long after the Cold War's[1] end, nations still send secret agents[2] across borders. But corporations, terrorists, and private investigators are also part of the sleuthing underground.

By Mckay Coppins

1   The startling discovery of an undercover Russian spy ring last month no doubt shocked many Americans who assumed that

international espionage was mostly a product of the Cold War and, these days, Hollywood[3].

2　　But intelligence experts weren't the least surprised. "We forget that states like Russia have been conducting espionage for centuries," says Peter Earnest, a former member of the CIA who is now director of the Spy Museum[4] in Washington, D. C. "It didn't stop with the Cold War and start again recently. It simply continued." Of course, diplomatic relations between the U. S. and Russia have improved in recent years, and Earnest says the two governments work together with an unspoken understanding that they are still spying on each other. "It's just the cost of doing business," he says.

3　　While professional spying was once about nation-states looking over other governments' shoulders, today it's largely about tracking terrorists' activities and monitoring public communications for suspicious chatter[5]. In fact, intelligence experts say espionage of all shades has actually increased since the Cold War, amplified by new technology and soaring demand for information in the public and private sectors. Just this week, The Washington Post reported that "some 1,271 government organizations and 1,931 private companies work on programs related to counterterrorism, homeland security, and intelligence in about 10,000 locations across the United States" as part of the paper's report on the top-secret world created by Washington after 9/11[6].

4　　Here's a look at who's spying on whom, circa 2010:

OTHER NATIONS

5　　When it comes to state-backed espionage, experts say the U. S. has focused much of its recent spying on Iran, North Korea, and China. And these countries, it appears, are returning the favor.

6　　Earnest says the U. S. is the recipient of "hundreds of thousands" of cyberattacks every day, many of which emanate from Beijing. "They want to find out if they can penetrate our firewalls and actually learn intelligence. We believe a good deal has been learned."

7   But, of course, computers and satellites can do only so much. Secret agents, like the ones recently deported to Russia, still play a significant role in international spy games, though Earnest says the number of "illegals" currently undercover in the U. S. is unknowable. "The problem with counting spies is that their nature is not to be counted," he says.

8   Even longtime strong allies may spy on each other. An Israeli report in 2008 documented a long history of American spying on Israel, particularly in regard to Israel's secret nuclear program. And there have been several known instances of Israel spying on America, including the famous case of Jonathan Pollard[7], a U. S. intelligence analyst sentenced to life in prison after an espionage conviction.

TERRORISTS

9   Many Americans are under the false impression that "cave-dwelling terrorists" are too primitive to support effective intelligence operations, Earnest says. The most dangerous spies, however, are often the ones not working for recognized governments (which are bound, at least theoretically, by diplomacy and international law).

10   Independent terror networks have proved adept at the art of deception and intelligence gathering. The 2008 attack on Mumbai[8], says Earnest, "required a tremendous amount of planning as well as some relatively low-tech, but well-used, technology." And this January, a double agent[9] of Al Qaeda[10] successfully infiltrated a CIA base in Afghanistan and killed seven agents in a suicide bombing, temporarily crippling America's intelligence operations in the country.

MAJOR CORPORATIONS

11   Spying isn't just the stuff of war and international politics. While researching his 2010 book *Broker, Trader, Lawyer, Spy: The Secret World of Corporate Espionage*[11], journalist Eamon Javers uncovered the dealings of private-sector spy firms employed by companies to detect deception in negotiators, surveil competing investors, and glean intelligence that could give them an edge in their dealmaking. Espionage has become so ubiquitous in the corporate world, Javers says, that

billion-dollar merger-and-acquisition deals are almost never made these days without highly skilled spies getting involved.

12   Using some of the most sophisticated technology in the world (like a laser that can record conversations from a kilometer away by picking up the slightest vibrations on an office window), these firms are staffed almost entirely by former military and intelligence officials, from the U. K.'s MI5 to Russia's KGB[12]. The CIA even has a policy that allows its analysts to "moonlight" for major corporations. And there's no shortage of demand. One hedge-fund executive told Javers he used corporate spies to keep tabs on the entire board of directors for every company he invested in[13]. "There is even a whole network of people who do nothing but track corporate jets," Javers says.

13   It's not only competitors snooping around these major corporations. Both Earnest and Javers say foreign governments regularly spy on U. S. companies. "The Chinese have an extremely elaborate intelligence network aimed at penetrating defense and technology firms," Javers says. "Every piece of technology they steal is a piece they don't have to invent for themselves."

PRIVATE INVESTIGATORS

14   The advent of the Internet transformed the private-eye industry, shifting its focus from background checks (which can now be completed for a small price on myriad Web sites) to surveillance[14].

15   Skipp Porteous, president of New York-based Sherlock Investigations, says much of his business is derived from spouses who suspect infidelity. "A lot of times we get calls from a wife whose husband is coming to New York, usually on business, and she's afraid he's going to fool around," Porteous says. "So she hires us and we get the goods." (Incidentally, Porteous says women are right in their suspicions about 90 percent of the time; when men think their wives are cheating, they're usually wrong.)

16   Sherlock dispatches teams of two licensed private investigators, experts at blending into crowds and going unnoticed, to follow the suspected cheater and snap photos. In one case, a woman from Bermuda hired Sherlock to follow her husband while he was in New York. Investigators took pictures of him with six prostitutes (at once) and

e-mailed them to their client before her spouse returned home.

17　　Additionally, since the Internet has enabled people to easily purchase illegal audio and video transmitters, Sherlock has seen a boom in "bug sweep" business[15], especially among celebrities who believe the paparazzi have infiltrated their homes or cars. As new technologies emerge, experts expect intelligence and counterintelligence methods to grow in sophistication, and generate even more job opportunities for a new generation of supersleuths. (From *The Daily Beast*[16], July 21, 2010)

New Words

adept /əˈdept/ *adj.* good at sth. that needs care and skill 熟练的, 擅长的, 内行的

advent /ˈædvent/ *n.* the time when sth. first begins to be widely used(重要事件、人物、发明等的)到来

Afghanistan /æfˈgænɪstæn/ *n.* a country in Asia that is west of Pakistan and east of Iran 阿富汗

amplify /ˈæmplɪfaɪ/ *v. fml.* to increase the effects or strength of sth. 增强

Bermuda /bə(ː)ˈmjuːdə/ *n.* a group of islands in the West Atlantic Ocean which is a popular place for tourists. Bermuda is a British colony, but has its own local government. 百慕大群岛(英国)

circa /ˈsɜːkə/ *prep.* used before a date to show that sth. happened close to but not exactly on that date(用在日期、数字等前面)大约在, 接近于

counterterrorism /ˌkaʊntəˈterərɪzəm/ *n.* a strategy intended to prevent terrorist acts or to get rid of terrorist groups 反恐怖主义

cripple /ˈkrɪpl/ *v.* to damage sth. badly so that it no longer works or is no longer effective 削弱, 使……瘫痪

deception /dɪˈsepʃn/ *n.* the act of deliberately making someone believe sth. that is not true 欺骗

deport /dɪˈpɔːt/ *v.* to force someone to leave a country and return to the country they originally came from, esp. because they do not have a legal right to stayor have committed crimes 驱逐出境

elaborate /ɪˈlæbəreɪt/ *adj.* carefully planned and organized in great detail 精心制作的

emanate /ˈeməneɪt/ *v.* to produce a smell, light etc., or to show a particular quality 散发, 发出

espionage /'espɪənɑːʒ/ n. the activity of secretly finding out secret information and giving it to a country's enemies or a company's competitors 间谍行为,谍报活动

firewall /'faɪəwɔːl/ n. （computing）a security system consisting of a combination of hardware and software that limits the exposure of a computer or computer network to attack from crackers; commonly used on local area networks that are connected to the internet 防火墙

glean /gliːn/ v. to find out information slowly and with difficulty 费力地收集,四处收集（信息、知识）

hedge-fund /'hedʒ'fʌnd/ n. a flexible investment company for a small number of large investors（usu. the minimum investment is $1 million) 对冲基金

infidelity /ˌɪnfɪ'delətɪ/ n. an act of sex with someone other than one's marriage partner(夫妇间的)不忠实,不贞行为

infiltrate /'ɪnfɪltreɪt/ v. to secretly join an organization or enter a place in order to find out information about it or harm it 渗透,潜入

intelligence /ɪn'telɪdʒəns/ n. information about the secret activities of foreign governments, the military plans of an enemy 情报,情报工作,情报机关

Israel /'ɪzreɪl/ n. a country on the eastern side of the Mediterranean Sea, surrounded by Egypt, Jordan, and Lebanon 以色列

moonlight /'muːnlaɪt/ v. to have a second job in addition to your main job, esp. without the knowledge of the government tax department （暗中)兼职,从事第二职业

Mumbai /mʌm'baɪ/ n. a city in western India and India's 2nd largest city(印度城市)孟买

myriad /'mɪrɪəd/ adj. very many 无数的

North Korea a country in East Asia, west of Japan and east of China, which is officially called the Democratic People's Republic of Korea 朝鲜

paparazzi /ˌpæpə'rætsɪ/ n. pl. photographers who follow famous people in order to take photographs they can sell to newspapers 狗仔队

penetrate /'penətreɪt/ v. to enter sth and pass or spread through it, esp. when this is difficult 穿透,渗透

primitive /'prɪmətɪv/ adj. belonging to a simple way of life that existed in the past and does not have modern industries and machines 原始的

prostitute /'prɒstɪtjuːt/ n. someone, esp. a woman, who earns money by having sex with men 卖淫者,娼妓

ring /rɪŋ/ *n.* a group of people who illegally control a business or criminal activity 团伙，帮派，集团
sleuth /sluːθ/ *v.* to track or follow; to act as a detective 跟踪，侦查
snap /snæp/ *v.* to take a photograph
snoop /snuːp/ *v.* to try to find out about someone's private affairs by secretly looking in their house, examining their possessions etc 窥探，打探
sophistication /səˌfɪstɪˈkeɪʃn/ *n.* the state of being developed or produced with a high level of skill and knowledge 复杂，尖端
staff /stɑːf/ *v.* to provide the workers for 为……配备职员
supersleuth /ˈsjuːpəsluːθ/ *n.* a special law-enforcement agent of the Federal Bureau of Investigation（美国联邦调查局）高级特工
surveil /sɜːˈveɪl/ *v.* to keep under surveillance 使受监视（或监督）
surveillance /sɜːˈveɪləns/ *n.* a close watch kept on someone, esp. someone who is believed to have criminal intentions（对有犯罪意图者的）监视
ubiquitous /juːˈbɪkwɪtəs/ *adj.* seeming to be everywhere, sometimes used humorously 普遍存在的，无所不在的
undercover /ˌʌndəˈkʌvə(r)/ *adj.* working secretly using a false appearance in order to get information for the police or government 秘密从事的，从事间谍活动的

Notes

1. Cold War — unfriendly and hostile relationship between the US and the Soviet Union after the Second World War(1947－1991)冷战(cf. cool /hot/ skooting war)
2. secret agents — someone whose job is to find out and report on the military and political secrets of other countries 特工人员，间谍
3. Hollywood — movie studios in Los Angeles, California where films are made, often used to refer to the U.S film industry in general 好莱坞
4. Spy Museum — a privately owned museum dedicated to the field of espionage located in Washington, D.C. 间谍博物馆
5. While professional spying ... for suspicious chatter. — Although in the past, the focus of professional spying had been investigating other governments' intelligence in all aspects for the sake of their sovereign nation, today, tracking terrorists' activities and monito-

ring public communications for anti-governments or suspicious comments had been a very important part of their undercover investigation. 虽然职业间谍的工作重点曾是为主权国家监视他国，但现在追踪恐怖分子的活动和监控公众通信中的可疑言论则成了他们隐秘调查的重头戏。

  look over one's shoulder — keep close watch over 严密监视

6. 9/11 — Also the September 11 attacks/September 11. It refers to a series of four coordinated terrorist attacks launched by the Islamic terrorist group al-Qaeda(基地组织) upon the United States in New York City and the Washington, D. C. area on September 11, 2001. 9·11事件

7. Jonathan Jay Pollard — 1954— , an American who passed classified information to Israel while working as an American civilian intelligence analyst. He pleaded guilty and received a life sentence in 1987. Because his crime occurred prior to November 1, 1987, he is eligible for parole(假释), and released on November 21, 2015.

8. The 2008 attack on Mumbai — The twelve coordinated shooting and bombing attacks across Mumbai by members of Lashkar-e-Taiba(虔诚军). The attacks, which drew widespread global condemnation, began on 26 November and lasted until 29 November 2008, killing 164 people and wounding at least 308. 孟买恐怖袭击(2008)

9. double agent — someone who finds out an enemy country's secrets for their own country but who also gives secrets to the enemy 双重间谍

10. Al Qaeda — also the Base, is a global militant terrorist organization founded by Osama bin Laden at some point between August 1988 and late 1989, with its origins being traceable to the Soviet War in Afghanistan. It has attacked civilian and military targets in various countries, including the September 11 attacks, 1998 U. S. embassy bombings and the 2002 Bali bombings(巴厘岛爆炸案).

11. *Broker, Trader, Lawyer, Spy: The Secret World of Corporate Espionage* — a book written by Award-winning reporter Eamon Javers. It is a penetrating work of investigative and historical journalism about the evolution of corporate espionage, exploring the dangerous and combustible power spies hold over international business.

12. KGB — the Committee for State Security, more commonly known

by its transliteration "KGB," was the main security agency for the former Soviet Union from 1954 until its collapse in 1991. (见 Lesson Eight "读报知识")

13. he used corporate spies to keep tabs on the entire board of directors for every company he invested in — For the company he invested in, the hedge-fund executive employed corporate spies to keep all the board members of these companies under his surveillance. 他利用公司探子监视他所投资公司的董事会。

    keep tabs on — to keep an eye on, watch attentively 监视

14. The advent of the Internet ... to surveillance. — With the Internet becoming widely used, the private detective industry has changed markedly. The focus of private detective agency had been investigating individuals' identity for security purposes before, such as membership in groups or organizations, criminal convictions, work experiences, education, etc., which can be done now on numerous websites for a small price. But nowadays its focus has been shifted to attentively observing a person or group, especially one under suspicion. 因特网的出现改变了私家侦探行业。他们的工作重点从背景调查(现在，背景调查只要付一点费用就可以在海量的网站上完成)变为监视。

15. "bug sweep" business — the business of detecting and sweeping away any concealed electronic listening devices equipped in a room or telephone circuit, etc. "清除窃听器"业务

16. *The Daily Beast* — "每日野兽"(thedailybeast.com)是美国曼哈顿的互联网公司 IAC/ InterActiveCorp 拥有的一家新闻报道和评论网站,成立于 2008 年 10 月 6 日,由《纽约客》和《名利场》前总编蒂娜·布朗(Tina Brown)创办,被称为"野兽"级《新闻周刊》。每日野兽的名字来自于伊夫林·沃(Evelyn Waugh's)的小说《独家新闻》(*Scoop*)中的一份虚构报纸。据美国《纽约时报》报道称,每日野兽拥有自己独特的客户群,每月大约有 300 万访问量,2010 年 11 月 12 日,每日野兽与美国新闻周刊合并,成立新闻周刊与每日野兽公司(The Newsweek Daily Beast Company)。该网站的新闻涉及政治、经济、娱乐、时尚、女性和艺术等领域,同时刊登《新闻周刊》电子版。以突发新闻和尖锐的时评著称。

Questions

1. Is espionage mostly a product of the Cold War? Why or why not?
2. What is the focus of modern professional spying?
3. How many "secret agents" are there currently undercover in the U.S.?
4. According to experts, who are the most dangerous spies?
5. What is the focus of modern corporation espionage?
6. According to the passage, what contributes most to modern espionage?

语言解说

间谍行话

　　间谍用语大多是从泛指到特指而词同义异的一些俚语行话,其中有不少是 CIAese, KGBese 等 spookspeak(间谍行话),一般词典大多语焉不详。例如本课第 7 段就有一字把编委将住了:… the number of "illegals" currently undercover in the U. S. is unknowable.

　　此处的"illegals"是何意?虽经编委劳顿也未能阐释其意,直至看了《导读》"间谍行话"和"报刊词典"才知非"非法移民"等意思。下面从《导读》附录"间谍行话"选若干词语,或许对读者看间谍书刊有参考价值:

agent of influence 旨在影响舆论(而不是从事破坏、暗杀等间谍活动)的特工;散布假情报、反宣传等活动的人员;在美收买权势人物的特工

agent provocateur（鼓励涉嫌者从事非法活动而加以逮捕的）坐探,密探

asset（尤指美国中央情报局在搜集情报的国家所建立的）关系,眼线

bagman 从事收买拉拢的特工

black bag (job) 黑袋(活计):指警察或特工人员为获取证据而"非法入室秘密搜查"。黑袋子是从事非法秘密搜查的象征,里面装着搜查用具。

blown（间谍）被发现的

boxed 被测谎过的

brainwashed（谍报人员的）心理经过调试的:如用测谎器就不一定能测准

burnt 身份暴露的,活动曝光的

compromised = burnt 可能死了

country team 见 U. S. country team

cut-off man（地方情报站的）联络员,交通

cut-out（情报联络或交易的）中间人

desk man（情报总局负责间谍活

动部门的)总管,主管

destabilize 颠覆

drop (间谍用于传递情报、转交赏金等的)"信箱":如树根、古庙等均可用作这样的地点;如"无人情报交接处"则为 **dead (letter) drop** (见 **dubok**);(为获取情报而进行的)成功讹诈

dubok (俄语)无人情报交接处,无人材料、信息交换处:一方将"信"放在隐蔽之处,另一方然后再去取,两方不见面。

Farm (中央情报局设在弗吉尼亚的)培训学校

field agent/man 外调特工,派遣特工

flaps and seals (美国中央情报局给学员开设的邮检)启封课:a ~ man 邮检专家

front (为非法活动、间谍活动而装的)门面,(作)掩护者

G-men 联邦调查局特工;美国特工处:源于一同名电影和美国特工处设在华盛顿G Street之故。

illegals (无外交身份和豁免权的)间谍(网),情报站

legals (具有外交官身份的)间谍(网)

legend 间谍的化名和伪造的履历

mole 鼹鼠,(打入敌对情报机关而)长期潜伏的间谍(见 **sleeper**)

naked 无掩护和支援的

nash 我们的一个人,我方的一员

onetime pad 简单的、只能用一次的编码法

paroles (未见过面的间谍接头时确认双方身份的)主要暗号

playback (被捕间谍)被迫继续向己方发送(情报)

plumbing (为进行颠覆等重大活动前而设的)秘密机构

resident director (驻在某国的)情报站站长,间谍网头头

safe house (接待或安排特情或投靠者用的)密点,秘密招待所,秘密旅馆,(旅馆的)秘密套间

secret secret service officer 秘密机关从事秘密工作的官员或人员,情报机关的情报人员或特工,保卫机关的安全人员。

... and it is likely that the former **secret secret service officer** [Peter Wright] with a Government pension of £ 2,000 a year (or 3,200) is already a millionaire. (The *Guardian*)

sleeper (随时待机活动的)潜伏间谍(见 **mole**)

stringer (非情报机关的)兼职间谍

swim (间谍的)外出活动,旅行

take (因间谍活动而取得的)情报成果

terminate with extreme prejudice (婉)暗杀,干掉:指美国中央情报局常选择"暗杀"政界要人甚至国家元首,原指其在越南战争期间"暗杀"北越村长

turned 被说服(而倒向另一方)或被收买的

U. S. country team 由驻某国大使和情报站长组成的美在驻在国的情报班子

walk-in 主动提供情报或支持的志愿人员

watcher 主管监视怀疑对象的情报人员

wet job (间谍进行的)流血行动，暗杀行动

Unit Four
Britain

Lesson 10

> 课文导读

在历史上,英国长期游离于欧洲之外。1973年加入欧共体后,英国在欧洲一体化进程中与其他欧洲国家始终不太融洽。欧盟建成后,英国拒绝加入欧元区和申根协定。在卡梅伦领导的保守党里,始终存在着很强的"疑欧主义"势力,使他不能不予以重视。同时,英国独立党的影响力日益增加,反映了英国公众强烈的疑欧情绪,英国政府必须做出回应。

2013年1月23日,卡梅伦正式就英国与欧盟关系前景发表讲话,承诺如果他赢得预定于2015年举行的大选,会在一年内批准所需法律,制定与欧盟关系的新原则,然后在2017年以前就脱欧问题举行全民公投,让人民有机会选择继续留在或退出欧盟。

英国当地时间2016年6月23日上午7点(北京时间6月23日下午2点)"脱欧"公投投票开始。结果,脱欧派获得了超过50%的投票。英国广播公司26日称,由于不满英国脱欧公投结果,当地民众发起联署签名请愿,要求英国议会重新考虑这次公投的有效性,呼吁二次公投。

事实上,卡梅伦本人希望英国留在欧盟,他曾多次表示,他认为留在欧盟符合英国的最大利益。2016年6月24日,英国通过民主投票宣布脱离欧盟后,卡梅伦宣布辞职。7月13日,卡梅伦正式卸任英国首相。9月12日,卡梅伦宣布辞去英国议会下议院议员职务,彻底退出英国政坛。2017年3月16日,英国女王伊丽莎白二世批准"脱欧"法案,授权英国首相特雷莎·梅正式启动脱欧程序。

Pre-reading Questions

1. How many member states are there in the EU?
2. Can you list some advantages and disadvantages of UK leaving the EU?

Text

Britain and the European Union: The Real Danger of Brexit[1]

Leaving the EU would hurt Britain — and would also deal a terrible blow to the West.

1   THE battle is joined, at last. David Cameron[2] has called a referendum on Britain's membership of the European Union for June 23rd, promising to campaign hard to stay in. What began as a gambit to hold together his divided Tory party[3] is turning into an alarmingly close contest. Betting markets put the odds that Britons opt to leave at two-to-one; some polls suggest the voters are evenly split; several cabinet ministers are campaigning for Brexit. There is a real chance that in four months' time Britain could be cast off from Europe's shores[4].

2   That would be grave news — and not just for Britain. A vote to leave would damage the economy, certainly in the short term and probably in the long run. (As financial markets woke up to the prospect, the pound this week fell to its lowest level against the dollar since 2009.) It would imperil Britain's security, when threats from terrorists and foreign powers are at their most severe in years. And far from reclaiming sovereignty, Britons would be forgoing clout, by giving up membership of a powerful club whose actions they can influence better from within than without. Those outside Britain marvelling at this proposed act of self-harm should worry for themselves, too. Brexit would deal a heavy blow to Europe, a continent already on the ropes. It would uncouple the world's fifth-largest economy from its biggest market, and unmoor the fifth-largest defence spender from its allies. Poorer, less secure and disunited, the new EU would be weaker; the West, reliant on the balancing forces of America and Europe, would be enfeebled, too.

Dreams, meet reality

3   The Brexiters' case is that Britain is held back by Europe: unshackled, it could soar as an open economy that continued to trade with the EU and all round the world. That is possible in theory, but as our briefing explains, it is not how things would work in practice. At a minimum, the EU would allow full access to its single market only in

return for adherence to rules that Eurosceptics[5] are keen to jettison. If Norway and Switzerland[6] (whose arrangements with the EU many Brexiters idolise) are a guide, the union would also demand the free movement of people and a big payment to its budget before allowing unfettered access to the market.

4 Worse, the EU would have a strong incentive to impose a harsh settlement to discourage other countries from leaving. The Brexit camp's claim that Europe needs Britain more than the other way round is fanciful: the EU takes almost half Britain's exports, whereas Britain takes less than 10% of the EU's; and the British trade deficit is mostly with the Germans and Spanish, not with the other 25 countries that would have to agree on a new trade deal.

5 To some Eurosceptics these hardships would be worth it if they meant reclaiming sovereignty from Europe, whose bureaucrats and judges interfere with everything from bankers' bonuses to working-time limits. Yet the gain would be partly illusory. In a globalised world, power is necessarily pooled and traded: Britain gives up sovereignty in exchange for clout through its memberships of NATO[7], the IMF[8] and countless other power — sharing, rule — setting institutions. Signing up to treaties on trade, nuclear power or the environment involves submitting to regulations set jointly with foreigners, in return for greater gains. Britain outside the EU would be on the sidelines[9]: notionally independent from, but in fact still constrained by, rules it would have no role in formulating. It would be a purer but rather powerless sort of sovereignty.

6 One exception is immigration, the area over which many Eurosceptics most long for control. Half of Britain's migrants come from the EU, and there is little the government can do to stop them. If Britain left the union, it could. But doing so would have a double cost. Gaining the right to stop immigration from the EU would almost certainly mean losing full access to the single market. And reducing the numbers of immigrants would hurt Britain's businesses and public services, which rely on French bankers, Bulgarian builders and Italian doctors.

A global concern

7 The longer-term costs would go beyond economics. Brexit might

well break up the United Kingdom itself. Scotland, more Europhile than England, is again agitating for a divorce[10]; if Britain decides to leave Europe, then the Scots may at last have a point. Brexit could also dangerously unsettle Northern Ireland[11], where the peace process over two decades has depended on the fact that both Ireland and Britain are members of the EU. The Irish government is among the most vocal foreign supporters of the campaign for Britain to stay in.

8   Ireland is not the only country that would suffer. European leaders know Brexit would weaken a club already in deep trouble over such issues as migration and the euro crisis. And Europe would be poorer without Britain's voice: more dominated by Germany; and, surely, less liberal, more protectionist and more inward—looking. Europe's links to America would become more tenuous. Above all, the loss of its biggest military power and most significant foreign — policy actor would seriously weaken the EU in the world.

9   The EU has become an increasingly important part of the West's foreign and security policy, whether it concerns a nuclear deal with Iran, the threat of Islamist terrorism or the imposition of sanctions against Russia. Without Britain, it would be harder for the EU to pull its global weight[12]— a big loss to the West in a troubled neighbourhood, from Russia through Syria to north Africa. It is little wonder that Russia's Vladimir Putin is keen on Brexit and that America's Barack Obama is not. It would be shortsighted for Eurosceptics to be indifferent to this. A weakened Europe would be unambiguously bad for Britain, whose geography, unlike its politics, is fixed.

10   A lot thus rests on the tight race now under way. For those who believe, as this newspaper does, in free trade and freedom of movement, the benefits to Britain of its membership of the EU have never been in much doubt. What more sceptical sorts must now recognise is that Brexit would also weaken Europe and the West. The stakes in Mr Cameron's great gamble are high; should he fail, the losses would be widely felt. (From *The Economist*, Feb. 27, 2016)

New Words

adherence/əd'hɪərəns/*n.* the action of continuing to support or be loyal to sth, esp. in spite of difficulties 坚持；遵循

agitate/'ædʒɪteɪt/*v.* to argue strongly in public for or against some political or social change 鼓动，煽动；宣传

Brexit/'breksɪt/*n. abbr.* Britain exiting (British exit) from the EU 英国退出欧盟的一种戏谑说法

briefing/'briːfɪŋ/*n.* an act of giving necessary instructions or information 情况简介；简明指示

Briton/'brɪtn/*n.* a British citizen, or a person of British origin

Bulgarian/bʌl'ɡeəriən/*adj.* 保加利亚的；保加利亚人的；保加利亚语的

bureaucrat/'bjʊərəkræt/*n. usu. derog.* a member of a bureaucracy 官僚，官僚主义者

clout/klaʊt/*n. slang* influence, esp. political influence 影响力；势力

enfeeble/ɪn'fiːbl/*v. fml* to make weak; cause to lose strength completely 使衰弱，使完全无力

Europhile//*adj. & n.* (a politician) strongly supporting the EU and believing that the UK should become more closely united with other European countries 亲欧派(的)，欧盟支持者(的)

Eurosceptic/jʊərəʊ'skeptɪk/*n.* Someone, esp. a British politician who dislikes the EU, and thinks that the UK should leave it or become less closely involved with it 疑欧派，欧盟怀疑论者

forgo/fɔː'ɡəʊ/*v.* to give up; (be willing) not to have (esp. sth pleasant) 放弃，弃绝

formulate/'fɔːmjuleɪt/*v.* to invent and prepare (a plan, suggestion, etc.) 制定；规划，构想

gambit/'ɡæmbɪt/*n.* an action made to produce a future advantage, esp. an opening move in a game, an argument, or a conversation 精心策划的第一招；开局；开场白

idolise//*v. BrE* (= idolize) to treat as an idol 把……当偶像崇拜；极度敬慕；热爱

impose/ɪm'pəʊz/*v.* to (use your authority to) force people to accept sth; to establish (an additional payment) officially 实施(新法律或规则)；征收(新税等) imposition *n.*

inward-looking/'ɪnwəd 'lʊkɪŋ/*adj.* (of a people or society) more interested in themselves than in other people or society. 对外界不关

心的

jettison/'dʒetɪsn/*v.* to throw away; get rid of 丢弃; 拜托

notionally/ˈnəʊʃənli/*adv.* based on a guess, estimate or theory; not existing in reality 概念上, 理论上

odds/ɒdz/*n.* the probability that sth will or will not happen, expressed in numbers when making a bet 可能性;（打赌时的）赔率

opt/ɒpt/*n.* a choice (esp. of one thing or course instead of another)

pool/puːl/*v.* to combine; share; bring together for the advantage of everyone in a group 合伙（集中）使用, 公用

protectionist/prəˈtekʃənɪst/*adj.* 贸易保护主义的

reclaim/rɪˈkleɪm/*v.* to ask for the return of

sanction/ˈsæŋkʃn/*n.* measures taken by countries to restrict trade and official contacct with a country that has broken international law 国际制裁

sceptical/ˈskeptɪkl/*adj.* BrE (skeptical AmE) unwilling to believe a claim or promise; doubting; distrustful

sovereignty/ˈsɒvrənti/*n.* complete freedom and power to act or govern; the quality of being an independent self-governing country 主权; 国家的独立自主

stake/steɪk/*n.* money risked on the result of sth, esp. a horse race; bet 赌注;（尤指赛马的）赌金

submit（to）/səbˈmɪt/*v.* to agree to obey 遵守; 服从

Syria/ˈsɪriə/*n.* 叙利亚

tenuous/ˈtenjuəs/*adj.* very thin; slight; insignificant 纤细的; 微弱的; 无力地

unambiguously/ˌʌnæmˈbɪgjuəsli/*adv.* clearly; that cannot be misunderstood 不含糊地; 明确地

uncouple/ʌnˈkʌpl/*v.* to separate (esp. joined railway carriages); free fro a fastening 使（连接的火车车厢）分开; 使分离

unfettered/ʌnˈfetəd/*adj.* fml free from control; not tied by severe rules 不受约束的, 自由自在的

unmoor/ʌnˈmʊə(r)/*v.* to unfasten (a ship, boat, etc.) 起锚; 解掉; 去掉

unsettle/ʌnˈset(ə)l/*v.* to make less calm, more anxious, dissatisfied, etc. 使不安宁, 使焦急; 搅乱

unshackle/ʌnˈʃækəl/*v.* to set free or release 解放; 使自由

vocal/ˈvəʊkl/*adj.* expressing oneself freely and noisily in words; telling people your opinions or protesting about sth loudly and forcefully 大声表达的；直言不讳的

Notes

1. Brexit — *abbr.* (also Brixit) British exit from the EU
2. David Cameron — the Prime Minister of the United Kingdom from 2010 to 2016. He has been associated with both economically liberal and socially liberal policies. His administration introduced large-scale changes to welfare, immigration policy, education, and healthcare. It privatised the Royal Mail and some other state assets, and legalised same-sex marriage. In 2016, to fulfil a manifesto pledge, he introduced a referendum on the UK's continuing membership of the EU. Cameron supported continued membership; following the success of the Leave vote, he resigned to make way for a new Prime Minister and was succeeded by Theresa May.（大卫·卡梅伦，英国前首相，2016 年英国脱欧公投后辞职。）
3. Tory party — the Conservative Party of the UK
4. Britain could be cast off from Europe's shores. — It is possible that Britain will be disconnected from other European countries.

    cast off — (of a boat or ship) to be set free on the water by a rope being untied（船只）解缆
5. Eurosceptics — Euroscepticism, i. e. the opposition to policies of EU institutions and/or opposition to Britain's membership of the European Union, has been a significant element in the politics of the UK. Levels of support for the EU have historically been lower in the UK than most other member states. UK citizens are the least likely to feel a sense of European identity, and national sovereignty is also seen as more important to British people than that of people from other EU nations.
6. Norway and Switzerland — Although the Kingdom of Norway is not a member state of the EU, it is closely associated with the Union through its membership in the European Economic Area (EEA), in the context of being a European Free Trade Association (EFTA) member. The relations between Switzerland and the EU are framed by a series of bilateral treaties whereby the Swiss Confederation has adopted various provisions of European Union law in order to

participate in the Union's single market.
7. NATO — the North Atlantic Treat Organization(北大西洋公约组织,简称"北约")
8. IMF — The International Monetary Fund is an international organization headquartered in Washington, D. C. , of "189 countries working to foster global monetary cooperation, secure financial stability, facilitate international trade, promote high employment and sustainable economic growth, and reduce poverty around the world."(国际货币基金组织)
9. on the sidelines — having no influence on an event 置身局外;处在旁观者的位置
10. Scotland, more Europhile than England, is again agitating for a divorce… —比英格兰更赞成留欧的苏格兰,再一次掀起了独立运动。
    a. -phile — *combining form* 爱好……的(人),亲……的(人),嗜……的(物)
    b. agitate for — protest or take part in political activity in order to get sth(为某事)进行鼓动,煽动;抗争
    c. divorce — here it refers to the independence of Scotland
11. Brexit could also dangerously unsettle Northern Ireland … — Possibly, Brexit will cause more troubles in Northern Ireland. (In Northern Ireland, a significant minority, mostly Catholics, were nationalists who wanted a united Ireland independent of British rule.)
12. Without Britain, it would be harder for the EU to pull its global weight — Without Britain, it would be more difficult for the EU to play its role in world affairs.
    pull one's weight — to do one's full share of work 做好本分工作

Questions

1. Why did David Cameron call a referendum on Britain's membership of the European Union?
2. Why does the writer say Brexit would deal a heavy blow to Europe?
3. What is the Brexiters' case?
4. Does the author agree with the Brexiters?
5. Why does the author say that Britain's gain by leaving EU would be

partly illusory?
6. How would Brexit seriously weaken the EU in the world?

读报知识

英国的议会、大选与全民公投

1. 议会

议会(Parliament)是英国最高立法机关,由英王、贵族院和平民院组成。英国政府的核心是议会,不仅拥有立法权,还有行政决策权。首相和内阁成员都由议会执政党产生,且都是议员。他们均可提出议案,一旦提出,一般都能顺利通过。不像美国那样,因党派之争而把议案修改得支离破碎,或是双方处于僵持状态,议案无法通过。这是因为英国的行政和立法不像美国那样独立分权,议会的多数党就是执政党,首相又是多数党党魁,普通议员必须接受党的领导和纪律,支持法案通过。因而,英国议会被视为一个高效的立法办事机构,能 get work done,不像美国的 don't-work Congress。但是有人批评说,这是以牺牲议员的自由意志为代价的。难怪 *The Economist* 评论说:(British) politics is based on the iron disciplines of the British party machine.

英国议会由贵族院(House of Lords, the Lords)和平民院(House of Commons, the Commons)组成。贵族院又称上院(the Upper House),形式上是英国最高立法机关,但实际上其立法权已被削弱,只能提出动议,对下院通过的法案表示赞同、反对或提出修改意见,并无决定立法的实权。上院议员主要由新封终生贵族、世袭贵族、上诉法院法官和教会首要人物组成。议长由大法官(Lord Chancellor)兼任。平民院又称下院(the Lower House),议员经选举产生,任期5年,主要职能为立法、监督财政和政府,较上院有实权。值得注意的是,报刊上常用缩略词 MP (member of Parliament),仅指下院议员。

2. 大选

英国的议会选举(parliamentary election),也称立法选举(legislative election),实际上就是下院选举,每5年举行一次。不过执政党可以通过内阁选择对自己有利的时机要求女王解散议会,提前选举。

英国的议会选举实行的是简单或相对多数制(plurality/simple majority system of voting),而不是非要获得过半数选票的多数(majority)。选举的原则是每一个选区都有数目相等的选民,每一个选民都有平等的选举权,即"一人,一票,一价"(one man/person, one vote, one value)。每一个选民只能投一票给一个候选人,在一个选区获得票数最多者当选为本区的下院议员。整个英国分为 646 个选区(parliamentary constituency),所以,下议院一共由 646 名成员组成。获得多数议员席位的政党便成为执政党,即得票多者当选的选举制度(first-past-the-post electoral system)。

议会选举结束后,国王或女王召见多数党领袖,请他出任首相并着手组阁,议会表决通过后,新政府即告成立。最大的在野党依法成为正式的反对党,组成"影子内阁"(shadow cabinet)。因此,英国的大选(general election)是议会选举和行政选举不分的。

3. 全民公投

通常的全民公决,又称全民投票或全民公投,是全体公民对重大问题投票作出决定。它起源于古希腊城邦雅典的公民大会。全民公决是一种直接民主形式,它是民主国家实行宪政制度的重要组成部分,是由选民通过直接投票的方式,对相关议题表达同意、反对或弃权的明确态度,然后根据表决结果达成决策的一种制度。它是人民自决权实施的一种特定程序选择,属于民主宪政的范畴。从性质上讲,它不是对代议制民主的否定,而是对代议制民主的补充和修正。

在英国历史上,共举行了三次全国性公投:分别在 1975 年、2011 年和 2016 年。其中两次是关于英国与欧洲关系问题的。1975 年,关于英国是否继续留在欧洲共同体(the European Communities,亦称 the Common Market)举行了公投,这是在英国 1973 年 1 月 1 日加入欧共体两年半后。另一次就是 2016 年的退欧公投了。2011 年的全国公投是关于选举制度改革的,也是唯一一次针对国内事务举行全国性的公投。

另外,英国还举行过 11 次区域性的公投,比如 1973 年关于北爱尔兰边境问题投票,还有最近的一次,2014 年苏格兰独立公投。

Lesson 11

课文导读

从常规衡量标准看,英国的报纸衰落了。自20世纪80年代中期起,英国出版的《每日快报》和《每日镜报》的发行量已锐减三分之二,年轻人因为电视和网络而摒弃了报纸,报纸衰亡似乎无可避免。事实真是如此吗? 本文独特的分析告诉我们一个恰好相反的动态:四面楚歌的英国报纸正引领世界报业革新,其实纸质和电子报纸各有千秋。

Pre-reading Questions

1. Do you often read newspapers? If you do, do you prefer a printed paper or an electronic one?
2. What do you think is the key reason for young readers to abandon regular newspapers?

Text

Britain's Embattled Newspapers Are Leading the World in Innovation

1   By most conventional measures, Britain's newspapers look doomed. Young readers are abandoning them for the Internet and television. The *Daily Express* and the *Daily Mirror*, both tabloids,

have shed about two-thirds of their circulation since the mid-1980s. Yet Evgeny Lebedev[1], co-owner of the *Independent* and the *Evening Standard*, is optimistic. "People are hailing the death of newspapers," he says. "But if you go into the Tube[2], you'll see almost everybody is reading one."

2   Britain's newspaper market is the world's most savage. It is unusually competitive: there are nine national daily papers with a circulation of more than 200,000. And advertising has migrated online more quickly than elsewhere. Since 2009 more advertising money has been spent on the Internet than on newspapers, according to ZenithOptimedia[3], a marketer. British papers receive no government funding (as is the case in France, for example). Indeed, they face a fearsome state-sanctioned competitor in the BBC[4].

3   Fierce competition has created a scrappy, sometimes immoral trade. This week the *News of the World*, a tabloid that has been caught up in a celebrity phone-hacking scandal, revealed it had suspended an editor. But Britain's papers are also exceptionally innovative, busily testing new format sizes and prices. Paul Zwillenberg of Boston Consulting Group[5] says they are now experimenting in dramatically different directions. There are three main trends.

4   The first is being driven from Wapping, London home of News Corporation. Its four British titles — the *Times*, the *Sunday Times*, the *Sun* and the *News of the World* — are moving behind an exceptionally tough online paywall.[6] Unlike the *Wall Street Journal*, also owned by News Corporation, the *Times* does not allow people to read any articles free on the web. Its prices are steep: £2 ($3.10) per week after the first month.

Not worth the paper they aren't reading

5   As online commentators and rivals have gleefully pointed out, News Corporation's paywalls have led to a drastic drop in traffic. A survey by Mark Oliver, a consultant, finds that only 14% of regular *Times* readers and just 1% of non-regular ones subscribe to the website in some form: upon hitting the paywall, most head for the BBC's free website instead. That does not worry News Corporation. It sees online advertising as an unreliable source of revenue. Online ad spending is

growing, but the number of ad slots available is rising much faster; as a result, prices are so low that a reader who visits a website once or twice a month is hardly worth having. The firm would rather extract more money from dedicated readers directly.

6   Thus the pages of the *Times* and *Sunday Times* are thick with in-house ads offering entertainments to readers, from iPad applications to theatre tickets and Italian holidays. Some 250,000 people buy from the *Times* wine club. These things tend to make money, but the main goal is to hook readers on a bundle of services. Katie Vanneck-Smith, chief marketing officer for News Corporation's British papers, wants to get to the point where a newspaper subscription is like its pay-television or mobile-phone equivalents: something it hurts to cancel. Rivals fear the firm will bundle newspapers with BskyB[7], a hugely successful satellite broadcaster that it controls and wants to take over completely.

7   Britain's second great innovator takes the opposite view. The *Daily Mail* contends that online advertising works fine — if you are huge. The paper has been one of the most consistent sellers in print over the past few years, crushing its nearest competitor, the *Daily Express*. But it is even mightier online. With 35m unique visitors each month, it is now the world's second-biggest newspaper website, according to comScore[8], which measures online traffic[9]. It may take the top spot[10] when the *New York Times* goes behind a paywall this year.

8   In contrast to the paper, which is conservative and often alarmist, the *Daily Mail*'s website is a breezy read. It is big on celebrity news, particularly reports involving attractive women in swimsuits. Lots of online news aggregators link to it. Executives claim that the website is now so successful that it competes not with other newspaper websites but with portals such as Yahoo! and MSN.com. The *Mail* is now steering readers to its iPhone application.

9   Perhaps the most counter-intuitive strategy is being pursued by Mr Lebedev and his father, Alexander, a Russian tycoon. In the past two years they have acquired the *Independent* and the *Evening Standard*, a London paper that they have made a freebie. In October they launched *i*, a cut-down *Independent*, priced at 20p — one-fifth the price of most quality daily newspapers. It is the first new national paper since 1986.

10   Not one of the Lebedevs' British papers has a compelling website.

They think young people do want to read newspapers — they just don't want to pay much, or anything, for them. The *Evening Standard*'s circulation has more than doubled since going free, to 700,000. Distribution costs have plunged. Papers are now handed out in central London and moved around the capital by Tube: because they are free, commuters often leave them on trains.

11   The *Independent* and *i* face a harder road. Because *i* is so cheap, newsagents make little money from sales. They often shelve it with bottom-feeding tabloids and the *Racing Post*. Yet *i* is an intriguing effort to prop up the *Independent*, which was nearing the point at which marketers were losing interest: now advertising often runs in both papers, which together offer a higher circulation. It costs little to assemble and may help keep alive the newspaper habit, by offering a halfway house[11] between free and premium papers.

12   The strategies being pursued by News Corporation, the Daily Mail and General Trust[12] and Lebedev Holdings rest on distinct assumptions about what readers want, what they will pay for, and the future of advertising. It is highly unlikely that all three experiments will work. It may well be that none of them does. But none can be faulted for lack of boldness.

13   The innovators also exude more confidence than others. The *Guardian*, which first championed a big, free online presence, has been overhauled by the *Mail*'s website.[13] It lacks News Corporation's expertise in bundling and is far more expensively staffed than the Lebedevs' outfits. It is a measure of how quickly things are moving that the newspaper closest to the cutting edge[14] a few years ago now seems most in need of a new strategy. (From *The Economist*, Jan 6, 2011)

New Words

aggregator /ˈæɡrɪɡeɪtə/ *n.* 聚合器（一种信息处理工具）
alarmist /əˈlɑːmɪst/ *adj.* making people feel worried about dangers that may or may not really exist
bottom-feeding /ˈbɒtəmˈfiːdɪŋ/ *adj. sl.* well-sold, widely required by readers
breezy /ˈbriːzɪ/ *adj.* fresh and animated; lively 清新的，活泼的
bundle /ˈbʌndl/ *n.* a number of articles tied, fastened, or held together
                  v. to sell several products or services together, package slae

捆绑销售

celebrity /sɪˈlebrətɪ/ *n.* a famous person, esp. in the entertainment sector 演艺界名人

circulation /ˌsɜːkjuˈleɪʃən/ *n.* the average number of copies of a newspaper, magazine etc that are regularly sold (报刊等的)发行量

contend /kənˈtend/ *v.* to claim; say or state strongly 宣称

equivalent /ɪˈkwɪvələnt/ *n.* sth that has the same value, purpose, job, etc. as sth else 类似,同样

exude /ɪɡˈzjuːd/ *v.* if you exude a particular quality, it is easy to see that you have a lot of it 充满,洋溢,充分显露(某一品质)

format /ˈfɔːmæt/ *n.* the size, shape, design, etc., in which sth. such as a book or magazine, is produced 格式,样式

freebie /ˈfriːbɪ/ *n. infml* sth. that you are given free, usu. by a company 免费赠品

gleeful /ˈɡliːfəl/ *adj.* very excited and satisfied

in-house /ˈɪnˈhaʊs/ *adj. & adv.* working within a company or organization 内勤

outfit /ˈaʊtfɪt/ *n. infml* a group of people who work together as a team or organization 整体(形象)

overhaul /ˈəʊvəhɔːl/ *v.* to catch up with; overtake

paywall /ˈpeɪˌwɔːl/ *n.* a program that stops people who have not paid a subscription from using a website 网站的收费墙

plunge /plʌndʒ/ *v.* if a price, rate, etc. plunges, it suddenly decreases by a large amount 下跌,颓市

portal /ˈpɔːtl/ *n.* a website that helps you find other websites 门户网站

premium /ˈpriːmɪəm/ *adj.* of very high quality

scrappy /ˈskræpɪ/ *adj. BrE* untidy or badly organized; *AmE infml* having a determined character and always willing to compete, argue, or fight 不整,零乱;好斗

shed /ʃed/ *v.* to drop sth or allow it to fall; to lose by natural process 放手,让其倒,下

slot /slɒt/ *n.* a short period of time allowed for one particular event on a program or timetable (广告)位,时段

steep /stiːp/ *adj.* steep prices, charges etc are unusually expensive; involving a big increase or decrease 急剧升降的(价格)

subscribe /səbˈskraɪb/ *v.* to pay money, usu. once a year, to have copies of a newspaper or magazine delivered to you, or to purchase some other service 订阅

suspend /sə'spend/ *v.* to officially stop sth from continuing, esp. for a short time

tabloid /'tæblɔɪd/ *n.* a newspaper that has small pages, a lot of photographs, and stories mainly about sex, famous people etc., rather than serious news; tabloid newspaper 小报(*cf.* broadsheet)

traffic /'træfɪk/ *n.* number of people or amount of goods moved from one place to another by road, rail, sea or air(公路、铁路、海上或空中人员或货物的)流量

tycoon /taɪ'kuːn/ *n.* one who is successful in business or industry and has a lot of money and power 产业大亨

Notes

1. Evgeny Lebedev — 叶夫根尼·列别捷夫(1980—), the Russian-born British co-owner of the *Independent* and the *Evening Standard*. Under Lebedev's tenure (任期), the *Evening Standard* became the first large-circulation newspaper in Britain to be distributed free, its circulation tripling to 600,000 copies. Lebedev is a supporter of the Arts and chairman of the Evening Standard Theatre Awards. He is a sponsor of the Moscow Art Theatre (莫斯科艺术剧院) and the Anton ChekhovYalta Theatre (安东尼·契科夫雅尔塔剧院). He is also the founder and chairman of the Raisa Gorbachev Foundation(赖萨·戈尔巴乔夫基金会).

2. the Tube — The London underground railway system, serving a large part of Greater London and some parts of Buckinghamshire (白金汉郡), Hertfordshire (赫特福德郡) and Essex (艾塞克斯郡).

3. ZenithOptimedia — a French multinational advertising and public relations company, headquartered in Paris, France. It is one of the world's three largest advertising holding companies (控股公司). The company owns several full-service advertising groups that undertake a range of media activities: mobile and interactive online communication, television, magazines & newspapers, cinema and radio, and outdoor ads. 实力媒体

4. a fearsome state-sanctioned competitor in the BBC — a competitor which is given official approval and so is very powerful and frightening. BBC is just such a competitor.

5. Boston Consulting Group — a global management consulting firm

with 78 offices in 43 countries. It is one of the largest private companies in the US. 波士顿咨询公司

6. The first is being driven from Wapping … an exceptionally tough online paywall. — 第一种趋势源自新闻集团驻伦敦办事处——沃平，它旗下四份报纸——《泰晤士报》《星期日泰晤士报》《太阳报》和《世界新闻》，正移至特别强大的网站收费墙之后。

News Corporation — a diversified multinational mass media corporation headquartered in New York City, the world's second-largest media group as of 2011 in terms of revenue, and the world's third largest in entertainment as of 2009, controlled by Rupert Murdoch and his family members. Its U. S. holdings include Fox News, *The Wall Street Journal* and Twentieth Century Fox. 新闻集团

7. BSkyB — British Sky Broadcasting Group, a British satellite broadcasting, broadband and telephone services company headquartered in London, with operations in the UK and Republic of Ireland, formed in 1990 by the equal merger of Sky Television and British Satellite Broadcasting, the largest pay-TV broadcaster in Britain and Ireland with over 10 million subscribers. It had a market capitalisation of approximately £11. 47 billion (US＄18 billion) as of 20 June 2012 on the London Stock Exchange. News Corporation owns a 39. 14 per cent controlling stake in the company. 英国天空广播公司

8. comScore — an Internet analytics company providing marketing data and analytics to many of the world's largest enterprises, agencies, and publishers. ComScore Networks was founded in August 1999 in Reston, Virginia. 康姆斯克互联网公司

9. online traffic — the flow of data across the Internet 浏览量

10. top spot — top of the list 顶尖，第一

11. halfway house — Usually, it refers to a place where people with mental disorders, victims of child abuse, orphans or teenage runaways can stay. However, a halfway house more usually refers to something combining features of two other things, for example a solution to a problem based on two ideas. 收容所；折中的解决方法

12. the Daily Mail and General Trust — a British media conglomerate （传媒集团），one of the largest in Europe. In the UK, it has interests in national and regional newspapers, television and radio.

The company has extensive activities based outside the UK. Its biggest markets apart from the UK are in the US, Central Europe, the Middle East, India and Australia. The head office is located in the Northcliffe House in Kensington, London Borough of Kensington and Chelsea. 每日邮报集团

13. the *Guardian*, which first … by the *Mail*'s website. — The *Guardian* was the first to publish its free online edition, which was very popular, but now the *Daily Mail*'s website is more popular.

14. the cutting edge — the most recent stage of development in a particular type of work or activity 最前沿,先锋地位

Questions

1. Why is Britain's newspaper market considered the world's most savage?
2. Do online paywalls do good to Britain's embattled newspapers? Why or why not?
3. Why is News Corporation's main goal to hook readers by means of a bundle of services?
4. How could the *Daily Mail*'s website be successful?
5. What are the three main trends of innovation in Britain's newspapers?

新闻写作

导语(Lead)

消息报道中的导语十分重要,一般在消息的第一个自然段,有时也由前两个或三个自然段组成。迅速点出新闻的主题,这是这种消息新闻体裁区别于其他体裁的一个重要特征。导语用三言两语写出消息中最主要的、最新鲜的事实,使读者先获得一个总的概念,再吸引读者继续看下去。可以说,导语是消息的概括,而标题又是导语的概括。

导语的作用是什么?美国新闻学家威廉·梅茨在《怎样写新闻》一书中认为有三点:(1)告诉读者这条消息的内容。(2)使读者愿意看下去。(3)必要时制造适当的气氛。还有人认为导语的作用可以概括为:(1)用简洁的文字反映消息要点,让读者大体了解消息的主要事实和主题思想。(2)引出主题以及阐述、解释这个主题的新闻主体。(3)唤起读者注意,吸引读者往下看。

一百多年来,导语产生了"两代"。什么是第一代新闻导语?如前所述,在导语里必须具备五个 W 和一个 H 要素(When, Where, Who, What, Why 和 How),即何时,何地,何人,何事,何故,如何。具体地讲,就是在什么时候发生的?在什么地方发生的?事情牵涉到什么人?发生了什么事?事情为什么会发生?事情是怎样发生和发展的?西方新闻学鼻祖之一戴纳提出,新闻导语必须回答五个 W 和一个 H。这个观点,曾经在相当长的时间里被认为是导语写作的金科玉律。这样的导语具有具体、完整的长处,看了导语,对消息的主要内容大体上都知道了。短处是内容太多,主次不清,重点不突出。再则,文字和重点易重复,展开难以顺畅。不适用于特写这样的软新闻体裁,缺乏悬念感。于是一些新闻工作者对导语进行改革。1954 年,《纽约时报》总编辑在采访部里贴出这样一个布告:"我们认为把传统五个 W 写在一个句子或一个段落里没有必要,也许永远没有必要。"这时顺便提醒一下读者,凡教过"托福"者无不知道,它的问答题往往都是这类问题。

通过改革,许多消息导语里只突出一两个新闻要素,其余新闻要素放在后面的主体或结尾,这样就可以更突出重点。这种出现在 20 世纪 50 年代至 70 年代的新闻导语,称为第二代导语。从导语的形式来分,有叙述式、设问式、评论式、结论式、描写式和对比式等。有的新闻专家列出 10 多种形式的导语,但不管多少种,都可归结为"direct lead"和"indirect lead"两种形式。不过这里要着重阐明倒金字塔式导语,五个 W 和一个 H 是构成一则完整的消息不可缺少的要素。以往直接的消息报道或纯消息一般采取"倒金字塔形式",其特点是将新闻报道最重要的五个 W 和一个 H 按重要性的顺序头重脚轻地安排,把新闻的高潮和结论放在最前面的导语里,然后按事实的重要性递减的顺序来安排(in the order of descending importance),由此突出最重要、最新的事实。

应该说明,新闻报道现在仍采用倒金字塔式结构形式为主,但不一定在导语里全部都包括五个 W 和一个 H,或许只有三个或四个 W,另一个或两个 W 出现在下面段落里,这是由于后来改革的结果。

由于导语形式多样,报道手法跟着翻新。如"时间顺序式"(Chronological Order Form)、"悬念式"(Suspended Interest Form)和"解释性报道式"(Interpretative Reporting Form)等。时间顺序式,有如香肠,一根接一根,所以又称为"香肠式"(Wiener Form)。时间顺序式多用于体育比赛,作案过程,厂家发展或名人讣告之类的消息报道。"悬念式"多用于特写。"解释性报道式"与纯新闻的客观报道不同,着重探讨理念、事情成败原因,寻求答案等。这种形式尤其在刊物中数量居多。(详见《导读》一章二节)

Lesson 12

课文导读

玛格丽特·撒切尔是英国保守党第一位女领袖,英国历史上第一位女首相,她创造了蝉联三届,雄踞政坛11年之久的记录,她始终不渝奉行强硬的保守派政策,被媒体喻为"铁娘子"。

在任英国首相期间,撒切尔大刀阔斧地进行改革。她主要采取四项措施:一是私有化,二是控制货币供应量,三是削减福利开支,四是打击工会力量。这一系列措施至今仍然影响着这个国家。

然而,读了此课,人们不禁感到这不但不像悼词,而是一篇声讨她的檄文。北爱尔兰新芬党党魁、工会和中右派都加入谴责她的队伍,而《卫报》此文也基本上支持他们的立场。客观地说,她从上台时把一个欧洲病夫的英国拯救出来是有功的,打击和压制工会也是有种种理由的。但她助富不济贫和极端自由派的经济政策是错误的。工党领袖布莱尔(Tony Blair)在1997年至2007年执政时基本上继承了她的经济政策,也执政达10年之久,所以我们要对她的功过加以分析,不被一人、一文的言论所左右。

Pre-reading Questions

1. Who is Margaret Thatcher, and what do you know about her?
2. Why is Mrs Thatcher called the "Iron Lady"?

Text

Little Sympathy for Margaret Thatcher[1] Among Former Opponents

Anger and regret rekindled in those who still feel that Thatcherism[2] ruined their lives and wrecked their communities

By Michael White

1   In death, as she had been in life, Margaret Thatcher proved to be a deeply divisive figure, with former opponents vocal in their criticism of

her on Monday.

Margaret Thatcher at Selby coalfield in 1980. Photograph: PA

2   To no one's surprise, news of her death prompted expressions of satisfaction and even delight on social media. "May she burn in hell fires," tweeted George Galloway, who also quoted an Elvis Costello protest song, "Tramp the dirt down."[3]

3   The Sinn Fein president, Gerry Adams[4], was among the first to react, offering a scathing assessment of Thatcher's political legacy. He said she had done "great hurt to the Irish and British people during her time as British prime minister. Here in Ireland her espousal of old draconian militaristic policies prolonged the war[5] and caused great suffering."

4   No amount of genuine dismay at such sentiments within the rival family of Thatcher admirers — those new mobile classes of the skilled and the newly rich identified by the BBC's social survey only last week — or Fleet Street's synthetic finger-pointing could inhibit the toasts and cheers[6]. Some people claim to have kept champagne bottles in the fridge for the occasion for decades.

5   Any satisfaction that Britain's first female prime minister — and their personal enemy — is dead mingled with burning anger and regrets rekindled in those who still feel that Thatcherism ruined their lives and wrecked their communities. The further north, the more visible it was among people who felt she cared nothing for them, their skills or values or for a slower, gentler world. In Scotland her legacy has crippled the Tory vote and may contribute to the breakup of Britain, one of many

ironies for her own declared values.

6 David Hopper, general secretary of the Durham Miners Association[7], now a shadow of its once mighty self, in part thanks to Thatcher's defeat of the miners union[8], spoke for millions — the white-collar teachers and clerical workers, nurses and bus drivers as well as former industrial workers — who blamed Thatcher for the loss of livelihoods that globalisation and technology might have taken anyway, but without her blunt coup de grace[9].

7 "It looks like one of the best birthdays I have ever had," said the ex-miner, 70 on Monday, who spent all of his working life at Wearmouth colliery[10]. "There's no sympathy from me for what she did to our community. She destroyed our community, our villages and our people. For the union this could not come soon enough and I'm pleased that I have outlived her."

8 Thatcher supporters will recoil from such sentiments as unfair and blind to economic realities and the selfish, sectional stranglehold then exercised by unions on behalf of their members. In 1979 it could take several months to obtain a phone — a landline installed by a state monopoly, the Post Office.

9 But such talk will not sway the likes of Hopper. "I imagine we will have a counter-demonstration when they have her funeral," he said.

10 "Our children have got no jobs and the community is full of problems. There's no work and no money and it's very sad the legacy she has left behind. She absolutely hated working people and I have got very bitter memories of what she did. She turned all the nation against us and the violence that was meted out[11] on us was terrible. I would say to those people who want to mourn her that they're lucky she did not treat them like she treated us."

11 It was Thatcher's misfortune that her insights were not tempered with much sympathetic imagination for people unlike herself — "is he one of us?" in the famous phrase — or by humour or emollient wit, by homely style or evident personal weakness.[12] She had tender feelings (her staff liked her), but rarely let them show in public until that last tear[13] after her party ejected her from power with a crude, male brutality she had not expected.

12 Even among the party faithful it made her more admired than loved.

On holiday among friends the restless workaholic was not easy company. Among those she worsted in political battles it all made it much easier to hate her. Few prime ministers in Britain have been burned in effigy[14].

13   The gay rights campaigner Peter Tatchell[15] said Thatcher was "an extraordinary woman but she was extraordinary for mostly the wrong reasons. During her rule, arrests and convictions for consenting same-sex behaviour rocketed, as did queer-bashing[16] violence and murder. Gay men were widely demonised and scapegoated for the Aids pandemic and Thatcher did nothing to challenge this vilification."

14   Ken Livingstone[17] also offered a critical assessment. He blamed Thatcher for causing unemployment and leaving people dependent on welfare: "She decided when she wrote off[18] our manufacturing industry that she could live with two or three million unemployed," he said.
(From *The Guardian*, April 8, 2013)

New Words

blunt /blʌnt/ *adj.* (of people, manner of speaking, etc.) lacking refinement or subtlety; straightforward and uncomplicated

colliery /ˈkɒliəri/ *n.* BrE a coal mine and the buildings around it 煤矿

consent /kənˈsent/ *v.* to give your permission for sth or agree to do sth

demonise /ˈdiːmənaɪz/ *v.* to convince sb that a person or thing is evil 将……妖魔化

dismay /dɪsˈmeɪ/ *n.* the worry, disappointment, or unhappiness you feel when sth unpleasant happens 哀伤

divisive /dɪˈvaɪsɪv/ *adj.* causing a lot of disagreement between people 引起分裂的,造成不和的

draconian /drəˈkəʊniən/ *adj.* very strict and cruel (法律等)严酷的,残酷的

effigy /ˈefɪdʒi/ *n.* a roughly made, usu. ugly, model of sb you dislike 肖像,画像

eject /ɪˈdʒekt/ *v.* to force sb to leave

emollient /ɪˈmɒliənt/ *adj.* making sb feel calmer when they have been angry 安抚的;抚慰的

espousal /ɪˈspaʊzl/ *n.* support for an idea, belief, etc., esp. a political one

finger-pointing *n.* the imputation of blame 相互指责

landline /ˈlændlaɪn/ *n.* telephone that is not a cell phone 固定电话,座机

militaristic /ˌmɪlɪtəˈrɪstɪk/ *adj.* (of groups, ideas, or policies) which support the strengthening of the armed forces of their country in order to make it more powerful 军国主义的

mingle /ˈmɪŋgl/ *v.* to bring or combine together or with sth else

monopoly /məˈnɒpəli/ *n.* a large company that controls all or most of a business activity 垄断

outlive /ˌaʊtˈlɪv/ *v.* to remain alive after sb. else has died 比……长寿

pandemic /pænˈdemɪk/ *n.* a disease that affects people over a very large area or the whole world 传染病

recoil /rɪˈkɔɪl/ *v.* to move back suddenly and quickly from sth you dislike or are frightened of 退缩,畏缩

rekindle /ˌriːˈkɪndl/ *v.* to make someone have a particular feeling, thought, etc. again 使重新激起

scathing /ˈskeɪðɪŋ/ *adj.* (of a remark) bitterly severe

stranglehold /ˈstræŋglhəʊld/ *n.* complete control over a situation, organization, etc.

sway /sweɪ/ *v.* to influence sb so that they change their opinion 动摇

temper /ˈtempə(r)/ *v. fml* to make sth less severe or extreme 调和,使缓和

tweet /twiːt/ *v.* to post (a message) on Twitter for (people) to read

vilification /ˌvɪlɪfɪˈkeɪʃn/ *n.* a rude expression intended to offend or hurt 诋毁;诽谤;中伤

worst /wɜːst/ *v.* to defeat thoroughly

Notes

1. Margaret Thatcher — 1925—2013,a British Prime Minister (1979—1990), Leader of the Conservative Party (1975—1990). She was the longest-serving British Prime Minister of the 20th century and the only woman to have held the office. 玛格丽特·撒切尔之所以在1990年被迫辞职是因为她在外交上对欧盟的前身欧共体(European Community)不合作和在国内执行的不分财富和收入一律按比例交人头税(poll tax)的问题上不得人心,党内不满而引起分裂,不得不将权交给她不喜欢的梅杰(John Major)。

2. Thatcherism — the system of political thought attributed to the governments of Margaret Thatcher. It is characterized by decreased state intervention via the free market economy, monetarist(以货币为基础的) economic policy, privatisation of state-owned industries,

lower direct taxation and higher indirect taxation, opposition to trade unions, and a reduction of the size of the Welfare State. 撒切尔主义是指撒切尔夫人上台后所推行的一套强硬的右翼政治、经济等政策,是当代西方"新自由主义"与"新保守主义"的混合物。如经济私有化,削减政府开支以减少赤字,控制货币供应量以降低通货膨胀率,大量限制工会权利等。她的这套政策使富人愈富,穷人愈穷,穷人的生活被毁掉了,各方面均无保障。此外,她与美国总统里根对经济不干预的极端自由派政策导致2008年后出现全球性经济危机和衰退。

3. "May she burn in hell fires" … "Tramp the dirt down" — George Galloway cursed Margaret Thatcher after her death that she would go to hell to be burned for her sins. And in Elvis Costello's song, "I'll stand on your (Thatcher's) grave and tramp the dirt down," he expressed his anger.

    a. George Galloway — (1954—) a British politician, author, journalist, and broadcaster, and the Respect Party Member of Parliament (MP) for Bradford West. 乔治·加洛韦

    b. Elvis Costello — (1954—) an English musician and singer-songwriter with Irish ancestry. 埃尔维斯·科斯特洛

    c. "Tramp the dirt down" — a fiery lament (哀悼词), depicting Costello's anger at the Thatcher government and its effect on Britain's society. In the song, Costello expresses his desire to live long enough to see Margaret Thatcher die and vows, "I'll stand on your grave and tramp the dirt down."

4. the Sinn Fein president, Gerry Adams — 新芬党领袖格里·亚当斯

    a. the Sinn Fein — the second-largest political party and the largest nationalist party in Northern Ireland. 爱尔兰民族主义政党。成立于1905年,建党之初,党员成分复杂,政见也较温和。它反对与英国妥协,主张依靠自己的力量谋求独立。英政界认为,它实际是爱尔兰共和军(IRA)的政治组织。新芬(Sinn Fein)英文意为"we ourselves"。

    b. Gerry Adams — an Irish Sinn Fein politician, the President of Sinn Fein since 1983

5. the war — 指当时英国政府与爱尔兰正在进行的关于北爱尔兰的地位归属问题的谈判,爱尔兰主张与爱统一,英却坚持由北爱全民公决,因北爱支持留在英国的新教徒占多数。支持统一的武装组织北爱尔兰共和军(Irish Republican Army)代表天主教徒早在20世纪50年代就

为统一而展开斗争,暴力不断。僵持不下时,英国就派军队镇压和维持秩序。IRA 的暴力行动一度渗透到英国,直至 1997 年 9 月 15 日它才最终宣布停火,采用政治手段达到目的。Adams 指的 war 外刊普遍用 troubles, violence, terrorist attack, terrorism 等字眼。

6. No amount of genuine dismay … or Fleet Street's synthetic finger-pointing … could inhibit the toasts and cheers. — no matter how sad people were,(such sadness)could not prevent some people from their celebration.

   a. no amount of sth can/will do sth — used to say that sth has no effect on sth 再多……也不

   b. Fleet Street — a street in the City of London named after the River Fleet. It was the home of British national newspapers until the 1980s. Even though the last major British news office, Reuters, left in 2005. The term Fleet Street continues to be used as a metonym for the British national press.

   c. synthetic finger-pointing — insincere criticism or blame

7. the Durham Miners Association — a trade union in the U. K. , founded in 1869 达拉谟矿工协会

8. Thatcher's defeat of the miners union — The Thatcher Government gradually reduced the power of the trades unions, and the greatest single confrontation with the unions was the NUM (National Union of Mineworkers) strike of 1984 to 1985, in which the union eventually had to concede(退让). Both Thatcher's approach to industrial relations(劳资关系)and the behaviour of the trades unions in the 1970s accelerated the departure from the British tradition of voluntarism (based on contract law, 唯意志论), bringing more and more aspects of labour relations into the sphere of government. 她打击和限制工会是因其好斗,动辄罢工,曾迫使过首相下台;是工党的坚定支柱。使它不得翻身,工党也因此在野十多年而不得掌权。

9. but without her blunt coup de grace — if she had not given a direct strike
   coup de grace — a hit or shot that kills sb or sth 致命的一击,决定性的一击

10. Wearmouth colliery — a major North Sea coal mine located on the north bank of the River Wear（威尔河）, located in Sunderland（巽得兰）. It was the largest mine in Sunderland and one of the most important in County Durham（达拉谟郡）in northeast England. 威

尔茅斯煤矿

11. mete out — *fml* to give sb, esp. a punishment（给予[惩罚]）

12. It was Thatcher's misfortune…by homely style or evident personal weakness. — 对于撒切尔来说,不幸的是她的远见毫不温和,不带有对与她不同的人的同情——比如,她的口头禅"他是我们的人吗?"——不幽默、没有抚慰人心的智慧,不亲切、没有表现出人性的软弱。

   "is he one of us?" — a phrase derived from Thatcher's Conservative Party Conference speech（Thatcher brooked [容忍] little criticism. She sacked party members who questioned her divisive practices. "Is he one of us?" became a stock [常备的] Thatcher question, asked of impartial civil servants [公务员] and even would-be bishops [主教].）

13. She…rarely let them show in public until that last tear — 她几乎从不将她柔情的一面示之与众,直到她辞职时,她才潸然泪下。1990年11月22日,撒切尔夫人发表声明决定退出党魁选举,这个决定使她长达11年半的首相生涯步上终结。

14. burned in effigy —（Thatcher's) portrait is damaged or destroyed by fire.

15. Peter Tatchell —（1952— ）an Australian-born British political campaigner best known for his work with LGBT (lesbian, gay, bisexual and transgender 同性恋、双性恋及变性者) social movements. 彼得·泰切尔

16. queer-bashing — an offensive term for the practice or an instance of committing unprovoked acts of violence against gay and lesbian people 酷儿打压（即打压同性恋）。"酷儿"（queer）由英文音译而来,原是西方主流文化对同性恋的贬称,有"怪异"之意。

17. Ken Livingstone —（1945— ）a British Labour Party politician. Livingstone has positioned himself on the hard left of the Labour Party. 肯·利文斯通

18. write off — to cancel; regard as cancelled or useless

Questions

1. After hearing of Mrs Thatcher's death, how did the media react?
2. How did Gerry Adams comment on Mrs Thatcher's political legacy?
3. What did David Hopper think of Mrs Thatcher's policies?
4. How do the party faithful feel about Mrs Thatcher?

5. How did Ken Livingstone think of Mrs Thatcher?
6. What do you think about Mrs Thatcher?

读报知识

英国政党简介

翻开英国近代史,人们可以看到,政府都由保守党和工党轮流执掌或联合执掌。两党制根深蒂固,第三党受到选举等限制难以壮大。

1. 工党和新工党

工党(the Labour Party)成立于1900年,原名"劳工代表委员会",1906年改用现名。第二次世界大战至2008年,工党已联合或单独组阁7次,是保守党的主要对手。它曾标榜"社会主义",主张通过"议会斗争"和"议会民主"方式进行改革。虽然工党党员大部分是工人,但领导人的行动和政治策略也代表富裕资产阶级的利益。工党原先一贯主张扩大国有化,限制资本外流。对外政策强调"国家利益"。自1979年以来工党一直在野,已在4次大选中败给保守党。英报认为,该党政策正在向右转,与撒切尔夫人推行的一些做法相似。后来改革派领袖史密斯出任领袖,1994年5月,正值声望上升之时,史密斯猝然去世。这样,工党又陷入了内部权力斗争,保守党获得急需的喘息机会。直至1995年以改革家著称的布莱尔(Tony Blair)出任该党领袖,并在1997年的大选中击败保守党,改写了该党在野18年的历史。

工党的胜利靠的是布莱尔的"走第三条道路"(the third way)和改旧工党为"新工党"(New Labour)。与此同时,布莱尔改革党章,放弃了党章第四条国有化的条款(Clause Four)。

2007年,布莱尔因在伊拉克开战等问题上追随美国,结果吃了大亏,声誉扫地,国内问题也不如意,被迫将首相一职交给财政大臣布朗(Gordon Brown)。由于经济不振,该党在2010年大选中败北。为省略,报刊常用Labour(工党),如Labour's plan。

2020年4月,基尔·斯塔默(Keir Rodney Starmer)当选现任领袖。

2. 保守党

保守党(the Conservative Party)的前身为1679年成立的托利党(the Tory Party),1833年改称保守党。1912年国家统一党并入保守党,称保守统一党(The Conservative and Unionist Party),简称保守党。为省略,报刊常用the Tories或the Conservatives(保守党)。在力量占优势的选区扎根深,自身又较能抑制内阁,屡次大选击败工党,从1951年至1964年和1979

年至 1997年曾长期执政。从不公布党员人数,据估计为180万左右,大多来自社会上层。保守党代表英国垄断资本家、大地主和贵族的利益。

1979年撒切尔夫人执政,大力推行"货币主义"经济政策(monetarist financial policies),通过严格控制货币供应量和减少公共开支等手段控制通货膨胀。反对削减个人所得税,主张加强法律和社会治安,限制工会权力,加速私有化,将某些国有企业恢复为私营,有走极端市场经济倾向。对外主张加强防务,增加军费,加强与欧盟前身欧洲共同体各国的合作,协调外交政策和欧美立场,加强大西洋联盟,尤其强调英美的"特殊关系"。

撒一意孤行,推行不分财富和收入多寡,一律按比例交税的人头税(poll tax)失去民心而被迫下台。

1990年梅杰接班上台,内外政策均有所调整。但因爆发"疯牛病"(mad-cow disease)跟欧洲联盟的关系紧张,党内又纷争不断,不如当年一致对外,加之梅杰能力平庸,政绩乏善可陈。结果在1997年大选中被工党击败。2010年大选,该党在下院650个席位中获306席,稍多于工党的258席,未能过半,卡梅伦(David Cameron)不得不与自民党组成联合内阁,出任首相。

2015年大选后,保守党重获多数,取得单独执政地位,卡梅伦连任首相,组成保守党政府。虽然卡梅伦不主张脱离欧盟,但迫于国内压力,同意举行"脱欧"公投。2016年6月,英国全民公投决定"脱欧",卡梅伦宣布辞职,特雷莎·梅(Theresa May)当选保守党魁,成为英国历史上第二位女首相。

2017年3月,英国正式启动"脱欧"程序。然而,在两年多的"脱欧"谈判过程中,英国议会一直未能通过"脱欧"协议,"脱欧"日期一再推迟。2019年6月7日,特雷莎·梅宣布辞职。7月,鲍里斯·约翰逊(Boris Johnson)当选保守党领袖,成为新一任首相,并在2020年1月31日带领英国正式脱欧。2022年10月,时任保守党党首里希·苏纳克(Rishi Sunak)成为英国第57任首相。

3. 自由民主党

自由民主党(the Liberal Democrats 或 the Liberal Democrat Party)常简称Lib Dems(自民党),是自由派的政党,英国第三大党。1988年由自由党和社会民主党内多数派组成,正式名称为社会自由民主党(the Social and Liberal Democrats)。该党实力尚不如保守党和工党,但很有前途。曾任副首相的尼克·克莱格(Nick Clegg)在2007年的党魁选举中获胜,担任党魁至2015年。在2017年大选中该党仅在国家议会(Parliament)中占有14席。(详见《导读》英国"政党")

Unit Five
World

Lesson 13

课文导读

近年来亚洲国家经济发展强劲而举世瞩目。越来越多的亚洲国家脱离赤贫状态，民众对国家福利制度的诉求越来越高。于是乎，亚洲大国诸如中国和印度的福利制度出现了高歌猛进式的发展。福利制度应跨越式发展，一蹴而就，还是应稳步推进呢？本文根据欧美国家福利制度的发展过程，指出了亚洲国家在福利制度的制定与实施过程中值得反思的问题和难点，提出了可资借鉴的经验教训和建议。亚洲国家如何能既保持强劲的经济发展势头，又能真正实现向福利国家的转变，这的确需要一场社会变革。

Pre-reading Questions

1. What do you think of China's social welfare? What benefits has it brought to the people?
2. How much do you know about the social welfare programs of other countries?

Text

Rethinking the Welfare State: Asia's Next Revolution
By Bob Dillon

1　　Countries across the continent are building welfare states[1] — with a chance to learn from the West's mistakes.

2　　Asia's economies have long wowed the world with their dynamism. Thanks to years of spectacular growth, more people have been pulled from abject poverty in modern Asia than at any other time in history. But as they become more affluent, the region's citizens want more from their governments. Across the continent pressure is growing for public pensions, national health insurance, unemployment benefits and other hallmarks of social protection. As a result, the world's most vibrant economies are shifting gear, away from simply building wealth towards building a welfare state.

3   The speed and scale of this shift are mind-boggling. Last October Indonesia's government promised to provide all its citizens with health insurance by 2014. It is building the biggest "single-payer" national health scheme[2] — where one government outfit collects the contributions and foots the bills — in the world. In just two years China has extended pension coverage to an additional 240 million rural folk, far more than the total number of people covered by Social Security, America's public-pension system[3]. A few years ago about 80% of people in rural China had no health insurance. Now virtually everyone does. In India some 40 million households benefit from a government scheme[4] to provide up to 100 days' work a year at the minimum wage, and the state has extended health insurance to some 110 million poor people, more than double the number of uninsured in America.

4   If you take Germany's introduction of pensions in the 1880s as the beginning and Britain's launch of its National Health Service[5] in 1948 as the apogee, the creation of Europe's welfare states took more than half a century. Some Asian countries will build theirs in a decade. If they get things wrong, especially through unaffordable promises, they could wreck the world's most dynamic economies. But if they create affordable safety nets, they will not just improve life for their own citizens but also become role models themselves. At a time when governments in the rich world are failing to redesign states to cope with

ageing populations and gaping budget deficits, this could be another area where Asia leapfrogs the West.

Beyond Bismarck and Beveridge[6]

5   History offers many lessons for the Asians on what to avoid. Europe's welfare states began as basic safety nets. But over time they turned into cushions. That was partly because, after wars and the Depression[7], European societies made redistribution their priority, but also because the recipients of welfare spending became powerful interest groups. The eventual result, all too often, was economic sclerosis with an ever-bigger state. America has kept its safety net less generous, but has made mistakes in creating its entitlements system[8]— including making unaffordable pension and health-care promises, and tying people's health insurance to their employment.

6   The record in other parts of the emerging world, especially Latin America, is even worse. Governments have tended to collect insufficient tax revenue to cover their spending promises. Social protection often aggravated inequalities, because pensions and health care flowed to affluent urban workers but not the really poor. Brazil famously has a first-world rate of government spending but third-world public services.

7   Asia's governments are acutely conscious of all this. They have little desire to replace traditions of hard work and thrift with a flabby welfare dependency. The region's giants can seek inspiration not from Greece but from tiny Singapore, where government spending is only a fifth of GDP[9] but schools and hospitals are among the best in the world. So far, the safety nets in big Asian countries have generally been minimalist: basic health insurance and pensions which replace a small fraction of workers' former income. Even now, the region's social spending relative to the size of its economies is only about 30% of the rich-country average and lower than any part of the emerging world except sub-Saharan Africa[10].

8   That leaves a fair amount of room for expansion. But Asia also faces a number of peculiarly tricky problems. One is demography. Although a few countries, notably India, are relatively youthful, the region includes some of the world's most rapidly ageing populations. Today China has five workers for every old person. By 2035 the ratio

will have fallen to two. In America, by contrast, the baby-boom[11] generation meant that the Social Security system had five contributors per beneficiary in 1960, a quarter of a century after its introduction. It still has three workers for every retired person.

9   Another problem is size, which makes welfare especially hard. The three giants — China, India and Indonesia — are vast places with huge regional income disparities within their borders. Building a welfare state in any one of them is a bit like creating a single welfare state across the European Union. Lastly, many Asian workers (in India it is about 90%) are in the "informal" economy[12], making it harder to verify their incomes or reach them with transfers.

Cuddly tigers, not flabby cats[13]

10   How should these challenges be overcome? There is no single solution that applies from India to South Korea. Different countries will, and should, experiment with different welfare models. But there are three broad principles that all Asian governments could usefully keep in mind.

11   The first is to pay even more attention to the affordability over time of any promises. The size of most Asian pensions may be modest, but people collect them at an early age. In China, for example, women retire at 55; in Thailand many employees are obliged to stop work at 60 and can withdraw their pension funds at 55. That is patently unsustainable. Across Asia, retirement ages need to rise, and should be indexed to life expectancy.

12   Second, Asian governments need to target their social spending more carefully. Crudely put, social provision should be about protecting the poor more than subsidizing the rich. In fast-ageing societies, especially, handouts to the old must not squeeze out investment in the young. Too many Asian governments still waste oodles of public money on regressive universal subsidies. Indonesia, for instance, last year spent nine times as much on fuel subsidies as it did on health care, and the lion's share[14] of those subsidies flows to the country's most affluent. As they promise a broader welfare state, Asia's politicians have the political opportunity, and the economic responsibility, to get rid of this kind of wasteful spending.

13   Third, Asia's reformers should concentrate on being both flexible and innovative. Don't stifle labor markets with rigid severance rules[15] or over-generous minimum wages. Make sure pensions are portable, between jobs and regions. Don't equate a publicly funded safety net with government provision of services (a single public payer may be the cheapest way to provide basic health care, but that does not have to mean every nurse needs to be a government employee). And use technology to avoid the inefficiencies that hobble the rich world's public sector. From making electronic health records ubiquitous to organizing transfer payments through mobile phones, Asian countries can create new and efficient delivery systems with modern technology.

14   In the end, the success of Asia's great leap towards welfare provision will be determined by politics as much as economics. The continent's citizens will have to show a willingness to plan ahead, work longer and eschew handouts based on piling up debt for future generations: virtues that have so far eluded their rich-world counterparts. Achieving that political maturity will require the biggest leap of all. (From *The Economist*, September 8, 2012)

New Words

abject /ˈæbdʒekt/ *adj.* the state of being extremely poor, unhappy, unsuccessful, pitiful etc 不幸的, 悲惨的

affluent /ˈæfluənt/ *adj.* having plenty of money, nice houses, expensive things etc; wealthy 富足的

aggravate /ˈæɡrəveɪt/ *v.* to make a bad situation, an illness, or an injury worse 雪上加霜

apogee /ˈæpədʒiː/ *n.* the most successful part of sth 最高点, 顶峰

beneficiary /ˌbenɪˈfɪʃəri/ *n.* someone who gets advantages from an action or change (遗嘱, 保险等的)受益人;(退休金等的)领受人

contributor /kənˈtrɪbjətə(r)/ *n.* someone who gives money, help, ideas etc to sth that a lot of other people are also involved in 贡献者

coverage /ˈkʌvərɪdʒ/ *n.* the protection an insurance company gives you, so that it pays you money if you are injured, or sth is stolen, etc. 费用的承担

crudely /ˈkruːdli/ *adv.* expressed in a simple way 简单表达

cuddly /ˈkʌdli/ *adj.* lovable; suitable for cuddling 可爱的, 想抱的

cushion /ˈkʊʃn/ *n.* sth esp. money, that prevents you from being

immediately affected by a bad situation 缓冲，解难
demography /dɪˈmɒrəfɪ/ *n.* the study of human populations and the ways in which they change, for example the study of how many births, marriages and deaths happen in a particular place at a particular time 人口学
disparity /dɪˈspærətɪ/ *n.* a difference between two or more things, esp. an unfair one 差距，悬殊
dynamism /ˈdaɪnəmɪzəm/ *n.* energy and determination to succeed 劲头，魄力
elude /ɪˈluːd/ *v.* (of a fact, answer etc.) to be difficult for (sb) to find or remember 把……难倒，记不起
entitlement /ɪnˈtaɪtlmənt/ *n.* the official right to have or do sth or the amount that you have a right to receive 应得的东西
eschew /ɪsˈtʃuː/ *v.* to deliberately avoid doing or using sth 避开；戒绝
expectancy /ɪkˈspektənsɪ/ *n.* the length of time that a person or animal is expected to live 生命预期
flabby /ˈflæbɪ/ *adj.* weak or not effective 无力的；软弱的
foot /fʊt/ *v.* to pay for sth esp. sth expensive that you do not want to pay for 结(账)，付(款)
gear /ɡɪə(r)/ *n.* an apparatus, esp. one consisting of a set of toothed wheels, that allows power to be passed from one part of a machine to another so as to control power, speed, or direction of movement 档位（汽车变速）
hallmark /ˈhɔːlmɑːk/ *n.* an idea, method, or quality that is typical of a particular person or thing 标志，特点
hobble /ˈhɒbl/ *v.* to deliberately make sure that a plan, system, etc. cannot work successfully 阻碍，阻挠
index /ˈɪndeks/ *v.* to arrange for the level of wages, pensions etc to increase or decrease according to the level of prices ⟨美口⟩按生活指数调整
insured /ɪnˈʃʊəd/ *n.* an insured person 被保险人
leapfrog /ˈliːpfrɒɡ/ *v.* to suddenly become better, more advanced etc than people or organizations that were previously better than you 跨越
mind-boggling /ˈmaɪndˌbɒɡlɪŋ/ *adj.* difficult to imagine and very big, strange, or complicated
minimalist /ˈmɪnɪməlɪst/ *adj.* deliberately designed to be as simple as possible; used esp. to describe the inside of someone's house where there is little furniture and very few patterns or decorations 简朴的

oodles /'uːdlz/ *n.* a large amount of sth 大量的
outfit /'aʊtfɪt/ *n.* a group of people who work together as a team or organization 群体
patently /'peɪtntlɪ/ *adv.* very clearly and obviously 明显地；赤裸裸地
pension /'penʃən/ *n.* a fixed sum of money paid regularly to a person by a government or company to sb. who is considered to be too old or too ill to work
portable pension pension that workers can keep when they move from one job to another 可转移的退休金
provision /prə'vɪʒn/ *n.* the act of providing 供给，服务
ratio /'reɪʃɪəʊ/ *n.* a relationship between two amounts, represented by a pair of numbers showing how much bigger one amount is than the other 比率
regressive /rɪ'ɡresɪv/ *adj.* returning to an earlier, less advanced state, or causing sth to do this
sclerosis /sklə'rəʊsɪs/ *n.* a disease that causes an organ or soft part of your body to become hard 僵化，硬化
severance /'sevərəns/ *n.* money paid by a company to one of their workers losing their job through no fault of their own, esp. when the job is no longer necessary because of reorganization in the company 离职补偿金
stifle /'staɪfl/ *v.* to stop sth from happening or developing 遏制，抑制
transfer /træns'fɜː(r)/ *v. & n.* to move money from one account or institution to another 转帐
ubiquitous /juː'bɪkwɪtəs/ *adj.* seeming to be everywhere
unsustainable /ˌʌnsə'steɪnəbl/ *adj.* unable to continue at the same rate or in the same way 不可持续的
verify /'verɪfaɪ/ *v.* to discover whether sth is correct or true
vibrant /'vaɪbrənt/ *adj.* full of activity or energy in a way that is exciting and attractive; lively 充满活力的
wow /waʊ/ *v. slang* to cause surprise or admiration 使人惊喜的，发出感叹
wreck /rek/ *v.* to completely spoil sth. so that it cannot continue in a successful way; ruin 致残，毁坏

Notes

1. welfare state — a concept of government in which the state plays a key role in the protection and promotion of the economic and social

well-being of its citizens. It is based on the principles of equality of opportunity, equitable distribution(机会平等、公平分配)of wealth, and public responsibility for those unable to avail(有助于)themselves of the minimal provisions for a good life. The general term may cover a variety of forms of economic and social organization. 福利国家。福利制度指的是国家或政府在立法或政策范围内为所有对象普遍提供在一定的生活水平上尽可能提高生活质量的资金和服务的社会保障制度。

2. "single-payer" national health scheme — a system in which the government pays for all health care costs. But the term "single-payer" only describes the funding mechanism — referring to health care financed by a single public body from a single fund. The healthcare services may be offered by either the government or private organizations. Usually, the fund holder is the state, but some forms of single-payer use a mixed public-private system. 单一支付方医疗体系是一种由政府作为唯一支付方,负责筹资和购买医疗服务的体系。在这种体系下,来自雇主、个人和政府的资金会由政府筹集起来统一管理,并用于支付每个公民的医疗开支。现在世界上很多国家都采用这种单一支付方体系,比如加拿大的医疗保险、英国的国民医疗保健制度等。

3. social security, America's public-pension system — 社会保障,即美国公共保险制度。起先由美国联邦政府于1935年实施,其中有退休、失业、残废等保险。后来,其中部分职能已转交或下放给地方政府,并在克林顿执政时期进行了大胆改革。它是一种公共福利措施。

4. government scheme — It refers to the Mahatma Gandhi National Rural Employment Guarantee Act (MGNREGA), an Indian job guarantee scheme, enacted by legislation on 25 August 2005. The scheme provides a legal guarantee for at least one hundred days of employment in every financial year to adult members of any rural household willing to do public work-related unskilled manual work at the statutory minimum wage(法定最低工资)of 120 rupees (US＄2.20) per day in 2009 prices. If they fail to do so the government has to pay the salary at their homes. 指印度议会2005年8月23日以口头表决的方式批准的政府提交的《全国农村就业保障法案》。根据此法案,印度政府今后将每年斥资4000亿卢比(1美元约合43卢比),以确保印度7.2亿农村人口中每个家庭每年都能获得

100 天的就业机会,并领取政府发放的最低日工资 120 卢比的报酬。
5. National Health Service — It may refer to one or more of the four publicly funded healthcare systems within the UK. The systems are primarily funded through general taxation rather than requiring private insurance payments. The services provide a comprehensive range of health services, the vast majority of which are free at the point of use for residents of the UK. The four systems are quite independent, and operate under different management, rules, and political authority. 英国医疗保健制度,1948 年建立,基本上是公费,并覆盖全民。
6. Beyond Bismarck and Beveridge — Here it means that the development of Asian countries' welfare states is beyond the imagination of Bismarck and Beveridge, both are authorities in this field. (小标题中提到这两个人正是照应了上一段的"If you take Germany's introduction of pensions in the 1880s as the beginning and Britain's launch of its National Health Service in 1948 as the apogee."他们的时代与此对应。)

  a. Bismarck, Otto von — (1815-1898) was a conservative German statesman who dominated European affairs from the 1860s to his dismissal in 1890. In 1871, he unified most of the German states into a powerful German Empire under Prussian leadership, which created a balance of power that preserved peace in Europe from 1871 until 1914. He designed and introduced social insurance in Germany to promote the well-being of workers in order to keep the German economy operating at maximum efficiency, thus creating a new nation-state and leading the way to the first welfare state. 俾斯麦是 19 世纪德国政治家,担任普鲁士首相期间通过一系列铁血战争统一德国,并成为德意志帝国第一任宰相。俾斯麦以保守专制主义者的身份,镇压了 19 世纪 80 年代的社会民主运动,但他通过立法建立了世界上最早的工人养老金、健康和医疗保险及社会保险制度。

  b. Beveridge, William — 1879-1963, was a British economist and social reformer. As one of the theoretical founders of the welfare states, he is best known for his 1942 report "Social Insurance and Allied Services" (known as the Beveridge Report) which served as the basis for the post-World War II welfare state. He was an authority on unemployment insurance from early in his career, served under Winston Churchill on the Board of Trade as Director of the newly created labor exchanges and later as Permanent Secretary of the Ministry of Food. 威廉·贝弗里奇是福利国家的理论建构者之一,他于1942年发表《社会保险报告书》,也称《威廉·贝弗里奇报告》,提出建立"社会权利"新制度,包括失业及无生活能力之公民权、退休金、教育及健康保障等理念。他是自由主义者,主张市场经济。他于1944年发表《自由社会的全面就业》一书,主张有国家及市场导向的私人企业来联合运作,对当代社会福利政策及保健制度具有深远影响。

7. the Depression — also "the Great Depression," a severe worldwide economic depression in the 1930s. It was marked by the Wall Street Crash of October 1929, wiping out 40 percent of the paper values of common stock. The market crash marked the beginning of a decade of high unemployment, poverty, low profits, deflation, plunging farm incomes, and lost opportunities for economic growth and personal advancement. The core of the problem was the immense disparity between the country's productive capacity and the ability of people to consume. The Depression caused huge political and economic changes in America and the world and was believed to be a direct contributor to World War II. 20世纪30年代的经济大萧条

8. entitlements system — the social security system or program(见"语言解说")

9. GDP — *abbr.* gross domestic product, the total value of all goods and services produced in a country in one year, except for income received from abroad. GDP per capita(人均GDP) is often considered an indicator of a country's standard of living. 国内生产总值

10. Sub-Saharan Africa — Geographically it refers to the area of the continent of Africa that lies south of the Sahara. Politically, it consists of all African countries that are fully or partially located south of the Sahara (excluding Sudan). It contrasts with North Africa, which is considered a part of the Arab world. 撒哈拉以南非洲,俗称黑非洲

11. baby-boom — a big increase in the number of babies being born within a certain period of time. Here it refers to the famous post-World War II baby boom in the US between about 1946 and 1964. Here in the article, the author means that thanks to this baby-boom which brought demographic bonus(人口红利) to America's

economy, there are still enough workers to support the retired people and the Social Security System. 美国第二次世界大战后出现的婴儿潮

12. informal economy — economic activities organized without government approval, outside mainstream industry and commerce, including barter of goods and services(易物交换), mutual self-help, odd jobs, street trading(沿街摆摊), and other such direct sale activities. Income generated by the informal economy is usually not recorded for taxation purposes, and is often unavailable for GDP computations. Informal employment are lack of protection in the event of non-payment of wages(拖欠工资), compulsory overtime or extra shifts(强制超时或加班), lay-offs without notice or compensation(无通知或补偿的辞退), unsafe working conditions and the absence of social benefits such as pensions, sick pay and health insurance. 非正规经济;零散的经济活动

13. Cuddly tigers, not flabby cats — 是幼虎而不是病猫,暗喻亚洲国家有很大的发展潜力

14. the lion's share — the largest portion

15. severance rules — 解聘规则(*cf.* severance pay 遣散费,解雇费)

Questions

1. What was the most important mission of the major Asian countries in the past decades? And what do their people concentrate on in recent years?
2. In building their welfare states, what achievements have the big giants of Asia accomplished and what problems have they got?
3. What lessons should the Asian countries learn from the western countries and what suggestions does the author offer?
4. Why does the author say that social protection often aggravated inequalities?
5. Do you agree with the author's opinion that different countries will and should experiment with various welfare models?

> 语 言 解 说

委婉语

委婉语多是报刊语言的一个特点,也是读报者理解上的一大难题。委婉语(euphemism)修辞格原本用来谈论生理及病、死、卖淫、同性恋等令人尴尬、不快或禁忌的话题,有的较文雅礼貌,有的含糊其辞,以使听者顺耳,读者舒服。各界都用委婉语,但用多了即成弊病。见本课第 5 段用的委婉语例句:

America has kept its safety net less generous, but has made mistakes in creating its **entitlements system** — including making unaffordable pension and health-care promises, and tying people's health insurance to their employment.

这句话的意思很清楚,社会安全网(safety net)不如应得权利制度覆盖的面广,但何谓这个拗口的制度或计划? 它包括 1. Social Security 和扶老医疗计划;2. 济贫医疗计划和生活费用、津贴等在内的 Public Welfare Programs。但多数情况下只指 Social Security(社会保障制度)。用 entitlement 这个字意为只要你够条件,就有权利得到联邦政府的津贴和补助,并非政府的施舍。1996 年《福利改革法》生效后,这些福利或大打折扣或无权得到了。句中的 entitlements system 指 Social Seurity System or Program,用在此处,语义更加委婉。

1. 社会领域委婉语

2007 年 10 月至 11 月,上海举办了一届智残者奥林匹克夏季运动会,2007 年 10 月 1 日出版的 *Newsweek* 上一篇题为"Shanghai Soften Up"的文章里用的是"the Special Olympics World Summer Games"。the Special Olympics 就是委婉语,在这篇文章中的其他委婉语还有 the less fortunate, special-needs pupils 以及:

Four years ago the city began setting up a network of "Sunshine Homes" to provide activities and vocational training for **mentally challenged** students aged 16 to 35.

(上海在四年前就开始为 16 岁至 35 岁的智残学生提供活动和职业训练而建立了一系列充满温暖的智残人场所。)

对于残疾人,报刊为不得罪任何一方读者,一般不会或不应该用 the retarded/disabled/deaf/crippled/deformed/disabled/handicapped 等,但可以用 people with mental retardation/disabilities 等。不过最受青睐的委婉用法是:physically/mentally/visually/vertically/challenged(身

体、智力、视力有缺陷及个子不高的）。此外，还有 physically inconvenienced（身体不便的）、partially sighted（只有部分视力的）、visually impaired（视力受损的）和 the otherly abled（有其他方面能力的人）等等。

2. 政治领域

委婉语成了政客歪曲事实、掩盖丑行、欺世盗名，奸商蒙骗消费者，记者追求语言新奇的手段，因而泛滥成灾，不少令受众不知所云。如老布什总统出尔反尔，承诺不增税，后来不明说 tax increase，而用了遭人讥讽的 revenue enhancement（岁入增加），人称 Bushisms。

战争不用 war 而用 future unpleasantness。为掩盖平民伤亡，政府不明言 civilian casualities/death 而用 collateral damage（附带性损伤），媒体将 terrorists 称之为 insurgents。美国对战俘施酷刑称之为 physical persuasion（或许是仿花钱打点的"currency persuasion"）。

以上有些是说话兜圈子（circumlocution syndrome）。难怪 2005 年 *U.S. News & World Report* 在一篇文章的漫画里讽刺说："能用拗口的委婉语，何必直说呢？"（Why say something clearly when you can use a jaw-breaking euphemism?）这与简明英语（plain English）运动背道而驰。（详见《导读》四章六节）

Lesson 14

课文导读

　　曾经的殖民地,如今的希望之洲,非洲正行进在崛起的路途上。历史、自然环境等因素导致非洲各国长期处于普遍的贫困状态,但依傍丰富的自然资源,国际上的友助,自身的拼搏,非洲在经历数十年的缓慢发展后,真正获得了发展的机会。非洲要真正崛起,前方还有哪些困难?需要解决哪些问题?本文对此进行了多层面的剖析。

Pre-reading Questions

1. Do you have any friends or relatives who have been to African countries?
2. What is their impression?

Text

The Hopeful Continent: Africa Rising

After decades of slow growth, Africa has a real chance to follow in the footsteps of Asia

1　　THE shops are stacked six feet high with goods, the streets outside are jammed with customers and salespeople are sweating profusely under the onslaught[1]. But this is not a high street[2] during the Christmas-shopping season in the rich world. It is the Onitsha market in southern Nigeria, every day of the year. Many call it the world's biggest. Up to 3m people go there daily to buy rice and soap, computers and construction equipment. It is a hub for traders from the Gulf of Guinea, a region

blighted by corruption, piracy, poverty and disease but also home to millions of highly motivated entrepreneurs and increasingly prosperous consumers.

2 Over the past decade, six of the world's ten fastest-growing countries were African. In eight of the past ten years, Africa has grown faster than East Asia, including Japan. Even allowing for the knock-on effect of the northern hemisphere's slowdown, the IMF expects Africa to grow by 6% this year and nearly 6% in 2012, about the same as Asia.

3 The commodities boom is partly responsible. In 2000—08 around a quarter of Africa's growth came from higher revenues from natural resources. Favourable demography is another cause. With fertility rates crashing in Asia and Latin America[3], half of the increase in population over the next 40 years will be in Africa. But the growth also has a lot to do with the manufacturing and service economies that African countries are beginning to develop. The big question is whether Africa can keep that up if demand for commodities drops.

Copper, gold, oil—and a pinch of salt[4]

4 Optimism about Africa needs to be taken in fairly small doses, for things are still exceedingly bleak in much of the continent. Most Africans live on less than two dollars a day. Food production per person has slumped since independence in the 1960s. The average lifespan in some countries is under 50. Drought and famine persist. The climate is worsening, with deforestation and desertification still on the march.

5 Some countries praised for their breakneck economic growth, such as Angola and Equatorial Guinea, are oil-sodden kleptocracies[5]. Some that have begun to get economic development right, such as Rwanda and Ethiopia, have become politically noxious. Congo, now undergoing a shoddy election, still looks barely governable and hideously corrupt. Zimbabwe is a scar on the conscience of the rest of southern Africa[6]. South Africa, which used to be a model for the continent, is tainted with corruption; and within the ruling African National Congress[7] there is talk of nationalising land and mines.

6 Yet against that depressingly familiar backdrop, some fundamental numbers are moving in the right direction. Africa now has a fast-growing

middle class: according to Standard Bank[8], around 60m Africans have an income of $3,000 a year, and 100m will in 2015. The rate of foreign investment has soared around tenfold in the past decade.

7　　China's arrival has improved Africa's infrastructure and boosted its manufacturing sector. Other non-Western countries, from Brazil and Turkey to Malaysia and India, are following its lead. Africa could break into the global market for light manufacturing and services such as call centres. Cross-border commerce, long suppressed by political rivalry, is growing, as tariffs fall and barriers to trade are dismantled.

8　　Africa's enthusiasm for technology is boosting growth. It has more than 600m mobile-phone users—more than America or Europe. Since roads are generally dreadful, advances in communications, with mobile banking and telephonic agro-info[9], have been a huge boon. Around a tenth of Africa's land mass is covered by mobile-internet services — a higher proportion than in India. The health of many millions of Africans has also improved, thanks in part to the wider distribution of mosquito nets and the gradual easing of the ravages of HIV/AIDS. Skills are improving: productivity is growing by nearly 3% a year, compared with 2.3% in America.

9　　All this is happening partly because Africa is at last getting a taste of peace and decent government. For three decades after African countries threw off their colonial shackles, not a single one (bar the Indian Ocean island of Mauritius[10]) peacefully ousted a government or president at the ballot box. But since Benin set the mainland trend in 1991, it has happened more than 30 times—far more often than in the Arab world.

10　　Population trends could enhance these promising developments. A bulge of better-educated young people of working age is entering the job market and birth rates are beginning to decline. As the proportion of working-age people to dependents rises, growth should get a boost. Asia enjoyed such a "demographic dividend"[11], which began three decades ago and is now tailing off. In Africa it is just starting.

11　　Having a lot of young adults is good for any country if its economy is thriving, but if jobs are in short supply it can lead to frustration and violence. Whether Africa's demography brings a dividend or disaster is largely up to its governments.

More trade than aid

12   Africa still needs deep reform. Governments should make it easier to start businesses and cut some taxes and collect honestly the ones they impose. Land needs to be taken out of communal ownership[12] and title handed over to individual farmers so that they can get credit and expand. And, most of all, politicians need to keep their noses out of the trough[13] and to leave power when their voters tell them to.

13   Western governments should open up to trade rather than just dish out aid. America's African Growth and Opportunity Act[14], which lowered tariff barriers for many goods, is a good start, but it needs to be widened and copied by other nations. Foreign investors should sign the Extractive Industries Transparency Initiative[15], which would let Africans see what foreign companies pay for licences to exploit natural resources. African governments should insist on total openness in the deals they strike with foreign companies and governments.

14   Autocracy, corruption and strife will not disappear overnight. But at a dark time for the world economy, Africa's progress is a reminder of the transformative promise of growth. (From *The Economist*, Dec 3, 2011)

New Words

Angola /æŋˈɡəʊlə/ *n.* a country in southwest Africa 安哥拉
autocracy /ɔːˈtɒkrəsɪ/ *n.* government by one person with unlimited power 专制, 独裁政治
ballot /ˈbælət/ *n.* a system of voting, usually in secret, or an occasion when you vote in this way 选票
bar /bɑː/ *prep.* except
Benin /beˈniːn/ *n.* a country in West Africa 贝宁
bleak /bliːk/ *adj.* (fig.) not hopeful or encouraging; dismal; gloomy 无望的; 阴郁的; 黯淡的
blight /blaɪt/ *v.* to ruin or destroy 损毁
boon /buːn/ *n.* sth very helpful and useful
bulge /bʌldʒ/ *n.* a sudden, usu. temporary increase in number or quantity
communal /ˈkɒmjʊnəl/ *adj.* shared by a group of people or animals, esp.

a group who live together 群体的

Congo /ˈkɒŋgəʊ/ *n.* a country on the Equator in the western part of central Africa 刚果

deforestation /diːˌfɒrɪˈsteɪʃən/ *n.* the cutting or burning down of all the trees in an area 大量砍伐

desertification /dɪˌzɛːtɪfɪˈkeɪʃn/ *n.* the process by which useful land, esp. farm land, changes into desert 土地的沙化

dismantle /dɪsˈmæntl/ *v.* to bring to an end (a system, arrangement, etc.), esp. by gradual stages

Equatorial Guinea /ˌekwəˈtɔːrɪəl ˈgɪnɪ/ *n.* a small country in west central Africa 赤道几内亚

Ethiopia /ˌiːθɪˈəʊpɪə/ *n.* a country in northeast Africa on the Red Sea 埃塞俄比亚

fertility /fəˈtɪlɪtɪ/ *n.* the ability to produce offspring; power of reproduction 生育能力；繁殖能力

hideous /ˈhɪdɪəs/ *adj.* extremely ugly or shocking to the senses; repugnant 极丑的，骇人听闻的 hideously *adv.*

kleptocracy /klepˈtɒkrəsɪ/ *n.* a government where officials are politically corrupt and financially self-interested 腐朽政府

oust /aʊst/ *v.* to force someone out and perhaps take their place 把某人撵走（以取代之）

profusely /prəˈfjuːslɪ/ *adv.* produced or existing in large quantities 大量生存地

ravage /ˈrævɪdʒ/ *v.* to ruin and destroy; devastate 破坏，毁坏

Rwanda /rʊˈændə/ *n.* a country in east central Africa 卢旺达

shackles /ˈʃæklz/ *n.* sth that prevents you from doing what you want to do 镣铐，禁锢

shoddy /ˈʃɒdɪ/ *adj.* unfair and dishonest 不公平，不诚实

slump /slʌmp/ *v.* to go down suddenly or severely in number or strength 暴跌，剧降

stack /stæk/ *v.* to put piles of things on or in a place 堆满，把……堆放在某处

strife /straɪf/ *n.* state of conflict; angry or violent disagreement; quarrelling 冲突；争斗；争吵

taint /teɪnt/ *v.* if sth bad taints a situation or person, it makes the person or situation seem bad 污染，玷污，（使）腐败

tariff /ˈtærɪf/ *n.* a tax on goods coming into a country or going out of a country 关税

trough /trɒf/ *n.* a long narrow open container that holds water or food for animals 水槽，饲料槽

Notes

1. salespeople are sweating profusely under the onslaught — They are sweating a lot because they are very busy with customers. 此处的"onslaught"不能死抠"a fierce attack"的意思，是指买卖人招揽顾客拼命推销商品，所以汗流浃背。词义要视上下文而定。
2. high street — the main street of a town where most of the shops and businesses are and people spend money in them 商业街
3. With fertility rates crashing in Asia and Latin America—As the birth rate drops in Asia and Latin America
   a. fertility rate — the birthrate of a population 生育率
   b. crash — to fail; become unsuccessful 跌，失败
4. a pinch of salt — used to describe a small amount of something. Here, it implies that although Africa is abundant in natural resources, it should be used in an economical way for, someday, it will be exhausted. 节俭方式，一点点
5. oil-sodden kleptocracies — Although some countries, such as Angola and Equatorial Guinea, are rich in oil resources, their government officials are politically corrupt and financially self-interested. 石油资源丰富，但是政府腐败。
   oil-sodden—covered with oil or full of oil 吸饱石油的
6. Zimbabwe is a scar on the conscience of the rest of southern Africa. —In Zimbabwe(津巴布韦), the Matabele unrest(马塔贝列人的动乱) led to what has become known as the Matabeleland Massacres(马塔贝莱兰大屠杀), which lasted from 1982 until 1985. Mugabe(津巴布韦总统穆加贝)ordered his North Korean-trained Fifth Brigade（第五旅）to occupy Matabeleland, crushing any resistance to his rule. It has been estimated that at least 20,000 Matabele were murdered and tens of thousands of others were tortured in military internment camps(俘虏收容所). The slaughter only ended after Nkomo and Mugabe reached a unity agreement in 1988 that merged their respective parties, creating the Zimbabwe African Union-Patriotic Front(津巴布韦非洲爱国阵线). In 1980s, such slaughter is indeed a scar on the conscience in such a civilized

world.（本文第5段及根据英文资料的释义充分说明西方对非洲国家反对殖民统治、种族歧视和隔离政策及独立自主充满不满和仇恨。）（见"读报知识"）

  a scar on the conscience — great sadness, guilt, etc. after the unpleasant experience left in the heart which is difficult to get rid of 心灵上的创伤

7. African National Congress — South Africa's governing political party, supported by its Tripartite Alliance（三方联盟）with the Congress of South African Trade Unions (COSATU)（南非工会大会）and the South African Communist Party (SACP)（南非共产党），since the establishment of non-racial democracy in April 1994.（南非）非洲国民大会

8. Standard Bank — The Standard Bank of South Africa Limited is one of South Africa's largest financial services groups. It operates in 30 countries around the world, including 17 in Africa.（南非）标准银行

9. telephonic agro-info — information related to agriculture given or obtained through telephoning 电话农业信息

  agro-info — 由"agricultural information"拼缀而成。

10. the Indian Ocean island of Mauritius — an island nation in the Indian Ocean about 2,000 kilometres (1,200 mi) off the south east coast of the African continent. 印度洋岛国毛里求斯

11. demographic dividend — a lot of advantages obtained from the population 人口红利，指一个国家的劳动年龄人口占总人口比重较大，抚养率比较低，为经济发展创造了有利条件。

12. communal ownership — an ownership of a territorial commune and its bodies of self administration. It is similar to municipal or public ownership, which is not part of state or private property. 群体所有

13. politicians need to keep their noses out of the trough — politicians should not interfere with government policies and practices.（This expression is a variant of the idiom "have one's nose in the trough," which means "to be involved in sth which you hope will get you a lot of money or political power."）

14. America's African Growth and Opportunity Act — a legislation that has been approved by the U.S. Congress in May 2000. The purpose is to assist the economies of sub-Saharan Africa and to improve economic relations between the United States and the

region. 美国非洲增长和机遇法案
15. Extractive Industries Transparency Initiative — an act to increase transparency over payments by companies from the oil and mining industries to governments and to government-linked entities, as well as transparency over revenues by those host country governments. 采掘业透明度行动计划

Questions

1. How is today's economic development in Africa compared with East Asia and the whole world?
2. When optimism is shown about Africa, what other obstacles is Africa facing now?
3. What is favorable to Africa's economic growth?
4. What measures should Africa take in order to achieve further development?
5. What are the main reasons leading to Africa's rising?

语言解说

Establishment

establishment 是报刊中常见的多义词,读者切忌见之就理解为"建立"。《泰晤士报》曾载文称,在现代报纸上,一个词有五六个意思是很平常的。见以下解说:

1. 界。作"界"讲,在美语里已成了贬义词,在英国却不然。

Intelligence **establishment** became intelligence community because establishment became pejorative. (*The New York Times Magazine*)

2. 建立起来的机构,单位

a. The hotel is a well-run **establishment**. (*Los Angles Times*)

b. "It is truly regrettable. It is deplorable that a diplomatic **establishment** has been mistakenly hit," Keizo Obuchi was quoted as saying by Kyodo News Agency. (*AP*)

3. 编制,建制

The Pentagon argues for a leaner military **establishment** ... (*Time*)

4. 当局，当权派，官方，统治集团。本课第四段中的"the political establishment"即为此义。

a. Indeed the West German **establishment**, like the Polishe and East German governments, seems to be cordially displeased with Judge Stern'sjudgment. (*Newsweek*)

b. Khomeini's curious blend of mysticism and activism still made him slightly suspect in the eyes of the Islamic **Establishment** — as a holy man who tried to run around with the Mob, one might say — but his following was growing steadily. (*Time*)

c. Some **establishment** figures remain wary of Byrne because she defeated their candidate, but the new mayor has moved to patch up differences. (*Time*)

5. 权势集团社会既成权力机构；门阀，财阀

a. Despite his contribution in the field of social progress President Johnson "was never accepted by the liberal Eastern **Establishment**," Carter said. "I don't know why." (*Washington Star News*)

b. The Church of England is the official (established) church of the United Kingdom, created in the 16th century as a protestant church by the Act of Supremacy. Its secular head is the sovereign, and its religious head, the Archbishiop of Canterbury. Its senior clergy — archbishops, bishops and deans — are appointed by the Prime Minister. It is one of the main forces of the **Establishment** in Britain. (*Adrian Room*)

Lesson 15

课文导读

　　叙利亚内战是从 2011 年初持续至今的叙利亚政府与叙利亚反对派之间的冲突,是阿拉伯之春运动的一部分。"阿拉伯之春"是西方媒体所称的阿拉伯世界的一次革命浪潮。自 2010 年 12 月突尼斯一些城镇爆发民主运动以来,阿拉伯世界一些国家民众纷纷走上街头,要求推翻本国的专制政体,并乐观地预见这个运动的前景是"一个新中东即将诞生",认为这个"阿拉伯之春"是"谙熟互联网、要求和世界其它大部分地区一样享有基本民主权利的年轻一代"。运动爆发后,西方国家扶持的叙利亚反对派要求总统巴沙尔·阿萨德下台,巴沙尔·阿萨德同意通过和谈解决叙利亚国内的矛盾,但遭到叙利亚反对派的拒绝。叙利亚的反政府示威活动于 2011 年 1 月 26 日开始并于 3 月 15 日升级,随后反政府示威活动演变成了武装冲突。叙利亚冲突既是一场内战,也是一场代理人战争。叙国内被撕裂为两派,一派为世俗政治拥趸,另一派为宗教势力拥趸,且双方各由敌对力量支持。

Pre-reading Questions

1. Do you know anything about the Arab world? How many countries does it consist of?
2. What do you think of the U.S. and Russian intervention in Syria?

Text

US Launches First Direct Military Action Against Assad[1]

　　Trump authorizes missile attack on government airfield in move Russia says is violation of international law. Bombing a 'significant blow to US-Russia relations', says Kremlin[2].

By Spencer Ackerman and Ed Pilkington in New York & Ben Jacobs and Julian Borger in Washington

1 The US military has launched a cruise missile attack on a Syrian airfield in response to Bashar al-Assad regime's use of chemical weapons this week[3], marking the first time the US has become a direct combatant against the Syrian regime.

2 The US move drew an angry response from Russia, which described the strike as an "aggression against a sovereign state in violation of international law".

3 The Russian foreign ministry has since announced that it was suspending a deal with the US to exchange information about military flights to avoid incidents in the crowded skies over Syria. Moscow has also called for a meeting of the UN security council to discuss the strikes.

4 Syrian officials said at least seven people were killed and nine wounded in US missile attack.

5 Russia's foreign minister said no Russian service personnel were hurt in the strike. Speaking during a trip to Uzbekistan, Sergei Lavrov[4] said the strike was launched on an "absolutely made-up pretext", adding: "It reminds me of the situation in 2003 when the United States and Britain, along with some of their allies, attacked Iraq."

6 He said Russia would demand Washington explain why it conducted the strikes. "I hope this provocation will not lead to irreparable damage [to US-Russian ties]," Lavrov said.

7 Donald Trump, who for years signalled he was comfortable with Assad remaining in power, abruptly switched course after seeing images of children gassed to death in Idlib province after Assad used chemical weapons against Syrian civilians.

8 The US strike saw 59 Tomahawk cruise missiles launched from the guided-missile destroyers USS Ross and USS Porter in the eastern Mediterranean.[5]

9 An airbase at Shayrat, near Homs[6], was targeted, signalling a limited initial engagement on a target the military said was used to launch the chemical attack.

10 Although the US targeted some of Syria's air defenses, it did not do so largely beyond Shayrat or in a sustained barrage, as it would

typically do before launching a concerted air campaign. Instead, the Pentagon said, it attacked "aircraft, hardened aircraft shelters[7], petroleum and logistical storage, ammunition supply bunkers, air defense systems, and radars" at the airfield.

11　　Russian state TV aired footage claiming to show the damage from the US strikes at the Syrian airbase. It showed craters and pockmarks left by explosions and said nine Syrian air force jets had been destroyed.

12　　Though Trump lacked congressional and international authorisation for the strike, prominent US politicians immediately gave him political cover.

13　　The president said on Thursday night at his Mar-a-Lago resort[8] that he had ordered a "targeted military strike on the airfield in Syria from where the chemical attack was launched".

14　　After a frantic day of consultation with his military advisers, including the defense secretary, James Mattis[9], and the national security adviser, HR McMaster[10], Trump said it was a "vital national security interest" of the US to prevent "the spread and use of deadly chemical weapons" after previous efforts to change Assad's behavior "had failed, and failed very dramatically".

15　　Trump also called on the international community to "join us in seeking to end the slaughter and bloodshed in Syria and also to end terrorism of all kinds and all types", leaving it unclear whether the US objective was retaliation for the chemical assault, destruction of Assad's chemical stockpiles or a push to oust Assad from power.

16　　For its part, the Pentagon said the strike "was intended to deter the regime from using chemical weapons again".

17　　Vladimir Putin's[11] spokesman, Dmitry Peskov, said in a statement carried by Russian news agencies that the president believed the US had carried out the strikes under a "far-fetched pretext". Russia has argued that the death of civilians in Khan Sheikhun[12] resulted from Syrian forces hitting a rebel chemical arsenal there, but the Guardian visited the attack site and found no evidence for this claim.

18　　Dozens of civilians, including 10 children, were killed, apparently by a chemical attack on Khan Sheikhun, in a region held by rebels who oppose Assad's regime.

19　　On Friday, sources told the Guardian US intelligence officials believed Russian personnel were at Shayrat airbase when the chemical agent was loaded on to a Syrian jet. They have not established whether the Russians knew it was happening.

20   The base covers an area of more than 8 sq km (3 sq miles) and has two runways and dozens of buildings, silos and storage facilities.

21   The sources said on both occasions a Russian Sukhoi aircraft[13] was monitored by ground radar and aerial reconnaissance flying over the town. Flashes had been detected on the ground indicating that ordnance had been dropped.

22   Trump had already warned that his view had been changed by the shocking images of children. The attack happened at 8.40pm eastern standard time[14] (4.40am in Syria) while Trump was hosting his Chinese counterpart, Xi Jinping, at Mar-a-Lago in Florida.

23   In 2013, Assad's forces used chemical weapons, including sarin and chlorine, killing more than 1,000 people. President Barack Obama threatened military action over Assad's use of sarin, an illegal weapon, but the US Congress balked and Russia intervened to make a deal in which Assad would hand over stockpiles of weapons.

24   Since Russia sent aircraft, troops and personnel to bolster Assad in late 2015, the Syrian president's fortunes have improved dramatically, and he has retaken territory from the beleaguered and fractious armed opposition. The Russian presence has raised the stakes dramatically for US military planners, as the prospect of accidentally killing Russian personnel and sparking a larger war with a nuclear power reduces the US room for manoeuvre.

25   However, according to the Pentagon spokesman Capt Jeff Davis, the US military notified Russian forces before the strike, using a communications channel set up to ensure US pilots who attacked Islamic State[15] targets in eastern Syria did not accidentally come into conflict with their Russian counterparts.

26   It is likely Russia would have passed the warning on to its Syrian allies. The US has roughly 1,000 troops in Syria, who may be at risk as a result of the strike.

27   For years, defense analysts have warned the US against attacking Assad without a plan for what it seeks to achieve or what a post-Assad Syria might look like.

28   Neither the US Congress nor the UN have authorized war against Assad. Mary Ellen O'Connell, an international law scholar at the University of Notre Dame[16], said Trump did not have a legal basis for military action.

29   For years, Trump rejected any attack on Assad as a strategic folly, despite repeated chemical assaults of the sort that prompted Thursday's missile strikes. After Russia's intervention in the conflict, Trump said rival Hillary Clinton's openness to strikes against Assad's forces were inviting conflict with Russia. Just days ago, his secretary of state and UN ambassador made statements indicating Trump was prepared to let Assad — who in November called Trump a "natural ally" — remain in power.

30   But earlier on Thursday, after Trump's public anger at Assad for the chemical assault, the secretary of state, Rex Tillerson[17], said there was "no role for [Assad] to govern the Syrian people" and called on Russia, where Tillerson will travel next week, to "consider carefully" its sponsorship of the Syrian dictator.

31   Tillerson suggested "steps are under way" to rally an international coalition to remove Assad diplomatically, a position long thwarted by Moscow and Beijing.

32   Trump and the military "sent an important message the United States will no longer stand idly by as Assad, aided and abetted by Putin's Russia, slaughters innocent Syrians with chemical weapons and barrel bombs[18]," the two Republican senators said in a joint statement.
(From *The Guardian*, April 7, 2017)

New Words

abet /ə'bet/ *v.* to help or encourage sb to do sth criminal or wrong 煽动；教唆；支持

agent /'eɪdʒənt/ *n.* a chemical that has a particular effect or is used for a particular purpose(化学)剂；药剂

ammunition /ˌæmjʊ'nɪʃn/ *n.* bullets, bombs, explosives etc, esp. things fired from a weapon 弹药

arsenal /'ɑːsənl/ *n.* a building where weapons and military equipment are made or stored; a store of weapons 兵工厂；军火库；一大批储存的

武器

authorize /ˈɔːθəraɪz/ *v.* to give formal permission to or for sth 授权，批准

balk /bɔːk/ *v.* not to want to do sth or let it happen 阻止，反对

barrage /bəˈrɑːʒ/ *n.* a continuous firing on an area with large guns and tanks 连续炮击；密集炮火，齐射式攻击

beleaguer /bɪˈliːgə(r)/ *v.* usu. pass. to surround with an army so as to prevent escape; besiege 围困；围攻

bolster /ˈbəʊlstə(r)/ *v.* to increase someone's confidence or courage; to strengthen one's position in a situation 增强；巩固；支持

bunker /ˈbʌŋkə(r)/ *n.* a place, usu. underground, that has been built with strong walls to protect it against heavy gunfire and bombing 地堡；弹药库

chlorine /ˈklɔːriːn/ *n.* a strong-smelling gas that is used to clean water and to make cleaning products 氯

combatant /ˈkɒmbətənt/ *n.* a person taking a direct part in fighting

concerted /kənˈsɜːtɪd/ *adj.* planned or done together by agreement; combined 商定的；一致的；协同完成的

cover /ˈkʌvə(r)/ *n.* sth that hides or keeps sth secret; the act of giving false information or not giving all the information you have, in order to protect someone who is doing sth secret or illegal 掩饰；包庇

crater /ˈkreɪtə(r)/ *n.* a round hole in a surface formed by an explosion, falling meteor etc (炸弹爆炸、流星坠落等在地上造成的) 坑

deter /dɪˈtɜː(r)/ *v.* to prevent from acting, esp. by the threat of sth unpleasant 制止，阻吓，使不敢

far-fetched *adj.* extremely unlikely to be true or to happen 不可信的，靠不住的，牵强的

folly /ˈfɒli/ *n.* a foolish act or way of behaving; an act of stupidity

footage /ˈfʊtɪdʒ/ *n.* a film or the part of a film which shows a particular event (描述某一事件的) 片段镜头

fractious /ˈfrækʃəsʊtɪdʒ/ *adj.* bad-tempered about small unimportant things and ready to quarrel 易怒的

logistical /ləˈdʒɪstɪkl/ *adj.* 后勤的；物流的

manoeuvre /məˈnuːvə(r)/ *n.* a skillful or carefully planned process intended to gain an advantage, to get out of a difficult situation etc 操控手段；策略，花招

ordnance /ˈɔːdnəns/ *n.* military supplies, esp. weapons 军火；大炮

pockmark /'pɒkmɑːk/ *n.* a hollow mark left on the skin where a small diseased area has been, esp. one caused by smallpox 痘痕，麻点

pretext /'priːtekst/ *n.* a reason given for an action in order to hide the real intention; excuse 借口

provocation /ˌprɒvəˈkeɪʃn/ *n.* a reason for someone else to react angrily, violently, or emotionally 挑衅

rally /'ræli/ *v.* to come or bring together (again) for a shared purpose or effort (为共同目的而)集合

regime /reɪˈʒiːm/ *n.* often derog. a particular (system of) government【常贬】政体，政权

retaliation /rɪˌtæliˈeɪʃn/ *n.* action against someone who has done something bad to you 报复；反击

sarin /'sɑːrɪn/ *n.* an extremely poisonous gas that is used in chemical weapons 沙林毒气；甲氟膦酸异丙酯（一种用作神经性毒气的化学剂）

silo /'saɪləʊ/ *n.* a specially built place underground where a nuclear missile is kept (核弹的)发射井

stockpile /'stɒkpaɪl/ *n.* a large store of goods, weapons etc for future use, esp. ones which may become difficult to obtain (准备应急或有可能短缺的)贮存物资；储备武器

suspend /səˈspend/ *v.* to stop or cause to be inactive or ineffective for a period of time

Syria /'sɪriə/ *n.* 叙利亚

Syrian /'sɪriən/ *adj.* 叙利亚的；叙利亚人的

thwart /θwɔːt/ *v.* to prevent sb from doing sth or from getting what they want 阻挠；挫败

Uzbekistan /ˌʌzbɛkɪˈstɑːn/ *n.* 乌兹别克斯坦

Notes

1. Assad — Bashar al-Assad (1965 —) is the 19th and current President of Syria, holding the office since 17 July 2000. He is also commander-in-chief of the Syrian Armed Forces, General Secretary of the ruling Arab Socialist Ba'ath Party and Regional Secretary of the party's branch in Syria. He is the second son of Hafez al-Assad, who was President of Syria from 1971 to 2000. 巴沙尔·阿萨德，现任叙利亚总统，阿拉伯复兴社会党总书记、叙利亚武装部队总司令，元帅军衔，是前任总统哈菲兹·阿萨德的次子。

2. Kremlin — the official residence of the President of the Russian Federation. It is often used metonymically to refer to the government of the Russian Federation. 克里姆林宫,位于莫斯科的心脏地带,是俄罗斯联邦的象征、总统府的所在地。常用来代指俄罗斯政府。

3. Bashar al-Assad regime's use of chemical weapons this week — 指 2017 年 4 月 4 日,叙利亚人权观察组织称,多架战机疑向叙利亚西北部一个市镇投掷毒气,造成至少 100 人死亡,约 400 人受伤,死者包括了 11 名儿童。叙利亚军方否认在反政府武装控制区使用毒气。

4. Sergei Lavrov — (1950 —   ) a Russian diplomat, and the Foreign Minister of Russia, in office since 2004. 谢尔盖·维克托罗维奇·拉夫罗夫,2004 年起至今担任俄罗斯外交部长,是普京的第一号外交心腹,以强硬著称。

5. The US strike saw 59 Tomahawk cruise missiles … in the eastern Mediterranean. — 美国在这次打击中发射了 59 枚"战斧"巡航导弹,这批巡航导弹是从美军停在东地中海区域的罗斯号和波特号驱逐舰上发射的。

6. an airbase at Shayrat, near Homs — 位于霍姆斯附近的沙伊拉特空军基地(Homs is a city in western Syria. Shayrat Airbase is home to the Syrian Air Force 50th Air Brigade located in Homs.)

7. hardened aircraft shelters — a reinforced hangar to house and protect military aircraft from enemy attack 加固的飞机掩体

8. Mar-a-Lago resort — an estate and National Historic Landmark in Palm Beach, Florida. In 1985, Mar-a-Lago was purchased by businessman Donald Trump. 海湖庄园,位于美国南部佛罗里达州棕榈滩,是美国前总统特朗普名下一处产业。特朗普就任总统后,在海湖庄园举行多场会客和外事活动,海湖庄园也因此有"冬季白宫"之称。2017 年 4 月 6 日至 7 日,中国国家主席习近平与美国总统特朗普在海湖庄园举行会晤。

9. James Mattis — (1950 —   ) the U.S. Secretary of Defense in the Trump Administration. Mattis is a retired US Marine Corps general (美国海军陆战队将军) who previously served as the 11th Commander of United States Central Command(美国中央司令部司令) and was responsible for American military operations in the Middle East, Northeast Africa, and Central Asia, from August 11, 2010, to March 22, 2013. 詹姆斯·马蒂斯,时任美国国防部长。

10. HR McMaster — Herbert Raymond McMaster (1962 —   ) was a

U. S. Army officer and the U. S. National Security Advisor during the Trump Administration. 赫伯特•雷蒙德•麦克马斯特,陆军中将,现任美国国家安全顾问。

11. Vladimir Putin — (1952 —) the President of the Russian Federation, holding the office since 7 May 2012. He was Prime Minister from 1999 to 2000, President from 2000 to 2008, and again Prime Minister from 2008 to 2012. 弗拉基米尔•弗拉基米罗维奇•普京,俄罗斯联邦总统。

12. Khan Sheikhun — a town in the southern Idlib Governorate(伊德利卜省)of northwestern Syria.

13. Russian Sukhoi aircraft — Sukhoi Company is a major Russian aircraft manufacturer, headquartered in Moscow, and designs both civilian and military aircraft. It was founded by Pavel Sukhoi in 1939 as the Sukhoi Design Bureau. 苏霍伊(1895-1975)是苏联著名飞机设计师,苏联喷气式超音速飞机的创始人之一。世界闻名的苏联苏霍伊飞机设计局,就是以他的名字命名。苏霍伊飞机实验设计局(简称苏霍伊设计局)于 1939 年组建,以设计战斗机、客机、轰炸机闻名于世。研制成功的著名机种有截击机苏-9,苏-15;歼击轰炸机苏-7,苏-17,苏-24,苏-30,苏-34;强击机苏-25;战斗机苏-27,苏-30,苏-33,苏-35,苏-37,与米高扬设计局齐名,是俄罗斯(苏联)著名的设计局之一。

14. eastern standard time — 美国本土横跨西五区至西八区,共四个时区,从东向西分别为东部时间(eastern standard time, EST)(西五区时间)、中部时间(central standard time, CST)(西六区时间)、山地时间(mountain standard time, MST)(西七区时间)、太平洋时间(西部时间)(Pacific standard time, PST)(西八区时间)。另外还有阿拉斯加时间(Alaska standard time, AKST)(西九区时间)和夏威夷时间(Hawaii standard time, HST)(西十区时间)。美国从每年 3 月的第二个星期日至 11 月第一个星期日采用夏令时(daylight saving time),夏令时比正常时间早一小时。

15. Islamic State — Also known as the Islamic State of Iraq and the Levant (ISIL), the Islamic State of Iraq and Syria (ISIS,), Islamic State (IS), is a jihadist (圣战的) unrecognised proto-state (准国家的) and militant group that follows a fundamentalist, Wahhabi (瓦哈比教派的) doctrine of Sunni (逊尼派) Islam. It gained global prominence in early 2014 when it drove Iraqi government forces out of key cities in its Western Iraq offensive (进攻伊拉克西部),

followed by its capture of Mosul（占领摩苏尔）and the Sinjar massacre. This group has been designated a terrorist organisation by the United Nations and many individual countries. 伊斯兰国,亦称"伊拉克和大叙利亚伊斯兰国",阿拉伯国家和部分西方国家称为"达伊沙"(DAESH),是一个自称建国的活跃在伊拉克和叙利亚的极端恐怖组织。2003年以前以"基地"组织伊拉克分支的名义开展活动。2017年11月21日,伊朗总统鲁哈尼宣布,极端组织"伊斯兰国"已经被剿灭。

16. University of Notre Dame —（美国）圣母大学(又音译为诺特丹大学),始建于19世纪中期,经历了一个多世纪的辉煌,享誉全美,是一所私立天主教大学、研究型大学,位于美国印地安纳州的南本德,本科教育稳居全美20所顶尖学府之列。

17. Rex Tillerson —（1952 — ）an American energy executive, civil engineer, and diplomat who is the 69th US Secretary of State. Tillerson joined ExxonMobil（埃克森美孚公司）in 1975 and rose to serve as the chairman and chief executive officer（CEO）of the company from 2006 to 2016. 雷克斯·蒂勒森,时任美国国务卿。

18. barrel bombs — an improvised unguided bomb（非制导炸弹）, sometimes described as a flying IED（improvised explosive device 简易爆炸装置）. They are typically made from a large barrel-shaped metal container that has been filled with high explosives, possibly shrapnel（弹片）, oil or chemicals as well, and then dropped from a helicopter or airplane. Due to the large amount of explosives（up to 1,000 kilograms）, their poor accuracy and indiscriminate use in populated civilian areas（including refugee camps）, the resulting detonations（爆炸）have been devastating. Critics have characterised them as weapons of terror and illegal under international conventions. 油桶炸弹

Questions

1. What is the response of the Russian government to the US attack on a Syrian airfield?
2. What was Donald Trump's attitude towards Assad before the attack? What made him change his mind?
3. Why did the US military target their missiles on the airbase at Shayrat?

4. Was Donald Trump supported by US Congress or the UN in launching the cruise missile attack on Syria?
5. What is implied by saying that Russian personnel were at Shayrat airbase when the chemical agent was loaded on to a Syrian jet?
6. What influence does the Russian presence have on US military planners?

语言解说

Presence

presence 的词义有时难以捉摸,只有先弄懂上下文,再作判断。在现代英语中,presence 并非只有"存在"一义,而是在不同的场合具有种种不同的含义。它是现代报刊用语中一个典型的舍具体求抽象的实例,这与西方人擅抽象思维和国人长于形象思维有关。本课第 24 段的"The Russian presence has raised the stakes dramatically for US military planners…"句中的"presence"即为"影响"或"干预"之义。下面见该词用于外交作"显示(军事)实力"(showing the flag)讲引申出的种种意义的例句:

1. 影响;实力,势力

a. Grassroots leaders are trying to step into the vacuum. Last fall former city councilman Ron Leeper founded Save the Seed, an organization that provides adult male mentors to African-American children. Fighting Back, a fledgling drug-and-alcohol-counseling group funded by a private grant, hopes to expand its **presence** in troubled west Charlotte. (*Newsweek*)

b. His price for a coalition arrangement would have been political autonomy for Scotland and Wales, with which Labour agreed, as well as electoral reform to make proportional representation the basis for future elections, which would give the Liberal Democrats a larger **presence** in Parliament. (*Time*)

2. 外交使团或机构

Britain is committed to maintaining a worldwide diplomatic **presence.** Diplomatic or consular relations are maintained with 183 countries and there are missions at nine international organisations or conferences. (*Britain News*)

3. 联合国"维和部队"

Indonesians opposed to **the UN presence** in East Timor protesting Friday outside UN offices in Jakarta. The UN said 20 more people died at the hands of militias in West Timor, but Indonesia denied the claim. (*International Herald Tribune*)

4. 驻扎，留驻

a. The Pentagon confirmed the **presence** of American troops in northern Afghanistan for the first time Tuesday and credited them with improving the effectiveness of U.S. bombing raids. (AP)

b. Despite the problems with civilian reconstruction and pressures from European governments to consider leaving a force behind after IFOR leaves, the White House — with an eye on the presidential election campaign — will not even discuss for now any possibility of an American troop **presence** in Bosnia past President Clinton's December deadline. (*U.S. News & World Report*)

5. （外来的）军事力量；军队；警察

The key decisions must still be made by and with Israel. The problem is how to give the Palestinians a homeland that would not pose a threat to Israeli security. Mr. Begin seems to think that this can be achieved only if Israel retains responsibility for security in the West Bank. This is not necessarily the case. An Israeli **presence** might exacerbate tension and provoke insecurity, whereas the Palestinians living on the spot, who have as great an interest in peace as the Israelis, might be able to police themselves more effectively. (*The Times*)

presence作为抽象意义的词可用来代表具体意义。这种虚实的转化会产生词义艰涩、含糊的新义，所以有时词义难以确定。还有的出于政治上的策略，如前联合国秘书长哈马舍尔德（Dag Hammarskjöld, 1905—1961）就喜欢此词的含糊其辞。他曾说："There is **a UN presence** wherever the UN is present."此处"a UN presence"指什么？"维和部队""外交官""外交使团"或"军事观察团"？此语妙在便于灵活掌握，使对手或政敌抓不住话柄。

以上可见，"a presence"可指"出访的外交官"、在海外的"航空母舰""永久性军事基地""军队"或"警察"等。（详见《导读》二章一节）

Unit Six
Society

Lesson 16

课文导读

手机时代,耳濡目染之下,未满周岁的幼儿抢过长辈的手机戳戳点点乃司空见惯。家长们无奈之中或许还有几分隐约的担忧。可谁曾料到,新一代少年网络安全奇才就在这种戳戳点点中诞生了。与互联网相伴的这一代孩子似乎把他们人生中的一切都记录在硅芯片中,保存在社交媒体上。然而,他们继承的这个庞大的数字生态系统却漏洞百出,侵犯敏感或机密信息成为普遍问题。在不远的将来,数字攻击可能引发下一场战争。而越来越多的少年开始利用他们的天赋和爱好致力于维护网络安全,他们中很多人还是戴着牙箍的中小学生,但已经开始搜寻软件漏洞、保护学校网络、帮助维护互联网安全。此篇出自美国《基督教科学箴言报》的报道就介绍了几位这样的天才少年。

Pre-reading Questions

1. Have you ever seen a baby fiddling with a smartphone?
2. Do you think it beneficial for a kid in a diaper to play with a smartphone?

Text

The Kids Who Might Save the Internet

A new generation of cybersecurity prodigies breaks into networks—just to make them safer. Meet the young hackers trying to keep the web from tilting to the dark side.

By Sara Sorcher

OCTOBER 31, 2016—Kristoffer Von Hassel could open smartphone apps before he could walk. By age 2, a time when most kids are still in diapers, he had bypassed the "toddler lock[1]" on his parents'

Android[2] phone. Then, at 5, young Kristoffer discovered how to outwit the parental controls on his father's Xbox One[3], which were meant to keep him from playing violent video games such as Call of Duty[4].

2 It wasn't a trivial discovery. He'd uncovered a serious security loophole in the game's software. When his dad, Robert Davies, found out, he laid out two options: They could expose the flaw on YouTube[5] to alert everyone else to the secret way in, or they could reveal it to Microsoft, which makes the Xbox.

3 Kristoffer thought about it and asked what bad guys would do if they learned about the workaround. "Somebody could steal an Xbox and use your bug to get on to it," Mr. Davies, a computer engineer, recalls telling him. "He said, 'Oh no, we can't have that. We've got to tell Microsoft.'"

4 Microsoft fixed the flaw within a week. And Kristoffer became known as the world's youngest hacker when he made the company's list of security researchers who had found dangerous vulnerabilities in Microsoft's products. "When I jammed the buttons, I probably saved Microsoft's b-u-t-t," says Kristoffer, now 8, from his bedroom, which is filled with space posters and coding books, in the family's San Diego apartment. "Thank goodness I found it, because it could have went into the wrong hands."[6]

5 Kristoffer is part of a new generation of wunderkinds, many of them lugging school backpacks and still wearing braces, that just might help save tomorrow's internet. Idealistic and computer savvy, they are mastering the mysterious numerical codes that underpin the digital world in the hope of making the web a more secure place.

6 Today, everything in kids' lives is captured in silicon chips and chronicled on Facebook[7]. As tweens and teens, they effortlessly swap selfies on Snapchat[8] and Instagram[9]. Most would rather text than talk.

7 Yet the massive digital ecosystem they inherited is fragile, broken, and unsafe. Built without security in mind, it's constructed on vulnerable code. As a result, malicious hackers are taking advantage. From Yahoo[10] to the US government, breaches of highly sensitive or highly personal networks have become commonplace. Stolen celebrity photos are the new tabloid staple. The insecurity of the internet is injecting itself into presidential politics ahead of the November election.

In the not too distant future, digital attacks may even set off the next war.

8   While Kristoffer's discovery may have been the result of a bit of serendipity-and youthful mischievousness-there's a whole community of brilliant young tinkerers intent on hacking the internet with the same exuberance. Only they aren't trying to break the web. They're trying to put it back together.

9   "CyFi" is a soft-spoken 15-year-old who is an avid skier and sailor and likes ripped jeans. She carries a two-foot-long pet snake named Calcifer almost everywhere she goes. By day, she totes a backpack to her experimental high school focused on technology in Silicon Valley. But she also has a secret identity: She's one of the most prominent young hackers in the country.

10 "Our generation has a responsibility to make the internet safer and better," says CyFi (who wants to keep her name anonymous and only go by her online moniker) in an interview at her high school where the hallways bustle with kids in Converse sneakers. "As the internet gets even more connected to our homes and our schools and our education and everything, there's going to be a ton more vulnerabilities."

11 CyFi first gained prominence in the tech press at age 10 when she hacked a kids' game on her iPad. That year, PC Magazine called her "a Girl Scout by day and a hacker by night." With the encouragement of her mother (who also works in the cybersecurity industry), CyFi took her talents to the vaunted DEF CON[11] hacker conference in Las Vegas, where she cofounded what's now known as r00tz Asylum, a hub for ethical hacking workshops for kids.[12]

12 As adults at DEF CON electronically infiltrate everything from ATMs to surveillance drones, r00tz is a "safe playground where [kids] can learn the basics of hacking without getting themselves into trouble," says CyFi. When launched in 2011, it drew about 100 kids. With CyFi as teacher and lead digital sleuth, the group uncovered 40 vulnerabilities in mobile apps. The next year, they found 180.

13 Now, r00tz Asylum has grown into a veritable security conference itself, drawing roughly 600 young people ages 8 to 16. This year at DEF CON, parents lined up all three mornings waiting to drop off their kids. In the sessions, youngsters rip apart smartphones, laptops, and other

gadgets at what's called the "junkyard" to learn how the devices work. Sparks fly as the young hackers solder hardware. Some of them march up on stage and, standing near the podium because they are too short to see over it, give speeches on hacking the video game Minecraft[13] and other tricks.

14   All around, they learn cryptography and simulate how they would thwart a real-world cyberattack. They're also developing a culture — with hacker names and sunglasses — to help protect themselves against the vast landscape of digital threats they face today, from internet thieves who want to steal their identity to data brokers who buy and sell their personal information, to companies that might want to sue them for exposing mistakes they made in their code. "You know how superheroes go by their superhero names, like Superman and stuff? It's good to have a hacker name," CyFi says, "so the villains don't know how to get you."

15   R00tz has become so big that it's drawing corporate sponsors such as AT&T, Adobe, and Facebook. Volunteers from well-known tech companies speak and teach at the sessions.

16   To ensure the kids only hack for good, there's a strict honor code, which includes the admonitions: "Only hack things you own. Do not hack anything you rely on. Respect the rights of others. Know the law, the possible risk, and the consequences for breaking it." The warnings are paired with encouragement. "R00tz is about creating a better world. You have the power and responsibility to do so. Now go do it!" the code says. "We are here to help."

17   In many ways, hacking has now become mainstream. Major tech companies such as Apple and Facebook are crowdsourcing their security, encouraging people to search for bugs in their products and report them so they can be fixed. Serious discoveries bring major rewards in the form of bounties. Some professional hackers earn as much as $100,000 a year just hunting for security flaws in tech products.

18   Kids are benefiting from this new security ethos, too. At r00tz, researchers set up devices for the kids to infiltrate.

19   CyFi says hacking into one of Samsung's newest smart TVs, as part of a bounty program set up by the company, was a "really

important moment for me." She was 12 at the time.

20   She entered a string of code that turned on the television's camera. This exposed the possibility of someone remotely hacking into a TV and being able to watch people while they sat on the couch viewing "Game of Thrones"[14] or "Madame Secretary."[15] Samsung awarded her $1,000 for exposing the flaw. "I think bug bounty programs[16] are really important," she says, "because it eliminates that worry of wondering, 'Oh, is this company going to be really mad about me poking around in their system?'"

21   Bug bounties are a great incentive for kids around the world. A 10-year-old from Finland, for instance, made headlines for winning $10,000 this May for finding a big security problem with the photo-sharing app Instagram.

22   Some of the most advanced kids are already becoming cybersecurity professionals, moving a step beyond taking computers apart in their basements and bedrooms like their predecessors. The upstairs bedroom of 14-year-old Paul Vann doubles as the worldwide headquarters of his company, Vann Tech. Next to his bed in Fredericksburg, Va., is a laboratory packed with devices designed to break into people's Wi-Fi networks, data analysis software, a computer loaded with advanced hacking tools, and a 3-D printer.

23   Paul's latest venture: a start-up that pushes the boundaries of how to test a company's security. "Once I have the funding, I think we need a building, and we definitely need more employees," says Paul, who talks — and thinks — at fiber-optic speed. "I can't be the only one developing projects."

24   On the side, Paul attends college courses in theoretical physics — but he's too young to get credit — and takes free math courses online through MIT. He is also trying to build an "invisibility cloak"[17] like the one in the "Harry Potter" books using theories rooted in acousto-optics.

25   Yet he has faced one recurring problem in his foray into adult capitalism: getting grown-ups to take him seriously. "They don't respect you as much as they would an adult," he says.

26   Paul, who has spoken at three different cybersecurity conferences, got into hacking after reading a book by self-described "break-in artist" Kevin Mitnick[18] called "Ghost in the Wires." It chronicles Mr.

Mitnick's escapades in two decades of hacking, which famously included stealing proprietary code from companies and snooping on the National Security Agency's phone calls in the 1980s and '90s.

27　But, Paul complains, "They never talked about how he did it." So he downloaded online hacking tools and started teaching himself through YouTube videos. "My first thing I wanted to learn was Wi-Fi [hacking] — that's the easiest way you can hack someone if you're not with them."

28　The tutorials were successful. Paul saw how he could break into Wi-Fi networks within a three-mile radius of his home. But Paul, who is close to becoming an Eagle Scout[19], also wanted to make sure he didn't do anything wrong. So he asked his neighbors, when they came over for dinner, for permission to hack into their home internet. "They said, 'Sure, as long as you don't do any damage.'"

29　As his parents and friends ate downstairs, Paul went to his bedroom laboratory. "I was finally able to break into something without getting into trouble," he says.

30　Paul understands the morality of hacking. "It's really important you consider ethics before you try to break into another system — and you want to make sure whatever you're doing is not going to harm that system," he says. "And whatever you do, tell the person."

31　In other words, don't wear an invisibility cloak. (From *The Christian Science Monitor*, October 31, 2016)

New Words

acousto-optics *n.* 声光学；光声学

admonition /ˌædməˈnɪʃn/ *n.* a warning or expression of disapproval about someone's behaviour 警告；告诫

Adobe /əˈdəʊbi/ *n.* (美国)奥多比公司(著名的图形图像和排版软件的生产商)

app /æp/ *n. abbr.* (= application program) 应用程序

AT&T *abbr.* (American Telephone and Telegraph Company) 美国电话电报公司

avid /ˈævɪd/ *adj.* doing sth as much as possible 劲头十足的；热衷的

bounty /ˈbaʊnti/ *n.* payment or reward for acts such as catching criminals or killing predatory animals 奖金；赏金

breach /briːtʃ/ *n.* an action that breaks a law, rule, or agreement

bustle /'bʌsl/ v. to move or cause to move energetically or busily in a hurried way 喧闹；忙乱；充满
bypass /'baɪpɑːs/ v. to avoid obeying a rule, system, or someone in an official position 绕过
chronicle /'krɒnɪkl/ v. to record events in the order in which they happened 按时序记载
cloak /kləʊk/ n. a warm piece of clothing like a coat without sleeves that hangs loosely from your shoulders 斗篷
Converse /kən'vɜːs, 'kɒnvɜːs/ n. an American brand of footwear 匡威（一美国运动品牌）
crowdsource /'kraʊdsɔːs/ v. to outsource work to an unspecified group of people, typically by making an appeal to the general public on the internet 众包；（尤指利用互联网）将工作分配给不特定人群
cryptography /krɪp'tɒgrəfi/ n. the science or study of analyzing and deciphering codes, ciphers, etc; cryptanalysis 密码学
escapade /'eskəpeɪd/ n. a wild and exciting undertaking (not necessarily lawful) 越轨行为；恶作剧
ethos /'iːθɒs/ n. the set of ideas and attitudes that is associated with a particular group of people or a particular type of activity. （某一团体或某类活动的）理念
exuberance /ɪɡ'zjuːbərəns/ n. joyful enthusiasm; behaviour that is energetic, excited, and cheerful 热情洋溢
fiber-optic /faɪbə 'ɒptɪk/ adj. 光学纤维的 n. 光纤，光纤技术
foray /'fɒreɪ/ n. a short attempt at doing a particular job or activity, esp. one that is very different from what you usually do 涉足，初次尝试
Fredericksburg /'frɛdrɪksbɜːrɡ/ n. 弗雷德里克斯堡（美国弗吉尼亚州东北部城市）
gadget /'ɡædʒɪt/ n. a small machine or device which does sth useful 小玩意；小器具
hacker /'hækə(r)/ n. someone who tries to break into computer systems, esp. in order to get secret information （电脑）黑客
jam /dʒæm/ v. to press tightly together
junkyard /'dʒʌŋkjɑːd/ n. a place where old machines such as cars or ships are destroyed and where useful parts are saved
loophole /'luːphəʊl/ n. a small mistake in a computer system that makes it possible to break into the system （计算机系统）漏洞

mischievousness /ˈmɪstʃɪvəsnɪs/ *n.* reckless or malicious behavior that causes discomfort or annoyance in others 恶作剧

MIT *n. abbr.* Massachusetts Institute of Technology 麻省理工学院

moniker /ˈmɒnɪkə(r)/ *n.* a nickname, esp. used humorously

outwit /ˌaʊtˈwɪt/ *v.* to beat through cleverness and wit 以智取胜

podium /ˈpəʊdiəm/ *n.* a platform raised above the surrounding level to give prominence to the person on it 表演台；讲台

prodigy /ˈprɒdədʒi/ *n.* a young person who has a great natural ability in a subject or skill 天才，神童

radius /ˈreɪdiəs/ *n.* the distance from the centre to the edge of a circle, or a line drawn from the centre to the edge(圆的)半径(长度)

Samsung /ˈsæmsʌŋ/ *n.* (韩国)三星电子公司

savvy /ˈsævi/ *adj.* having practical knowledge and ability 有见识的，懂实际知识的

selfie /ˈselfi/ *n.* a type of self-portrait photograph, typically taken with a hand-held digital camera or smartphone 自拍照

serendipity /ˌserənˈdɪpəti/ *n.* good luck in making unexpected and fortunate discoveries(有趣或有价值事物的)碰巧发现，机缘巧合

silicon /ˈsɪlɪkən/ *n.* [化学] 硅

sleuth /sluːθ/ *n.* a detective who follows a trail 侦探；警犬

solder /ˈsəʊldə(r)/ *v.* to join two pieces of metal together by melting a small piece of soft metal and putting it between them 焊接，焊合

staple /ˈsteɪpl/ *n.* theme; the topical subject

tilt /tɪlt/ *v.* to move or make sth move into a position where one side is higher than the other(使)倾斜

tinkerer /ˈtɪŋkərə(r)/ *n.* a person who enjoys fixing and experimenting with machines and their parts 喜欢捣鼓小器具、小发明的人

tote /təʊt/ *v. infml* to carry sth, esp. regularly

underpin /ˌʌndəˈpɪn/ *v.* to support from beneath

vaunted /ˈvɔːntɪd/ *adj.* being praised or talked about too much in a proud way 自夸的；大肆吹嘘的；受追捧的

veritable /ˈverɪtəbl/ *adj.* genuine; authentic 真正的，名副其实的

villain /ˈvɪlən/ *n.* a wicked or evil person; someone who does evil deliberately 坏人，恶棍

vulnerability /ˌvʌlnərəˈbɪləti/ *n.* the quality or state of being exposed to the possibility of being attacked or harmed, either physically or

emotionally 缺陷,弱点;易损性
Wi-Fi/ˈwaɪfaɪ/*n. abbr.* wireless fidelity 无线保真技术;无线上网技术
workaround/ˈwɜːkəraʊnd/*n.* a method to achieve sth in a computer program or system when the normal method is not successful(计算机程序或系统)变通办法
wunderkind/ˈwʊndəkɪnd/*n.* a person who, at an early age, develops one or more skills at a level far beyond the norm for their age 天才,神童

Notes

1. toddler lock — a technical measure by the parents to prevent their children from playing online games 幼儿锁
2. Android — a mobile operating system developed by Google 安卓系统
3. Xbox One — a line of home video game consoles developed by Microsoft, announced in May 2013, first released in North America, parts of Europe, Australia in November 2013, later in China in September 2014. 微软发售的家用游戏机
4. Call of Duty — a first-person shooter video game franchise. The series began on Microsoft Windows, and later expanded to consoles and handhelds. Several spin-off games have been released. 由 Activision 公司于 2003 年最初制作发行的系列游戏《使命召唤》,目前已发布作品十三部。
5. YouTube — an American video-sharing website headquartered in San Bruno, California. The service was created by three former PayPal employees in February 2005. Google bought the site in November 2006 for US＄1.65 billion. YouTube now operates as one of Google's subsidiaries. YouTube allows users to upload, view, rate, share, add to favorites, report, comment on videos, and subscribe to other users.
6. "When I jammed the buttons, I probably saved Microsoft's b-u-t-t," ... because it could have went into the wrong hands." — 文中几处直接引用天才少年接受采访时的原话,在语法上并不完善,恰恰表明他们仍处在成长期。
   jam the buttons — hit the keyboard
7. Facebook — an American online social media and social networking service based in Menlo Park, California. The Facebook website was launched on February 4, 2004, by Mark Zuckerberg, along with his

fellow Harvard College students. The Facebook name comes from the face book directories often given to U. S. university students. Facebook has more than 2 billion monthly active users as of June 2017. Its popularity has led to prominent media coverage for the company, including significant scrutiny over privacy and the psychological effects it has on users. In March 2018, Facebook was accused of having violated FTC privacy deal for providing information from 50 million Facebook users to Cambridge Analytica, a British political consulting firm. 美国社交网络服务网站"脸书"

8. Snapchat — an image messaging and multimedia mobile application created by Evan Spiegel, Bobby Murphy, and Reggie Brown, former students at Stanford University, and developed by Snap Inc., originally Snapchat Inc. One of the principal concepts of Snapchat is that pictures and messages are only available for a short time before they become inaccessible. "阅后即焚"照片分享应用。利用该应用程序,用户可以拍照、录制视频、添加文字和图画,并将他们发送到自己在该应用上的好友列表。这些照片及视频被称为"快照"("Snaps"),而该软件的用户自称为"快照族(snubs)"。该应用最主要的功能便是所有照片都有一个1到10秒的生命期,用户拍了照片发送给好友后,这些照片会根据用户所预先设定的时间按时自动销毁。

9. Instagram — a mobile, desktop, and Internet-based photo-sharing application and service that allows users to share pictures and videos either publicly or privately. After its launch in 2010, Instagram rapidly gained popularity, with 700 million registered users as of April 2017. 照片墙(一款运行在移动端上的社交应用,2012年10月被Facebook 以 7.15 亿美元收购。)

10. Yahoo — a web services provider, one of the pioneers of the early Internet era in the 1990s. 雅虎

11. DEF CON — one of the world's largest hacker conventions, held annually in Las Vegas, Nevada 黑客大会

12. ... she cofounded what's now known as r00tz Asylum, a hub for ethical hacking workshops for kids. — 她和其他人共同创办了"r00tz Asylum"。这是为诚信的少年黑客开展活动的工作室。也有人称该组织为 DEF CON 的儿童分会。

13. Minecraft — a sandbox video game created and designed by Swedish game designer Markus "Notch" Persson, and later fully developed

and published by Mojang. The creative and building aspects of Minecraft enable players to build constructions out of textured cubes in a 3D procedurally generated world. 《我的世界》，一款风靡全世界的沙盒游戏。玩家可以独自一人或与朋友们一起自由冒险，探索随机生成的世界，创造令人惊叹的奇迹。

14. 《Game of Thrones》— an American fantasy drama television series 《权力的游戏》
15. 《Madame Secretary》— an American political drama television series. The series primarily describes main character Dr. Elizabeth McCord's fight to balance her family and her work as the US Secretary of State. 《国务卿女士》
16. bug bounty programs — A bug bounty program is a deal offered by many websites and software developers by which individuals can receive recognition and compensation for reporting bugs, especially those pertaining to exploits and vulnerabilities. 漏洞赏金计划
17. invisibility cloak — a magical artefact used to render the wearer invisible, a specific instance in the Harry Potter series 隐身衣
18. Kevin Mitnick — an American computer security consultant, author and hacker. He is the co-author with William L. Simon, of *Ghost in the Wires*: *My Adventures as the World's Most Wanted Hacker*, published in 2011. 凯文·米特尼克（美国著名网络黑客）
19. Eagle Scout — the highest achievement or rank attainable in the Boy Scouting program of the Boy Scouts of America (BSA). The designation was founded over one hundred years ago. Only four percent of Boy Scouts are granted this rank after a lengthy review process. The requirements necessary to achieve this rank take years to fulfill. 鹰级童子军

Questions

1. What did Kristoffer do at the age of 5?
2. What is your first impression about CiFi?
3. How did CiFi gain prominence in the tech press at the age of 10?
4. What is r00tz Asylum?
5. How did Paul get into hacking?
6. According to the text, what is the morality of hacking?

语言解说

cyber 和 virtual

近年来,由于科技的飞速发展,科技新词层出不穷,造词能力出众,还有旧词不断引申出新义。本书第八课和本课中的 cyber 就是一个典型例子。

1995 年 5 月出版的一期《时代》周刊提到 cyber 时说:"Cyber has become the prefix of the day."*The New Oxford Dictionary of English* 的释义是:"relating to electronic communication networks and virtual reality",即"与电子通讯网络系统和虚拟现实有关的"。

请看这两课中用 cyber 组成的新词:cyberattack(网络攻击),cyberspace(网络空间),cyberwarfare(网络战争),cyberweapon(网络武器),cybersecurity(网络安全)。cyber 还以独立的单词形式出现,如第八课第 4 段中的"While cyber may not look or smell exactly like a fighter aircraft or a bomber aircraft..."此处作名词,意为"网络";另外,cyber 独立作形容词的用法也多次出现,如 cyber programs, cyber training, cyber capabilities, cyber domain, cyber techniques, cyber power 等,这反映了它从构词成分演化成词的过程。

我们再看几个常用的用 cyber 构成的词:cyberland(网络天地),cybercommunity(交互网络社会),cybercafe(网络咖啡屋),cyberspeak(网络用语或术语),cybercrime(网络犯罪),cyberbullying(网上欺凌),cyberpunk(数字朋客),cyber-violence(网络暴力)等。

virtual 是相当流行的科技用语,是一个旧词引申出新义的典型例子。我们常说的"VR"即"virtual reality(虚拟现实)"之缩写。

virtual 用于计算机领域,其英文释义是"in computing: not physically existing but made to appear so from the point of view of users; involving the replication of a physical object by an electronic equivalent",因此译为"虚拟的"。随着此词的出现而造出许多新词,如 virtual reality/environment/landscape/space/sex/shopping/therapy/world 等。virtual newsland 指互联网上的"新闻传真天地";virtual institution 指"虚拟(或网上)教育机构或大学";virtual surgery 是"远程遥控手术";virtual doctor 指"远程问诊大夫"。由此可见,要真正理解和译对 virtual 这个词并非易事。(见《导读》"科技用语")

Lesson 17

课 文 导 读

　　互联网的发展催生了以交流为目的的亿万网民,进而催化了婚恋交友网站的发展和繁荣。自 1995 年美国人创建婚恋交友网站 Match. com 至今,网上婚恋市场以欣欣向荣、势不可挡的态势蔓延至全球,婚恋网站已经发展成为利润丰厚的产业。在现实生活中,人们的社交圈狭窄,多元化的社交方式不足,而生活的压力又让人们少有空闲去体验传统的交友方式。网络的快捷和多元化恰恰提供了一个不错的交友平台,去交友网站寻求意中人逐渐成为一种选择方式,人们的婚恋观念也从传统的相亲模式向网络交友转变,因此也就有了对网络结识和传统结交的比较,哪一种方式更容易找到意中人呢? 网络世界使你有机会结识更多的人,是否就意味着你的候选意中人就更多了? 是否也意味着在道德问题上出轨更多? 值得探讨。其实,要找到匹配的另一半,网上约会与传统约会方式各有利弊,不可一概而论。《时代》周刊的《网站约会让找意中人变得更难吗?》一文,从其独特的角度探讨了这一社会热点问题。

Pre-reading Questions

1. Do you know something about online dating?
2. Are there any of your friends or relatives who have met their spouse online?

Text

Does Online Dating Make It Harder to Find "the One"?
By Alice Park

1　　Everyone knows someone who met their spouse online. A friend of mine whom I hadn't seen in years told me recently that she, too, met her husband on an Internet dating site. They're happily married, just moved into a new house, and are now talking about starting a family[1].

2　　When I asked her if she thought online matchmaking was a better way than offline dating to find guys who were more compatible with her — and, therefore, better husband material — she laughed. "No, because I couldn't stand him when I first met him," she says of her husband. She thought he was full of himself and rude during their first encounter. It definitely wasn't love at first sight, she said — that took a while.

3　　In other words, according to my friend, Internet dating is just as unpredictable as the non-digital version[2]. You never know how things are going to evolve until they do. But the benefit, she says, is that dating online gives you access to a lot more people than you'd ordinarily ever get to meet — and that's how she connected with her future husband.

4　　These observations have been borne out[3] in a new study by social psychologists collaborating across the country. The extensive new study published in the journal *Psychological Science in the Public Interest*[4] sought to answer some critical questions about online dating, an increasingly popular trend that may now account for[5] 1 out of every 5 new relationships formed: fundamentally, how does online dating differ from traditional, face-to-face encounters? And, importantly, does it lead to more successful romantic relationships?

5　　For their 64-page report, the authors reviewed more than 400 studies and surveys on the subject, delving into[6] questions such as whether scientific algorithms — including those used by sites like eHarmony, Perfect Match and Chemistry[7] to match people according to similarities — can really lead to better and more lasting relationships (no); whether the benefits of endless mate choices online have limits (yes); and whether communicating online by trading photos and emails before meeting in person can promote stronger connections (yes, to a certain extent).

6   Overall, the study found, Internet dating is a good thing, especially for singles who don't otherwise have many opportunities to meet people. The industry has been successful, of course — and popular: while only 3% of Americans reported meeting their partners online in 2005, that figure had risen to 22% for heterosexual couples and 6% for same-sex couples by 2007－09. Digital dating is now the second most common way that couples get together, after meeting through friends. But there are certain properties of online dating that actually work against love-seekers[8], the researchers found, making it no more effective than traditional dating for finding a happy relationship.

7   "There is no reason to believe that online dating improves romantic outcomes," says Harry Reis, a professor of psychology at University of Rochester[9] and one of the study's co-authors. "It may yet, and someday some service might provide good data to show it can, but there is certainly no evidence to that right now."

8   One downside to Internet dating has to do with one of its defining characteristics: the profile. In the real world, it takes days or even weeks for the mating dance to unfold, as people learn each other's likes and dislikes and stumble through the awkward but often rewarding process of finding common ground. Online, that process is telescoped and front-loaded, packaged into a neat little digital profile, usually with an equally artificial video attached.

9   That leaves less mystery and surprise when singles meet face to face. That's not necessarily a bad thing, as profiles can help quickly weed out[10] the obviously inappropriate or incompatible partners (who hasn't wished for such a skip button on those disastrous real-life blind dates[11]?), but it also means that some of the pleasure of dating, and building a relationship by learning to like a person, is also diluted.

10   It also means that people may unknowingly skip over potential mates for the wrong reasons. The person you see on paper doesn't

translate neatly to a real, live human being, and there's no predicting or accounting for the chemistry[12] you might feel with a person whose online profile was the opposite of what you thought you wanted. Offline, that kind of attraction would spark organically.

11 The authors of the study note that people are notoriously fickle about what's important to them about potential dates. Most people cite attractiveness as key to a potential romantic connection when surveying profiles online, but once people meet face to face, it turns out that physical appeal doesn't lead to more love connections for those who say it is an important factor than for those who say it isn't. Once potential partners meet, in other words, other characteristics take precedence over the ones they thought were important.

12 "You can't look at a piece of paper and know what it's like to interact with someone," says Reis. "Picking a partner is not the same as buying a pair of pants."

13 Making things harder, many sites now depend on — and heavily market — their supposedly scientific formulas for matching you with your soul mate based on similar characteristics or personality types. It may seem intuitively logical that people who share the same tastes or attitudes would be compatible, but love, in many cases, doesn't work that way.

14 Some online dating sites, for example, attempt to predict attraction based on qualities like whether people prefer scuba diving to shopping, or reading to running, or whether they tend to be shy or more outgoing. But social science studies have found that such a priori predictors[13] aren't very accurate at all, and that the best prognosticators of how people will get along come from the encounters between them. In other words, it's hard to tell whether Jim and Sue will be happy together simply by comparing a list of their preferences, perspectives and personality traits before they meet. Stronger predictors of possible romance include the tenor of their conversations, the subject of their discussions, or what they choose to do together.

15 "Interaction is a rich and complex process," says Reis. "A partner is another human being, who has his or her own needs, wishes and priorities, and interacting with them can be a very, very complex process for which going through a list of characteristics isn't useful."

16   The authors also found that the sheer number of candidates that some sites provide their love-seeking singles — which can range from dozens to hundreds — can actually undermine the process of finding a suitable mate. The fact that candidates are screened via their profiles already sets up a judgmental, "shopping" mentality that can lead people to objectify their potential partners.[14] Physical appearance and other intangible characteristics may certainly be part of the spark that brings two people together, but having to sift through[15] hundreds of profiles may become overwhelming, forcing the looker to start making relationship decisions based on increasingly superficial and ultimately irrelevant criteria.

17   "And remember", says Reis, "online dating sites have a vested interest[16] in your failure. If you succeed, the site loses two paying customers."

18   Communicating online before meeting can help counter some of this mate-shopping effect, but it depends on how long people correspond electronically before taking things offline. A few weeks of email and photo exchanging serves to enhance people's attraction when they finally meet, researchers found, but when the correspondence goes on too long — for six weeks—it skews people's expectations and ends up lowering their attraction upon meeting. Over time, people start to form inflated or overly particular views about the other person, which leaves them at risk for being disappointed in the end.

19   Considering the many pitfalls, what accounts for the enduring popularity — and success — of online dating sites? Part of it may be the fact that singles who use online dating sites are a particularly motivated lot. Their desire to find a spouse and get married may make them more likely to actually find a life partner on the site, or believe that they have. And they're also probably more likely to believe that the matchmaking algorithms that power so many sites really can find them that person who's "meant to be."

20   It also offers an attractive solution for an age-old problem for singles — where to meet potential mates. As more people delay marriage, either for financial or professional reasons, and with more people constantly moving around to find better jobs, disrupting their social networks, the easily accessed digital community of like-minded singles becomes a tantalizing draw.

21   Still, those who go online looking for love are left navigating a minefield of odds — not unlike dating in the non-digital realm. But at least there's solace in matches like my friend's[17]. If there's one thing online dating does better than any matchmaker or network of friends who are eager to set you up with that "someone who's perfect for you," it's finding you lots and lots of candidates. "Like anything on the Internet, if you use online dating wisely, it can be a great advantage," says Reis. You just have to accept that not all of your matches will be your Mr. or Ms. Right. (From *Time*, February 7, 2012)

New Words

algorithm /ˈælgərɪðəm/ *n.* a set of rules that must be followed when solving a particular problem 算法；计算程序

chemistry /ˈkemɪstri/ *n.* kind of attraction sparked organically between two people（常指两性之间强烈的）吸引力

collaborate /kəˈlæbəreɪt/ *v.* to work together with sb in order to produce or achieve sth 合作

compatible /kəmˈpætəbl/ *adj.* having a good relationship with sb because of similar opinions and interests 情投意合的；般配的

criteria /kraɪˈtɪəriə/ *n.* a standard or principle by which sth is judged or with the help of which a decision is made 标准

date /deɪt/ *n.* a romantic meeting *v.* to have a romantic relationship with sb

delve /delv/ *v.* to try to discover new information about sth 探究，钻研

dilute /daɪˈluːt/ *v.* to make a liquid weaker by adding water or another liquid to it 稀释

disastrous /dɪˈzɑːstrəs/ *adj.* extremely bad; terrible 糟糕的

disrupt /dɪsˈrʌpt/ *v.* to make it difficult for sth to continue in the normal way

downside /ˈdaʊnsaɪd/ *n.* the negative part or disadvantage of sth

draw /drɔː/ *n.* a performer, place, event etc. that a lot of people come to see

fickle /ˈfɪkl/ *adj.* changing often and suddenly 变幻无常的；善变的

front-load /ˈfrʌntləʊd; ˈfrɒntˌləʊd/ *v.* to assign costs or benefits to the early stages of（装载）置前；(喻)提前

heterosexual /ˌhetərəˈsekʃuəl/ *adj.* sexually attracted to people of the

opposite sex 异性恋的
inappropriate /ˌɪnəˈprəʊpriət/ *adj.* not suitable; *cf.* appropriate
incompatible /ˌɪnkəmˈpætəbl/ *adj.* different in important ways, and do not suit each other or agree with each other; *cf.* **compatible**
inflated /ɪnˈfleɪtɪd/ *adj.* ideas, opinions etc about sth make it seem more important than it really is 夸张的；过高的
intangible /ɪnˈtændʒəbl/ *adj.* difficult to describe, define or measure 不易捉摸的；难以确定的
intuitive /ɪnˈtjuːɪtɪv/ *adj.* showing or formed by the power of understanding or knowing sth without reasoning or learned skill 直觉的；直观的
match /mætʃ/ *n.* a marriage union or two people who are married
mentality /menˈtæləti/ *n.* attitudes and way of thinking 心态；思维方式
objectify /əbˈdʒektɪfaɪ/ *v.* to treat sth or sb as an object 将……物化，对……进行人格物化
overwhelming /ˌəʊvəˈwelmɪŋ/ *adj.* having such a great effect on you that you feel confused and do not know how to react 令人困惑的；不知所措的
pitfall /ˈpɪtfɔːl/ *n.* a danger or difficulty, esp. one that is hidden or not obvious at first
profile /ˈprəʊfaɪl/ *n.* a short description that gives important details about a person 人物简介
prognosticator /prɒgˈnɒstɪkeɪtə/ *n.* one who foretells sth will happen in the future 预言者
property /ˈprɒpəti/ *n.* a stated quality, power, or effect that belonging naturally to sth 特性
scuba /ˈskjuːbə/ *n.* a portable apparatus containing compressed air and used for breathing under water 便携式水下呼吸器
skew /skjuː/ *v.* to change or influence sth with the result that it is not accurate, fair, normal, etc. 歪曲；曲解
sift /sɪft/ *n.* to examine and sort carefully
solace /ˈsɒləs/ *n.* a feeling of emotional comfort when sb is sad or disappointed. 安慰
stumble /ˈstʌmbl/ *v.* to put one's foot down awkwardly while walking or running and nearly fall over 跌跌撞撞地走
tantalizing /ˈtæntəlaɪzɪŋ/ *adj.* making you feel a strong desire to have sth that you cannot have 逗引人的；撩拨心弦的
telescope /ˈtelɪskəʊp/ *v.* to make a process seem to happen in a shorter time

tenor /ˈtenə(r)/ *n.* the general meaning or mood of sth spoken 大意；要领

vested /ˈvestɪd/ *adj.* settled, fixed

Notes

1. start a family — to have a baby
2. non-digital version — traditional, face-to-face dating
3. These observations have been borne out. — These observations have been proved right.
   bear out — to show that sb is right or sth is true 证实；证明
4. Psychological Science in the Public Interest — PSPI, an academic journal of the Association for Psychological Science（美国心理学协会）that is published three times a year by SAGE Publications（塞奇出版社）《公众利益心理学》杂志
5. account for — If a particular thing accounts for a part or proportion of sth, that part or proportion consists of that thing; amount to（数量或比例上）占
6. delving into — searching thoroughly 钻研；深入研究
7. eHarmony, Perfect Match and Chemistry — the names of three well-known international online dating websites
8. there are certain ... against love-seekers ... — Online dating weakens one's social or traditional morality because, with the objective of developing a personal, romantic, or sexual relationship, it usually prevents love-seekers from finding their true love...
9. University of Rochester — a private university, founded in 1929, located in Rochester, New York 罗切斯特大学
10. weed out — to remove or get rid of people or things from a group because they are not wanted
11. blind dates — dates between persons who have not previously met
12. accounting for the chemistry — the reason for mutual attraction（此处 account for 意为 to explain or give the necessary reason or information about, 有别于第四段中的 account for）
13. a priori predictor — 推断出的预示因素
    a. a priori — using facts or principles that are known to be true in order to decide what the probable effects or results will be 推理的；从事实推断结果

b. predictor — sth that helps you preclict sth that will happen in the future 借以作出预测的事物

14. The fact that candidates are screened ... objectify their potential partners. — 候选对象的个人资料在网上进行筛选，这就形成了一种判断式的"购物"心态，它使人们对潜在伴侣进行了人格物化。

15. sift through — to make a close and thorough examination of (things in a mass or group) 筛选

16. vested interest — If you have a vested interest in sth happening, you have a strong reason for wanting it to happen because you will get an advantage from it 既得利益

17. in matches like my friend's — like my friend who has found her life partner or got married

Questions

1. Is online matching a better way than traditional dating according to the writer's friend who met her husband online?
2. What benefits does online dating create?
3. Does online dating lead to more successful romantic relationships?
4. How do you understand that one of the disadvantages of online dating is the profile?
5. Although there are many pitfalls occurring in the online dating websites, why does its popularity keep rising?
6. Why does online dating appeal so much to people delaying their marriage?

语言解说

借喻词和提喻词（I）

　　报刊中多借喻词和提喻词，与委婉语、竞选用语和法律语言等相比较易理解，不过读者需具有较广泛的文化背景知识。

　　凡世界各国首都均可指代所在国及其政府，凡战争地、协议签订地和重要机构的总部所在地也均可用来喻指此战争、协议和该机构。地名是这两种修辞格里用得较多的。如第1课中用"Washington"指"美国"或"美国政府"，就是典型的例子。

一、借喻法

1. 常见借喻法

借一事物的名称指代另一事物,称为借喻或借代法(metonymy),如以 the Crown 喻指"皇室事务",Pentagon 指代"美国防部",the blue helmets 喻"联合国维和部队"等。英语中往往用一个词代表整个事件或背景。在现代英美报刊语言中常见到以地名或国名代表整个事件。① 如 Vietnam/Viet Nam 指"越南战争",Bosnia 是"波黑"的简称,喻"波黑战争",Hungary 指"匈牙利事件",the Gulf"海湾战争",Dayton"代顿协议"或代顿和平协议,Post-Soviet 苏联解体后,等等。见例句:

(1) Yet in the years since **Vietnam**, critics in and out of uniform have repeatedly charged that too many officers have become cautious bureaucrats, adept at Pentagon politics perhaps, but interested more in advancing their careers than in preparing for the brutal exigencies of combat. (*Time*)

然而,自从**越南战争**开始以来的这些年,军内外批评家一再指责道……

(2) Once the political chaff is dusted away, the minidebate over **Bosnia** is instructive. Both Bush and Clinton were saying the same thing. (*Time*)

这是《时代》周刊报道 1992 年美国大选时,老布什代表共和党总统候选人与民主党候选人克林顿进行电视总统候选人的辩论,此例中的 Bosnia 就是借喻"波黑战争"。political chaff 指的是"竞选废话"。

(3) Washington concluded after **Dayton**, when NATO bombers seemed to bring him [Milosevic] to the negotiating table… (*Time*)

Dayton 为美国俄亥俄州一城市,是波黑和平协议签订地。此例不能说"代顿后美国断定……"这里的 Dayton 是指 1995 年关于结束波黑内战和版图划分等而达成的协议,称为 the Dayton (Peace) Accords,"代顿(和平)协议"。这样就好理解了。其正式名称应是"Bosnia and Herzegovina Peace Agreements"。

2. 另类借喻法

陆国强先生在论及借代曾举 November 等词语为例说明:"在涉及美国初选或大选时,报刊常以词代事的方式进行报道。"②

用年份(缩略词)可指代选举及经济情况,如"The Economy Sucks.

---

① 陆国强:现代英语词汇学,上海外语教育出版社,1983 年,第 66 页。
② 同上书,第 67 页。

But Is It '92 Redux?"(2008/1/21 *Newsweek*)(经济不振,是否这是 1992 年大选时经济情况和大选形势的翻版? 当时因老布什执政时经济衰退,竞选连任败给了克林顿)。此外,还可借喻战争。如:

The decisive step toward victory in Iraq, say military officials, will be to crush Saddam's elite Republican Guard. At least three Guard divisions are massed outside Baghdad, facing the American invaders. In **'91**, the Americans used air power and their superior armor to badly maul some of these same Republican Guard divisions. But it is often overlooked that several of the Guard battalions stood and fought and then made an orderly retreat, living to fight again another day. (2003/4/7 *Newsweek*)

此例中的"'91"指 1991 年以美国为首的联军发动的第一次伊拉克战争。这种以年份或日期指代战争或事件如英文里用 9/11 指 2001 年 "9·11"恐怖袭击事件,也是报刊中常用的一种形式。

二、提喻法

以局部代表全体,或以全体喻指部分,称为提喻或举隅法(synecdoche),报刊中较普遍,例如:Bosnia 代表"波黑",London 代表英国,Kremlin(克里姆林宫)代表(前)苏联,(现)俄罗斯,Washington 代表美国,还可代表东部,如 Washington mafia,喻指东部权势集团,cutthroat 代表 assassin(暗杀)或 murder。

三、一词数义

为避免用词重复、使读者产生联想等原因,作者常使用这两种修辞手段。在报刊文章中,为简约、换词等目的,这两种喻词用得尤其多。如 Foggy Bottom(雾谷),是美国首都华盛顿一地名,国务院所在地,喻"国务院",在修辞格里称借代法。又因其外交政策像雾蒙蒙的深山低谷一样模糊不清,令人难以捉摸,颇像"'雾'底洞",因此又用做隐喻(metaphor)来比喻"国务院的政策"。再如 Washington 做借喻指"美国或联邦政府",做提喻指"美国",做隐语可比喻为"贪污腐败(corruption)、尔虞我诈(fraud)和铺张浪费(waste)的官场"。

Lesson 18

> 课文导读
>
> 社会在思想意识激烈的碰撞中不断前进。年轻人总是站在思潮的前列，推陈出新，在各方面对社会作出贡献。20世纪六七十年代的嬉皮士与主流文化和传统观念背道而驰，而80年代的雅皮士却热衷于追求财富、事业成功与物质享受，这一趋势在X一代和Y一代身上达到顶点。
>
> Yawns与他们前辈的思想和言行大相径庭。他们年轻、富裕、事业有成，但并不追求物质享受，相反却具有强烈的社会责任感和环保意识，提倡救困济贫，过着简朴、节俭的生活。学了这一课我们会得到很多启示，是向往奢华的生活方式，还是以俭朴为荣？

Pre-reading Questions

1. What is the most valuable thing in your life?
2. What is your ideal way of life?

Text

Yawns[1]: A Generation of the Young, Rich and Frugal
By Evelyn Nieves

1   SAN FRANCISCO — They drive hybrid cars, if they drive at all, shop at local stores, if they shop at all, and pay off their credit cards every month, if they use them at all.[2]

2   They may have disposable income, but whatever they make, they live below their means in a conscious effort to tread lightly on the earth[3].

3   They are a new breed of Gen X'ers and Y's[4], Young and Wealthy but Normal, or Yawns.

4   The acronym comes from *The Sunday Telegraph* of London, which noted that an increasing number of rich young Britons are socially

aware, concerned about the environment and given less to consuming than to giving money to charity.[5]

5   Yawns sound dull, but they are the new movers and shakers[6], their dreams big and bold. They are men and women in their 20s, 30s and 40s who want nothing less than to change the world and save the planet.

6   Take Sean Blagsvedt, who moved from Seattle to India in 2004 to help build the local office of Microsoft Research. Moved by young children begging on the streets, Blagsvedt quit Microsoft and launched two networking sites, babajob.com and babalife.com, to link India's vast pool of potential workers with the people who need labor. The larger goal — to reduce poverty.

7   Far from the techie cafe life[7], Blagsvedt, 32, lives at babajob's headquarters in Bangalore, a 3,000-square-foot apartment where his mother and stepfather also live and 15 workers come and go every day.

8   "I'm a happy person," he said. "It's great to do something that you believe in doing."

9   The high-tech world has spawned its share of Yawns, but they can sprout anywhere.[8] In fact, Yawns are a subset of a growing global movement of the eco-socially aware. The state of the economy and the state of the planet have inspired people to consider what they buy and how they spend in ways not seen since the "Small is Beautiful"[9] and ecology movements of the 1970s[10].

10   The movement makes perfect sense, said David Grusky, a sociologist at Stanford University, since society tends to follow cycles — with anti-materialist periods like the hippie movement[11] generating a pro-materialist reaction — the yuppie period[12], and so on. Not to mention, he adds, that the evidence of major climate change and a concern with terrorism gives rise to more interest in spiritual as opposed to material objectives.

11   The upshot, he said, is that "a cultural and demographic perfect storm[13] may well push us decisively toward an extreme form of post-materialism in the coming period."

12   That helps explain why Earth Day[14] has become so big again, why products are all going "green" and why freecycle.org[15], an Internet community bulletin board where members offer items for free, has grown in five years from a dozen members in Tucson, Ariz., to a

network of more than 3,000 cities in 80 countries.

13 Deron Beal, the site's founder, counts 4 million members, and growing by 20,000 to 50,000 members each week.

14 "People have many reasons for freecycling," said Beal. "But the biggest reason is environmental-reusing and recycling instead of helping create more waste."

15 Could it also be that we are sick to death of buying stuff?

16 Pam Danziger, a consumer trends expert, thinks so. "The green thing is just a small part of it," said Danziger, whose firm, Unity Marketing, has new research showing luxury spending is way down. "Americans have been on a buying binge for the last 10 years," she said. "Our closets are full. Our attics are full. Our garages are full. Enough already!"

17 Yawns live small, but they already own whatever they want.

18 Rik Wehbring, a 37-year-old dot-com millionaire — he worked for multiple startups — limits himself to living on $50,000 a year. That's no chump change but well below what he could spend in San Francisco, where his rent eats up 40 percent of his allotted spending.

19 Wehbring doesn't own a television, his mp3 player cost $20 ("and it works just fine") and he drives (when he drives) a Toyota Prius[16].

20 He buys most of his food from local farmers' markets, is leaving the bulk of his estate to various environmental organizations and donates money to what he considers worthy causes. Everyday, he grapples with "how to live a low-carbon life."

21 But Wehbring doesn't buy clothes, or much of anything.

22 "I don't need a lot of material possessions," he said. "I haven't had to buy anything in a while."

23 Such frugality seems to run in his circle.[17]

24 Brad Marshland, 44, the husband of Wehbring's cousin, is a successful filmmaker living near Berkeley. He and his wife and two sons, ages 10 and 12, dry their clothes on a line, grow their own vegetables and buy what they need at garage sales and secondhand stores. (Secondhand stores are to Yawns what The Gap was to Yuppies.[18])

25 "We're pretty low on the stuff scale[19]," Marshland said.

26   Marshland offsets his family's "carbon footprint"—how much energy it uses—by donating money to environmental groups online.

27   Yawns hate ostentation.

28   When Ray Sidney, a software engineer at Google, cashed in his stock options[20] in 2003, they yielded him more money than he could ever burn through[21] in his lifetime. (Billions? He won't say.) But instead of building himself a 10,000-square-foot mansion in the Googledom of Silicon Valley[22], he retired to a four-bedroom house in Stateline, Nev., and started giving money away.

Ray Sidney poses for a photograph at his home in Stateline, Nev. Sidney, a software engineer at Google, cashed in his stock options in 2003 and shares the money with local organizations where he lives and to a variety of charities. By Jim Grant, AP

29   He has given $400,000 to a local arts council to help build a new arts center, $1 million to a bus company to help launch a route so that casino workers wouldn't have to rely on private transportation to get to and from work, and $1.7 million for a new football field and track at a local high school, for example.

30   Sidney also donates millions to charities that try to cure diseases or save the world.

31   His one rich-guy, carbon hogging guilt trip[23]: a single engine plane he flies about once a week to see his girlfriend in San Francisco.

32   But his pet project these days is pure Yawn. He is building what he calls "an environmentally friendly affordable housing development" on 100 acres near his home in Stateline.

33   "This world and our society and the people in it are good and worthwhile," he said, "and I think it's worth spending money to keep it around and try to improve it." (From The Associated Press[24], May 4, 2008)

New Words

acronym /ˈækrənɪm/ *n.* a word made up from the first letters of the name of sth such as an organization 首字母缩略词

affordable /əˈfɔːdəbl/ *adj.* that can be afforded; able to spend, give, do etc, without serious loss or damage

allot /əˈlɒt/ *v.* to decide officially to give sth to sb or use sth for a particular purpose 分配；拨出

Ariz. *abbr.* Arizona, a state in the SW of the US, north of Mexico, known for containing a large area of desert 亚利桑那州（美国）

attic /ˈætɪk/ *n.* the room in a building just below the roof 阁楼

Bangalore /ˌbæŋɡəˈlɔː/ *n.* a city of south-central India. It is a major industrial center and transportation hub in India. 班加罗尔（印度）

Berkeley /ˈbɜːklɪ/ *n.* a city on the eastern side of the San Francisco Bay area in California 伯克利（美国西部加利福尼亚州）

binge /bɪndʒ/ *n. infml* a short period when you do too much of sth, esp. drinking alcohol ［非正式］（短期的）狂欢作乐；大吃大喝

Briton /ˈbrɪtən/ *n. fml* someone from Britain ［正式］英国人

bulk /bʌlk/ *n.* the main or largest part of sth（某物的）主要部分；大半

bulletin board notice board; a board on a wall which notices may be fixed to 布告牌

carbon footprint a measure of the amount of carbon dioxide produced by a person, organization, or location at a given time. It describes the environmental impact of carbon emissions. 二氧化碳排放量（的测量单位）

casino /kəˈsiːnəʊ/ *n.* a place where people try to win money by playing card games or roulette 赌场

chump change *slang* a small amount of money 一小笔钱

council /ˈkaʊnsɪl/ *n.* a group of people appointed or elected to make laws, rules, or decisions, or to give advice 委员会

cycle /ˈsaɪkl/ *n.* a number of related events happening in a regularly repeated order 循环，周而复始

demographic /ˌdiːməˈɡræfɪk/ *adj.* of or related to the study of human populations and the ways in which they change 人口学的，人口统计学的

disposable income the amount of money you have left to spend after you have paid your taxes, bills, etc. 可支配收入；税后收入

donate /ˈdəʊneɪt/ *v.* to give sth, esp. money, to a person or an organization in order to help them 捐赠，捐献

dot-com /dɒt-kʌm/ *n.* a company that does all or most of its business on the Internet 网络公司

estate /ɪsˈteɪt/ *n.* all of someone's property and money, esp. everything that is left after they die 个人全部财产（尤指遗产）

frugal /ˈfruːɡəl/ *adj.* careful to only buy what is necessary 节俭的 **frugality** /fruːˈɡælɪtɪ/ *n.*

garage sale a sale of used household belongings, typically held outdoors or in a garage at the home of the seller（在住宅车库里进行的）旧物出售

grapple (with) /ˈɡræpl/ *v.* to try hard to deal with (a difficult problem); to search mentally, with uncertainty and difficulty 尽力解决（难题等）；费力思考

hog /hɒɡ/ *v.* to keep or use all of sth in a selfish or impolite way 贪心地攫取，把某物占为己有

hybrid /ˈhaɪbrɪd/ *adj.* consisting of or coming from a mixture of two or more other things; of mixed origin（两种或两种以上东西）混合的 **hybrid car** 混合动力车

mansion /ˈmænʃən/ *n.* a large house, usu. belonging to a wealthy person

multiple /ˈmʌltɪpl/ *adj.* including many different parts, types, etc. 多样的，多重的

Nev. *abbr.* Nevada, a state in the western US

offset /ˈɒfˌset/ *v.* to make up for; to balance 补偿，抵消

ostentation /ˌɒstenˈteɪʃən/ *n.* unnecessary show of wealth, knowledge etc （财富、知识等的）卖弄，炫耀

pet /pet/ *adj.* of sth (usu. a theory, project, subject, etc) that you have particularly strong feelings about or particularly like or support 宠爱的；最喜欢的，最珍视的

recycling /ˌriːˈsaɪklɪŋ/ *n.* the activity of reusing things that have already been used 回收利用

San Francisco a city and port in California, US 旧金山

Seattle /sɪˈætl/ a city and port in Washington State 西雅图

sociologist /ˌsəʊsɪˈɒlədʒɪst/ *n.* a social scientist who studies the institutions and development of human society 社会学家

sprout /spraʊt/ *v.* to grow, appear, or develop 生长；发芽；发展

startup /ˈstɑːtəp/ *n.* a small business or company that has recently been started by someone 新兴公司

subset /ˈsʌbset/ *n.* a set that is part of a larger set 分支，（一）小部分

techie /ˈtekiː/ *n.* a person who knows a lot about computers and electronic equipment

tread（on） /tred/ *v.* to put one's foot when walking; to step 踩，踏
upshot /'ʌpʃɒt/ *n.* the result in the end; outcome 结果，结局
way /weɪ/ *adv.* far 远远地，大大地

Notes

1. Yawns — 在本文中，这是"the Young and Wealthy but Normal"的首字母缩略词（acronym），指"年轻、富裕，但是生活节俭的一代人"。

2. They drive hybrid cars … if they use them at all. — 他们如果开车，就开混合动力车；如果购物，就去本地商店；如果使用信用卡，就每个月还清其欠款。此句中的三个条件从句都使用了 at all，强调所陈述条件可能性较小，即他们很少开车，很少购物，也很少使用信用卡。

3. tread lightly on the earth — move on the earth in a gentle way so that the earth is not disturbed

4. Gen X'ers and Y's — Generation X（Gen X）is a term used to describe the generation following the post-World War II baby boom（生育高峰期），especially people born from the early 1960s to the late 1970s. Generation X is generally marked by its lack of optimism for the future, nihilism（虚无主义），cynicism（犬儒主义），skepticism（怀疑论），alienation（疏远）and mistrust in traditional values and institutions. Gen Y is the generation following Gen X. They are primarily children of the Baby boomers, especially people born from the early 1980s to the late 1990. Generation Y are labeled for seeking instant gratification. X 一代人和 Y 一代人。X 一代可称为"后雅皮士时代"，他们收入较高，花钱比较随意。在心理上，这一代人由于面临种种社会问题而有明显的悲观主义色彩，大多数没有明确的生活目标。Y 一代人的父母是生育高峰期出生的人，因此他们处于又一个生育高峰，面临着吸毒、肥胖、教育费用增加以及不善于交流等问题。

5. The acronym comes from … giving money to charity. — 这个首字母缩略词来自于伦敦出版的《星期日电讯报》，其中指出越来越多的年轻富裕的英国人具有社会责任感，他们关心环境，喜欢把钱捐给慈善事业而不是自己消费。

（be）given to — to be in the habit of or have a tendency to 习惯于；有……癖好；倾向于

6. movers and shakers — opinion leaders; people who have power and influence, esp. those who are political or economic activists

7. techie café life —— 此处指把全部时间都花在工作上的一种生活方式。

    techie —— a term derived from the word *technology*, for a person who displays a great, sometimes even obsessive, interest in technology, as well as high-tech devices, particularly computers 高科技（或计算机）迷

8. The high-tech world … sprout anywhere. —— Although the high-tech industry has produced a large number of yawns, more and more are appearing in all walks of life.

9. "Small is Beautiful" —— *Small Is Beautiful: Economics As If People Mattered* is a collection of essays by British economist E. F. Schumacher. First published in 1973, *Small Is Beautiful* brought Schumacher's ideas to a wider audience. It was released during the 1973 energy crisis and emergence of globalization and dealt with the crisis and various emerging trends (like globalization) in an unusual fashion. *The Times Literary Supplement*（《泰晤士文学副刊》）ranked *Small Is Beautiful* among the 100 most influential books published after World War II.

10. ecology movements of the 1970s —— Ecology became a central part of the World's politics as early as 1971, when UNESCO（联合国教科文组织）launched a research program called *Man and Biosphere*（人类与生物圈）, with the objective of increasing knowledge about the mutual relationship between humans and nature. A few years later it defined the concept of Biosphere Reserve（生物圈保护区）. In 1972, the United Nations held the first international Conference on the Human Environment in Stockholm（斯德哥尔摩）. This conference was the origin of the phrase "Think Globally, Act Locally."

11. the hippie movement —— It was a peace movement during the Vietnam war, when people began to hate the war. On 5 September 1965, in an article in the *San Francisco Examiner*, Michael Fallon labeled the new "Bohemians（不受传统束缚者）"or "hippies." The label stuck and was thereafter applied to any young person who experimented with drugs, exhibited an unconventional appearance, enjoyed new forms of music and art, expressed disdain（轻蔑）for mainstream values and institutions, investigated exotic religions, or espoused（信奉）a philosophy that combined the beats' existentialism（垮掉的一代的存在主义哲学）with a colorful, expressive joie de vivre

（人生的乐趣）all their own. Now a hippy generally refers to a person who opposes and rejects many of the conventional standards and customs of society, especially one who advocates extreme liberalism in sociopolitical attitudes and lifestyles, often having long hair, wearing brightly-coloured clothes, taking illegal drugs, and rejecting middle-class materialism. 嬉皮士运动。流行于 20 世纪六七十年代。嬉皮士对社会现实不满，厌弃传统生活方式，实行群居，自由性爱，反对越南战争，主张和平。留长发，穿奇装异服，吸毒。

12. the yuppie period — The yuppies came into vogue in the 1980s. The term "yuppie" was derived from "young, urban professional person（城市少壮职业人士）". The yuppie population consists of that group of people in their thirties who are advancing rapidly in economic and social standing, having well-paid professional jobs and affluent lifestyles, and who represent a target audience for some advertisers, such as BMW automobiles or Fila sportswear. The term has come to have a somewhat pejorative connotation（贬义）, particularly when applied to a specific individual. 雅皮士时期。雅皮士具有较强的职业意识，追求高待遇工作，注重物质享受，住在环境幽雅的市郊。

13. a cultural and demographic perfect storm — a combination of violent changes in cultural and demographic trends

14. Earth Day — Apr. 22, a day to celebrate the environment. The first Earth Day was organized in 1970 to promote the ideas of ecology, encourage respect for life on earth, and highlight growing concern over pollution of the soil, air, and water. Earth Day is now observed in 140 nations with outdoor performances, exhibits, street fairs, and television programs that focus on environmental issues. 世界地球日

15. freecycle.org — 始于 2003 年的全球性环保网站。人们可以通过网站将自己不用的物品送与他人，也可免费得到自己想要的物品。

16. Toyota Prius — 丰田公司生产的世界首款油电混合动力量产车，是环保理念与高科技结合的产品。

17. Such frugality seems to run in his circle. — It seems that all the people connected with him are as frugal as he is. 在他的朋友圈中，节俭似乎很流行。

18. Secondhand stores are to Yawns what The Gap was to Yuppies. —

Yawns like secondhand stores as much as Yuppies like The Gap.

 The Gap — 嘉普(财富500强公司之一,总部在美国,主要经营服装零售)

19. We're pretty low on the stuff scale — We have little demand for material possessions.
20. stock options — options giving the holder, usually an officer or employee, the right to buy stock of the issuing corporation at a specific price within a stated period 优先认股权,股票期权。一般是指企业在与经理人签订合同时,授予经理人将来以签订合同时约定的价格购买一定数量公司普通股的选择权,经理人有权在一定时期后出售这些股票,获得股票市价和行权价之间的差价,但在合同期内,期权不可转让,也不能得到股息。
21. burn through — consume freely
22. The Googledom of Silican Valley — Googledom 一般指 google.com 通过网站链接和各项服务所提供的包罗万象的信息资源(the all-encompassing informational domain created by google.com's many websites and services),这里指 Google Inc. 位于硅谷的总部。
23. carbon hogging guilt trip — 带着因尽情消耗能源而产生的负疚感
   guilt trip — an experience of feeling guilty about sth, esp. when such guilt is excessive, self-indulgent, or unfounded(对某事的)内疚感,负罪感
24. Associated Press(*abbr.* AP) — 美联社,成立于1848年,总部设在纽约市。1976年就已有1,181家美国日报和约3,462家广播电台和电视台接受该社提供的新闻服务,现在已成为世界最大的通讯社。

Questions

1. What are the main characteristics of Yawns?
2. What is their dream?
3. What social-economic background has given rise to the consumer trends of Yawns?
4. How do you understand "post-materialism"?
5. What does "freecycling" mean? What's the most important reason for freecycling?
6. What do you think of the Yawns' life style?

语言解说

Generation 何其多？

Generation 虽不再时髦仍见诸报端，并造出新词。如 Generation O 即奥巴马(Obama)一代，虽然以前吸过毒，孩提时代不爱学习犹如 Generation Jones(1954 年至 1965 年出生)，但从 2009 年起这些人却在奥政府内领导着美国。有篇文章"The N. B. A. and China Hope They've Found the Next Yao"居然还有 Generation Yi(易建联一代)。肥胖的人多了，也称之为一代。

社会学家在总结和描写历史时，往往将有共性、出生同时代的某一特定群体称为"代"(generation)。如美国根据时间先后顺序就可从南北战争到现在分为诸如 Missionary/Lost/G. I. /Silent/Babyboom/Beat/Thirteenth/Millennial Generation 等这几代人。这里的所谓"代"是特指某一群体，并非一代。本课标题中的"A generation of the young, rich and frugal"即为"年轻、富有、节俭的一群人"之义。

因此有的学者认为是用词不当。2001 年《美国新闻与世界报道》发表的一篇题为"'××一代'的说法恰当吗？"的文章指出，"代"常把某个小群体的经历和人生态度强加给同时期出生的整整一代人而无视其地区、种族、阶层等重大差异。马萨诸塞大学的一位教授主张摒弃这种不科学的提法。再则，即使这样划分，有的也含糊不清。由于社会学家这么用，记者用不着动脑子，也纷纷效仿，出现了诸如 Generation XXL 等滥用的现象。

Lesson 19

课文导读

在搜索引擎上输入关键词,搜寻自己想要知道的信息;在社交网络上发布文章和照片,分享自己的心情和生活……你可知道,这些在网络时代人们习以为常的活动,是由遍布全球的互联网公司及其数据中心所支撑的?而互联网公司及其数据中心要使用惊人的能耗,无论用户需求多寡,各大网站的数据中心均全天 24 小时不间断运作,这些数据中心的服务器机群是增长最快的二氧化碳排放源之一。尽管搜索引擎巨头谷歌也是此类污染制造大户,但它正致力于改变目前造成污染的状况。早在 2007 年,谷歌公司就开始进行实现碳中和的尝试,并决意打造全美第一家零碳排放公司。其努力和尝试,是否能真正实现它宣称的零碳排放的目标?是否能成为其他互联网公司仿效的对象?且看本文作者如何评说。

通过本课的阅读,读者可以学到一些环保词语和知识。

Pre-reading Questions

1. What do you know about zero carbon?
2. Do you think real zero carbon is possible?

Text

Google's Zero-carbon Quest

The search giant has an ambitious plan to achieve its goal:
becoming the world's most energy-efficient company.
By Brian Dumaine

1   As the double-decker bus turns onto Charleston Road and starts winding through Google's Mountain View, Calif.[1], campus, I stretch out in the business-class-size seat, admiring the smoothness of the black leather and the plush gray carpeting at my feet. A spacious table expands to hold a laptop, which can connect to the vehicle's Wi-Fi

system[2]. This ＄800,000 luxury double-decker is one of 73 buses that Google owns and operates. (It leases 26 others.) Each day the fleet transports about 4,500 employees, or about a third of those working at the Googleplex[3], as the company's headquarters is known.

2   It turns out that Google (GOOG) isn't offering a free ride simply as an employee perk — the buses actually save the company money. Yes, there's the added productivity of 4,500 employees working an extra couple of hours each day while riding to and from work. But Google's bus service is about much more than that. Real estate in Mountain View is expensive. Underground parking spaces cost as much as ＄85,000 to construct. (Really!) If Google had to build a parking space for each of the bus riders, the price tag would run to almost ＄400 million. And that's not counting the lost opportunity cost[4] of not using that land for new office buildings.

3   Google has made other investments in transportation too. If, during the day, a Google-ite[5] needs to run an errand or pick up a sick kid at school, he or she can hop into one of 52 electric and hybrid cars parked on campus. The company also encourages employees to drive electrics. It has spent an estimated ＄3 million to ＄4 million to install 395 chargers — the largest corporate electric-vehicle infrastructure in the country.

4   Finding creative solutions to energy issues has become a major

priority for Google co-founder and CEO Larry Page[6] in recent years. For the obvious reasons — a growing population, increasingly scarce resources, and climate change — he believes that the corporate world needs to operate more sustainably, and he is determined to build the nation's first zero-carbon company. This means a business that ultimately is so energy efficient and uses so much clean power that it emits no greenhouse gas — a very tall order indeed. Experts aren't sure whether it's even possible for a company to emit no carbon, but Google is trying to come as close to that goal as possible. "As we became a bigger user of energy, we wanted to make sure we were not just part of the problem, but part of the solution," says Urs Hölzle, Google's employee No. 8 and a senior vice president[7] who oversees the company's green initiatives.

5　　To reach its audacious zero-carbon goal, Google is taking a three-pronged approach. First, it's making its server farms, office buildings, and commuting habits more energy efficient. (Apparently Page's Boeing 767, which he owns with co-founder Sergey Brin[8], doesn't get counted in the equation.) Then the company is investing heavily — $915 million to date — in solar and wind producers to make clean energy more available. And finally it is buying enough carbon offsets[9] to make the company carbon neutral[10] — at least on paper — until it can meet its overall goal.

6　　If the plan works, Page will have created a blueprint that other companies can use to reduce their own energy use and — as important — save money at the same time. But Google has already learned some hard lessons.

7　　In June 2007, Page and his top execs issued a staff memo declaring that the company would become carbon neutral. The catch? The existing power infrastructure is so dependent on fossil fuels that no major company in the world has yet achieved this goal without buying carbon credits[11]. Page began buying carbon credits from organizations that, say, capture methane from landfills to offset the greenhouse gas Google emits. Then he set the company on a long march to reduce the amount of energy it consumes while increasing its use of carbon-free wind and solar power.

8   Later that year Page, to the amazement of many in the IT industry, also announced that Google was getting into the clean-energy business. In a Nov. 27, 2007, press release, the company introduced an additional initiative based on the formula RE < C, which translates as "renewable energy is cheaper than coal." Page believed Google could become carbon neutral faster by applying the formidable brainpower of its engineers to the problem. He wanted to help produce one gigawatt of renewable power — about the equivalent produced by a nuclear power plant — that was cheaper than coal within a few years. This goal, however, turned out to be more devilish than anyone thought.

9   Page asked his managers to focus on a basic question: How much carbon are we emitting? Google's executives started asking themselves how they could use less power in their data centers, how they could make their office buildings more efficient, and where they could buy clean energy for their operations.

10   Becoming a zero-carbon company is no easy task. In 2011 — some four years after Page's memo — Google reported that it still had emitted 1.5 million tons of carbon in the previous year. It was the first time Google had publicly revealed its carbon footprint[12]. To put that in perspective, Google's 30,000 employees and its fleet of data centers last year emitted the same amount of CO_2 as a city the size of Fargo, N. D. (pop. 202,000)[13]. The good news: If the company hadn't embarked on Page's quest to become carbon neutral, the numbers would have been much worse. That 1.5 million tons of carbon is more than Google emitted in 2007, but much less than would have been expected

considering that the company's annual revenue since then has more than doubled, to $38 billion.

11 Google's largest source of greenhouse gas emissions is its data centers — those buildings stuffed with computers that handle each of the 3 billion searches its customers perform every day. According to Jonathan Koomey, a Stanford professor, server farms account for about 2% of America's total electricity use. (That's roughly the same greenhouse gas impact as the airline industry's.) However, they are one of the fastest-growing sources of CO_2 emissions.

12 Server farms also account for Google's biggest use of energy. One thing the company realized early on is that the managers in charge of building data centers were not the same people who operated them. "It's incredible how much people waste in a company," says Google executive Hölzle. "The facility department pays construction costs and utility bills, but the IT people buy the servers, so they don't care about how much electricity they use."

Server farms: not green but grey

To eliminate that conflict, Google made sure that the person paying the utility bills and the one buying the computers was the same.

13 Now the economic incentive exists to cut energy use. Typically a server farm consumes as much energy for lighting and cooling as for the computers themselves. By using customized hardware and applying innovative cooling techniques, the need for air conditioning is reduced. Joe Kava, Google's director of data center operations, cites as an example the search giant's new server farm in Finland — on the site of a former paper mill — that sits on the Gulf of Finland[14] and uses seawater in its cooling system.

14 No matter how efficient Google makes its server farms, it will still need clean power to meet its zero-carbon goals. Soon after Page launched the RE < C program in 2007, he set up a handful of green skunkworks projects[15] and created a team to make venture investments in green energy. Google put money into promising companies like BrightSource Energy[16], which is building a cutting-edge, solar thermal

plant in the Mojave Desert[17]. The search giant even had an internal engineering team working to improve a type of concentrating solar power technology called the solar power tower. It invested in AltaRock[18] to foster innovations in geothermal energy. It also sponsored research to develop the first geothermal map of the U. S. to better understand the potential for geothermal energy.

15 Driving the price of renewables below that of fossil fuels is an ambitious goal, especially for a company that has no background in power generation. The energy field, as Google eventually learned, is much more capital-intensive and has a far longer time horizon than is typical in Silicon Valley — where a new company with a garage full of software geeks can scale to billions in revenue seemingly overnight. After four years of effort, Google quietly dropped its RE $<$ C program in late 2011.

16 Google execs explain that relatively speaking, not much money was invested — perhaps $50 million. (Google has kept its equity investments in BrightSource and AltaRock but has disbanded its green-tech engineering efforts.) It couldn't have helped that the company had been taking flak from a group of shareholders who didn't understand why Google was spending money on clean tech. In 2011, Justin Danhof, the general counsel of a conservative think tank, the National Center for Public Policy Research[19], filed a shareholder proposal criticizing Google's lack of transparency about its green investments. (It didn't pass.)

17 While Google has abandoned its quest to be an innovator in clean-energy technology, it hasn't stopped investing in green power. Today Google has signed contracts to buy about 12% of its total energy from wind and solar farms, up from 4% just two years ago. (Add in existing sources of clean energy on the grid, and that number rises to 27%.) "As a company we are looking at ways we can support the renewables industry," says Rick Needham, Google's director of energy and sustainability. "We have a long vision of being a company powered by renewable energy, but how do we get from here to there?" Google pays more for clean energy than it would for power off the grid. However, it has locked into long-term pricing contracts for renewables and expects those contracts to eventually make money as conventional power becomes more expensive over time.

18   Google has also been investing directly in wind and solar projects to the tune of $915 million. It began in 2008 by financing a couple of wind farms — in North Dakota and Oregon — in need of funding after the financial meltdown had frozen the capital markets. A key to Google's strategy is that it wants the money it invests to expand utilities' solar and wind operations; otherwise it won't be adding capacity to the system. As the wind projects become operational and begin selling electricity to big utilities, Google gets a piece of the cash flow. This type of deal — a form of tax equity investment — gets sweetened by federal tax credits.

19   Google was one of the first companies — if not the first — outside the banking, energy, and utility sectors to start investing in these tax deals. Instead of keeping its cash in the corporate treasury and earning only 1% or 2% on it, it can earn as much as 15% to 20% through the tax credit investments, says Google.

20   The company may be increasingly cleaning up its act, but it is still a polluter. In the meantime, it continues to buy carbon offsets. Carbon offsets, however, are controversial. One common way is to, say, pay an organization to plant a tree to offset the carbon you emit when you fly cross-country. But how do you know if the tree ever gets planted or if someday a drought kills it? Some criticize offsets as just a guilt-free way to indulge in polluting habits.

21   Well aware of the problems posed by offsets, Google searched for ones that were verifiable and additional — meaning that the reduction in carbon is real and wouldn't have happened without Google's buying the offset. It decided the best way to create carbon offsets was to pay for reductions in methane emissions from landfills and swine farms. Says Jolanka Nickerman, Google's program manager for carbon offsets: "The gold standard for offsets is methane gas, which is 20 to 25 times more potent than carbon dioxide." These methane-capture projects can cost anywhere from $500,000 to $1 million. In Yadkinville, N.C.[20], Google, in partnership with Duke Energy[21] (DUK) and Duke University[22], helps the Loyd Ray Farms, home to 9,000 hogs, capture methane from manure to power its operations.

22   So far the company has spent upwards of $15 million investing in or purchasing carbon credits for dozens of such projects. That will

offset about 5 million tons of CO_2 — more than enough to make Google a carbon-neutral company on paper.

23   When asked how long it will take to become a truly zero-carbon company, Google execs say they don't really know. What they do know is that the green program has made the company stand for something more than just making money. That's a message that Google's bus riders are reminded of each day. (From *Fortune*, July 12, 2012)

New Words

audacious /ɔːˈdeɪʃəs/ *adj.* showing great courage or confidence in a way that is impressive or slightly shocking 大胆的, 雄心勃勃的

campus /ˈkæmpəs/ *n.* the land and buildings belonging to a large company (包括土地和建筑物在内的属于大公司的)园区

catch /kætʃ/ *n. usu. sing.*, *infml* a hidden problem or difficulty 诀窍, 关键

cutting-edge /ˈkʌtɪŋˈedʒ/ *adj.* in accordance with the most fashionable ideas or leading in nature 尖端的, 前沿的

devilish /ˈdevəlɪʃ/ *adj.* very bad, difficult, or unpleasant 阴暗, 魔鬼般的

electrics /ɪˈlektrɪks/ *n.* electric cars 电动车

embark /ɪmˈbɑːk/ *v.* to start sth, esp. sth new, difficult, or exciting 启动新奇事物

equation /ɪˈkweɪʒn/ *n.* the set of different facts, ideas, or people that all affect a situation and must be considered together (涉及平衡的)影响因素, 综合体

equivalent /ɪˈkwɪvələnt/ *n.* sth that has the same value, purpose, job etc as sth else 等同物, 等价物, 对应物

exec /ɪɡˈzek/ *n.* an informal word for executive 行政长官; (公司的)经理、管理人员

facility /fəˈsɪlətɪ/ *n.* rooms, equipment, or services that are provided for a particular purpose (为某种目的而提供的)设施; 设备

flak /flæk/ *n. infml.* strong criticism 强烈的反对

fleet /fliːt/ *n.* a group of vehicles that are controlled by one company, motorcade (某家公司控制的)车队

formidable /ˈfɔːmɪdəbl/ *adj.* very powerful or impressive, and often frightening 令人敬畏的, 可怕的

geothermal /ˌdʒiː(ː)əʊˈθəməl/ *adj.* relating to or coming from the heat inside the earth 地热的

grid /ɡrɪd/ *n.* the network of electricity supply wires that connects power stations and provides electricity to buildings in an area 电力网，输电网

hog /hɒɡ/ *n. esp. AmE.* a large pig that is kept for its meat 肉(肥)猪

hybrid /ˈhaɪbrɪd/ *n.* sth that consists of or comes from a mixture of two or more other things (两种或两种以上不同事物组成的)混合体；混合动力汽车

initiative /ɪˈnɪʃətɪv/ *n.* the ability to make decisions and take action without waiting for sb to tell you what to do 主动，首先发起

lease /liːs/ *v.* to grant the temporary possession or use of (lands, tenements, etc.) to another, usu. for compensation at a fixed rate 出租，租用

manure /məˈnʊə, -ˈnjʊə/ *n.* waste matter from animals or human droppings that are mixed with soil to improve the soil and help plants grow 粪肥，有机肥

meltdown /ˈmeltdaʊn/ *n.* a situation in which prices fall by a very large amount or an industry or economic situation becomes much weaker(价格的)暴跌；(行业或经济的)崩溃

methane /ˈmiːθeɪn/ *n.* a gas that you cannot see or smell, which can be burned to give heat 甲烷，沼气

neutral /ˈnjuːtrəl/ *adj.* neither moral nor immoral; neither good nor evil, right nor wrong 中性的；中和的

North Dakota /nɔːθ dəˈkəʊtə/ a state in the Midwestern region of the U.S., along the Canadian border(美国)北达科他州

offset /ˈɒfset/ *n.* a compensating equivalent 抵消，补偿

Oregon /ˈɒrɪɡən/ a state in the Pacific Northwest region of the U.S.(美国)俄勒冈州

perk /pɜːk/ *n.* sth that you get legally from your work in addition to your wages, such as goods, meals, or a car (工资以外的)额外收入，津贴

plush /plʌʃ/ *adj. infml* very comfortable, expensive, and of good quality 高贵而舒适的

potent /ˈpəʊtnt/ *adj.* powerful and effective 强有力的，有能力的

prong /prɔːŋ, prɒŋ/ *n.* one of two or three ways of achieving sth which are used at the same time (**three-pronged** *adj.* 三方面的)

scale /skeɪl/ *v.* to climb to the top of sth that is high and difficult to climb 攀登

sustainable /səˈsteɪnəbl/ *adj.* able to continue without causing damage to the environment (sustainably *adv.* sustainability *n.*) 可持续的

utility /juːˈtɪləti/ *n. usu. pl.* a service such as gas or electricity provided for people to use 公用事业(如煤气、电力等)

verifiable /ˈverɪfaɪəbl/ *adj.* capable of being tested (verified or falsified) by experiment or observation 可考验的

Notes

1. Mountain View, Calif. — a city in Santa Clara County, California. It is named for its views of the Santa Cruz Mountains. Situated in Silicon Valley, Mountain View is home to many high technology companies. Today, many of the largest technology companies in the world are headquartered in the city, including Google, Symantec(赛门铁克,美国著名软件公司), and Intuit(直觉软件公司). 山景城

2. Wi-Fi system — also spelled Wifi or WiFi, short for wireless fidelity(无线保真技术), and a trademark of the Wi-Fi Alliance 无线网络系统

3. Googleplex — the corporate headquarters complex(建筑群)of Google, Inc., located at 1600 Amphitheatre Parkway in Mountain View, Santa Clara County, California. "Googleplex" is a blend of "Google" and "complex", and a reference to "googolplex"(1 后跟着 10 的 100 次方个零,指巨大得无法想象的、天文数字), the name given to the large number 10 googol(10 的 100 次方). 谷歌公司总部

4. opportunity cost — a key concept in economics, which refers to benefit that could have been gained from an alternative use of the same resource. The notion of opportunity cost plays a crucial part in ensuring that scarce resources are used efficiently. Thus, opportunity costs are not restricted to monetary or financial costs: the real cost of output forgone, lost time, pleasure or any other benefit that provides utility should also be considered opportunity costs. 机会成本

5. Google -ite — 谷歌人,谷歌员工
   -ite — *suf.* a follower, supporter

6. Google co-founder and CEO Larry Page — (1973—   ) an American computer scientist and Internet entrepreneur. In 1998, Sergey Brin and Larry Page founded Google, Inc. Page ran Google as co-president along with Brin until 2001 when they hired Eric Schmidt as Chairman and CEO of Google. On April 4, 2011, Page took on the

role of chief executive officer of Google, replacing Eric Schmidt. As of 2012, his personal wealth is estimated to be $20.3 billion, ranking him #13 on the Forbes 400 list of richest Americans. 劳伦斯·"拉里"·佩奇

7. Urs Hölzle, Google's employee No. 8 and a senior vice president — Hölzle(乌尔斯·霍泽尔)is Senior Vice President(高级副总裁)for Technical Infrastructure at Google. In this capacity Urs oversees the design, installation, and operation of the servers, networks, and data centers that power Google's services. As the No. 8 of Google's first ten employees and its first VP(副总裁)of Engineering, he has shaped much of Google's development processes and infrastructure.

8. Sergey Brin — (1973—) a Russian-born American computer scientist and Internet entrepreneur who, with Larry Page, co-founded Google. Together, Brin and Page own about 16 percent of the company. 谢尔盖·布林

9. carbon offsets — reduction in emissions of carbon dioxide or greenhouse gases made in order to compensate for or to offset(补偿)an emission made elsewhere 碳补偿

10. carbon neutral — the achieving of net zero carbon emissions by balancing a measured amount of carbon released with an equivalent amount of offset 碳中和

11. carbon credits — a highly regulated medium of exchange used to offset, or neutralize(中和)carbon dioxide emissions. A single carbon credit generally represents the right to emit one metric ton of carbon dioxide or the equivalent mass of another greenhouse gas. 碳信用

12. carbon footprint — the measure given to the amount of greenhouse gases produced by burning fossil fuels, measured in units of carbon dioxide (i.e. Kg) 碳足迹

13. Fargo, N.D. (pop. 202,000) — Fargo is the largest city in the U.S. state of North Dakota, accounting for nearly 16% of the state population.

14. the Gulf of Finland — the easternmost arm of the Baltic Sea(波罗的海). It extends between Finland (to the north) and Estonia(爱沙尼亚) (to the south) all the way to Saint Petersburg(圣彼德堡) in Russia. 芬兰湾

15. green skunkworks projects — projects typically developed by a small and loosely structured group of people who research and develop projects primarily for the sake of radical innovation. 绿色臭鼬工厂项目
16. BrightSource Energy — an Oakland, California, corporation that designs, builds, finances, and operates utility-scale solar power plants（太阳能电厂）. Greentech Media（绿色科技媒介公司）ranked BrightSource as one of the top 10 greentech startups（创业公司）in the world in 2008. 亮源能源公司
17. the Mojave Desert — an area that occupies a significant portion of southeastern California and smaller parts of central California, southern Nevada, southwestern Utah and northwestern Arizona in the U.S. It is named after the Mohave tribe of Native Americans. 莫哈维沙漠
18. AltaRock — AltaRock Energy Inc., headquartered in Seattle, Washington and having a technology development office in Sausalito, California, is a privately held corporation that focuses on the development of geothermal energy resources and Enhanced Geothermal Systems (EGS). 艾塔洛克能源公司
19. a conservative think tank, the National Center for Public Policy Research — 保守智库, 美国全国公共政策研究中心

　　think tank — a group of people with experience of knowlege of a particular subject, who work to produce ideas and give advice reports on the implications.
20. Yadkinville, N.C. — a town in Yadkin County, North Carolina, U.S. It is the county seat and largest city of Yadkin County. 北卡罗来纳州亚德金维尔市
21. Duke Energy — the largest electric power holding company in the U.S. It is headquartered in Charlotte, North Carolina, with assets also in Canada and Latin America. 杜克能源公司
22. Duke University — a private university, located in Durham, North Carolina. 杜克大学

Questions

1. Why does Google offer the free ride of luxury double-decker buses to its employees on Mountain View campus?

2. What makes Larry Page determined to build the nation's first zero-carbon company?
3. How is Google going to reach its audacious zero-carbon goal?
4. What green powers are mentioned in the passage? And what is the conventional power?
5. What has Google done to make it a carbon-neutral company? Do those measures really work?

新闻写作

报刊文体

根据《现代汉语词典》的定义,文体是文章的体裁;体裁指的是文学作品的表现形式。中外对 style 历来争议不断,如文体即形式或修辞、解说技巧等,约有二三十个定义,真是众说纷纭,莫衷一是。报刊文体大致有如下几种定义或说法:

1. 新闻体

journalese(新闻体),尤指 type of news reporting,是最常见的含有贬义的定义,即指报道性文章多陈词滥调,行文仓促,思想性或说理性肤浅,还不时夹着口语(*Webster's Dictionary*)。这个定论是以往受传统偏见的约束,瞧不起报刊英语,把它跟粗俗低级语言画等号。现在报刊质量早已大大提高,语言简明实用,富有创意,这是不争的事实。所谓行文仓促是不得已而为之,日报得天天出,与期刊有别。但现在罕见 Alan Warner 写的 *Short Guide to English Style* 一书中举例文章 "Zoo Mountain Goat Leaps Lions' Enclose Rescued by Keepers" 那样,充斥着如 lions and elephants 比作 "monarches of the wilds"(与 "King of beast" 一样)、"brute creation"(无理性之动物)、"sawdust Caesar"(喻马戏团训狮员)等夸张或陈腐之词。至于夹着口语,这与为了表明"客观公正",记者以第三者口气论述有关(见"报刊语言主要特点""常用套语")。只要读了《导读》"新闻体裁"所举三篇文章,便知一二。

2. 综合体

报刊是由消息、特写、社评、采访、杂文、传记等多种体裁组成的,甚至还有散文、日记、游记和小说连载等等,无所不包,集多种体裁与题材之大成,所以说它是综合体。还有人无奈地称之为特殊文体。

3. 实用文体

报刊题材多样,语言紧贴当今现实而又简明,学了就能用。

4. 文学文体

四川大学曹明伦教授根据 19 世纪英国诗人、社会评论家马修·阿诺德(Matthew Arnold)所说的"Journalism is literature in a hurry"(报刊新闻是匆匆写出的文学作品)这句话,将报刊新闻定义为文学作品。还有的学者也将这种新闻急就章归类为文学。既然是文学,那又是何种文学文体? 值得探讨。

以上说明,要给报刊文体下一个众所接受的定义并非易事,这与人们从不同角度审视报刊和文体有关。

Unit Seven
Business & Science

Lesson 20

课文导读

模特在许多人眼中是美丽的代名词。美女模特在T型台上吸引众人的眼球。她们是世界时尚的弄潮儿,给人一种神秘高雅的感觉。然而个中滋味只有她们自知。

面对全球化的发展,这一行业正在慢慢发生变化。一批有才华的模特和全球化的模特圈正在改变T型台,受过良好教育的年轻女性纷纷入行。以往模特的职业生涯通常很短,薪水也低,现在却涌现出许多高收入的超模群体。以前的模特追求的是0号身材,瘦骨嶙峋;鉴于全球化的影响,现在的模特公司在世界范围内寻求体态强壮、高大健美的模特。然而,"骨模"仍有市场。现在该行业竞争激烈,要立于不败之地并非易事,时尚大牌和艺术总监不总是定海神针,模特自身的智慧才是不可或缺的。

通过学习此课,同学们可以了解西方模特现状和学习若干专有名词,如一般文章上很少出现的名模名字、时尚品牌和公司等。我们阅读各种题材的文章,能扩大视野,获得更广泛的知识。

Pre-reading Questions
1. Do you think modelling is attractive?
2. What kind of life do you think models live?

Text

Model Economics: The Beauty Business

Brainy models and a global talent pool are changing the catwalk

1 On February 17th London's spring fashion week[1] begins. Across the capital, young women in vertiginous shoes and skimpy dresses will be teetering along catwalks. And thousands of young doughnut-dodgers[2] will be inspired to queue outside agents' offices for the slim

chance of becoming the next Kate Moss[3].

2   Careers in modeling are typically short-lived, badly paid and less glamorous than pretty young dreamers imagine. Yet the business is changing. For one thing, educated models are in. This may sound improbable. In the film *Zoolander*[4], male models are portrayed as so dumb that they play-fight with petrol and then start smoking. But such stereotypes are so last year.[5]

3   Lily Cole, a redheaded model favoured by Chanel[6] and Hermès[7], recently left Cambridge University with a first-class degree in history of art. Edie Campbell, a new British star, is studying for the same degree at the Courtauld Institute[8] in London. And Jacquetta Wheeler, one of Britain's established catwalkers, has taken time out from promoting Burberry[9] and Vivienne Westwood[10] to work for Reprieve, a charity which campaigns for prisoners' rights.

4   Natalie Hand of London's Viva model agency, who represents Ms Campbell, says there has been a shift away from the "very young, impressionable models," who were popular in the past ten years, to "more aspirational young women.""There is an appetite now for models to be intelligent, well-mannered and educated," says Catherine Ostler, a former editor of *Tatler*, a fashion and society magazine.

5   This is new. The best-known models of yesteryear often led rags-to-riches lives, courtesy of the rag trade.[11] Twiggy, a star of the 1960s, was a factory worker's daughter. Ms Moss's mother was a barmaid.

6   But the big fashion houses and leading photographers are tiring of the drama that comes with plucking girls as young as 15 from obscurity

and propelling them to sudden stardom. Too often, models were showing up to photo-shoots hours late or drug-addled. This wasted a huge amount of time and money. Fashion houses are now keen to avoid trouble. Many find that educated models show up to work on time and don't go doolally as often.

7   Trends in the modelling business also follow those in the global economy. From the 1960s to the 1990s, America reigned supreme. The hottest "supermodels" were Americans such as Cindy Crawford and Christy Turlington. They were figures whose glossy confidence mirrored America's[12]. They never woke up for less than $10,000. They were cultural icons, too, celebrated in songs such as Billy Joel's "Uptown girl," the video of which starred Christie Brinkley, who became his wife[13].

Fat cheques
The world's best-paid models

Name	2011 earnings, $m	Comments
Gisele Bündchen	45	Giraffe-legged Brazilian; owns global underwear franchise. Has promoted Dior, Versace and Procter & Gamble's Pantene shampoo
Heidi Klum	20	Small-town German; has conquered America. Hosts "Project Runway" TV series
Kate Moss	14	Chirpy Brit from Croydon. Launched "heroin chic" look in 1993. Honoured with gold statue in British Museum
Adriana Lima	8	Brazilian newcomer; her GQ cover was the biggest-selling ever; Super Bowl ad hinted that flowers buy sex
Doutzen Kroes	6	Dutch ex-skater, known as "Helen of Troy" for launching so many products. Less well-known for promoting Friesian language

8   As in so many fields, the rewards for a handful of stars have shot up. Contracts are wrapped in secrecy, but sources say that a one-off deal for a shoot with a top model can begin at $75,000, rising to $1.5m for a global advertising campaign. For advertisers, the right face is lucrative. Procter & Gamble's campaign featuring Gisele Bündchen is said to have raised sales of its Pantene shampoo in Brazil by 40%.[14]

9   The stars pull in more from sidelines such as franchising goods in their own name (Elle Macpherson's underwear, Kate Moss's lipstick). Heidi Klum, a German model, serves as a judge on "Project Runway," a televised fashion-talent contest.[15]

10   Pay for lesser models has fallen sharply, however. This is partly because the labour pool has globalised and therefore grown much bigger. International agencies now scout for talent in emerging

economies[16]. In the 1990s they hired hordes of high-cheeked Slav teenagers. Now the hottest hunting-ground is Brazil, which produces Amazonian height and athletic looks.

11   Ashley Mears, an American sociologist and author of "Pricing Beauty," a study of the economics of modelling[17], says that although the industry has grown in the past decade, individual contracts have shrunk. Too many faces are chasing too few lenses.

12   Television fees have fallen, not least because technologies like TiVo[18] allow audiences to skip commercials. One British model told your correspondent that rates for the major fashion shows have roughly halved in recent years, and that many careers are now over in two seasons (a calendar year) rather than around six. The Model Alliance[19], an outfit that agitates for higher wages, estimates that the average regularly-employed model makes $27,000 a year. Part-timers and men make less.

13   The juiciest prize is to become the face of a luxury brand such as Dior or Burberry[20]. To have any chance, a model must first have magazine shoots under her designer belt. This fact allows fashion magazines to pay peanuts, even for a cover-shoot.[21]

14   There remains an iron divide between "editorial" models, who appeal to the expensive designers, and "catalogue" models, who are often slightly larger and more conventionally pretty. The catalogue models pose in normal clothes, which is less glamorous. But they earn a steadier income, and are less likely to be dropped by the time they reach their late 20s.

15   Agents take around 20% of a model's fee, plus another 20% from the client. Despite these high levies, agencies struggle. Since the financial crash, clients have been scrimping. And agencies must find models whose faces somehow capture the Zeitgeist, as defined by the big brands and their capricious artistic directors.

16   Large agencies are competing with a crowd of smaller upstarts, such as Viva London[22] and DNA[23] in New York. The giant Elite Model Management agency lost an American antitrust case on price-fixing in 2004[24] and drowned in a sea of recriminations. It has since been refounded under new ownership, though its Dutch branch faces a fresh lawsuit, brought by the winner of a contest who claims the agency

sacked her for putting on weight.

17 The sheer randomness of fashion makes it a tough business. Change is more predictable in other industries. IT firms, for example, can safely assume that computers will keep getting faster. But foreseeing next year's hot look is impossible. No one could have anticipated Kate Moss's early "grunge" look, which set a fashion for tangled long hair, boyish hips and pale complexions. Now the fashion is for models who look a little healthier, such as Doutzen Kroes[25], a former speedskater.

The exquisitely sensitive Karl Lagerfeld[26]

18 Despite angry campaigns against the cult of "Size 0"[27], skinny models are still in demand. This is partly because designers think clothes look better when there is no distracting flesh beneath them. Ms Mears adds that the industry keeps models thin to "signify elite luxury distinctiveness." Rough translation: if normal women have curves, then the elite want something different. This infuriates those who blame fashion for fostering eating disorders among the young. But the attitude shows little sign of shifting. Karl Lagerfeld, a designer, made headlines this week by describing Adele[28], a pop singer, as "fat."

19 Power in the fashion business depends on fame. "Super-brands" such as Gucci[29] and Burberry don't hesitate to throw their weight around[30]. Gucci flustered London's fashion week last autumn by ordering a clutch of the "mega-girls" to leave London early and fly to Milan for a more commercially important show.

20 Marc Jacobs[31], a prominent New York designer, caused a further shortage of models for British shows by detaining some prospective bookings in New York. Agents complained, but Mr Jacobs is bigger than any of them. "Where's the camaraderie?" asked Carole White of Premier Model Management[32], a London agency. On the catwalk, you walk alone. (From *The Economist*, February 11, 2012)

New Words

aspirational /ˌæspəˈreɪʃənl/ *adj.* having strong desire to do sth or have sth important or great 有志向的，有抱负的

addled /ˈædld/ *adj. infml* (of sb's brain) having become confused

agitate /ˈædʒɪteɪt/ *v.* to argue strongly in public for or against some political or social change 鼓动，煽动，宣传

Amazonian /ˌæməˈzəʊnjən/ *adj.* strong and aggressive (used of women) 常作 amazonian（指妇女）男子气概的，强壮且咄咄逼人的

antitrust /ˌæntɪˈtrʌst/ *adj.* against trust or business monopolies 反托拉斯的，反垄断的

barmaid /ˈbɑːmeɪd/ *n.* a woman who serves drinks in a bar

brainy /ˈbreɪnɪ/ *adj.* intelligent; smart

capricious /kəˈprɪʃəs/ *adj.* changing often, esp. suddenly and without good reason 反复无常的

catwalk /ˈkætwɔːk/ *n.* a narrow raised footway sticking out into a room for models to walk on in a fashion show（时装表演时模特走的）T 型台

camaraderie /kɑːməˈrɑːdərɪː/ *n.* the friendliness and goodwill shown to each other by friends, esp. people who spend time together at work, in the army, etc.

complexion /kəmˈplekʃn/ *n.* the natural color and appearance of the skin, esp. of the face 面色，气色

cult /kʌlt/ *n.* a system of worship, esp. one that is different from the usu. and established forms of religion in a particular society 狂热的崇拜，迷信

detain /dɪˈteɪn/ *v.* to keep from proceeding; delay or retard 阻止，拖延

doolally /duːˈlælɪ/ *adj. infml* crazy

established /ɪˈstæblɪʃt/ *adj.* well-known and recognized by the public

exquisitely /ekˈskwɪzɪtlɪ/ *adv.* intensely, greatly（感觉）强烈的，剧烈的

feature /ˈfiːtʃə(r)/ *v.* to have or include as a prominent part or characteristic 由……主演；包含……作为主要部分或特点的

franchise /ˈfræntʃaɪz/ *v.* authorize someone to sell or distribute a company's goods or services in a certain area（授予出售或发行的）特许经营或销售权

fluster /ˈflʌstə(r)/ *v.* to cause to be nervous and confused

glamorous /ˈɡlæmərəs/ *adj.* full of or characterized by glamour 充满魅力的

glossy /ˈɡlɒsɪ/ *adj.* having a smooth, shiny, lustrous surface 表面光滑的，有光泽的；表面上时髦动人的

grunge /ɡrʌndʒ/ *n.* a style of fashion, popular with young people in the early 1990s, of wearing clothes that look dirty and untidy 邋遢装时尚

horde /hɔːd, həʊrd/ *n.* a large moving crowd, esp. one that is noisy or disorderly

icon /ˈaɪkɒn/ *n.* one who is the object of great attention and devotion; an idol

impressionable /ɪmˈpreʃənəbl/ *adj.* capable of receiving an impression; plastic 可塑的；有可塑性的

infuriate /ɪnˈfjʊərɪeɪt/ *v.* to make someone extremely angry

juicy /ˈdʒuːsɪ/ *adj.* yielding profit; rewarding or gratifying

levy /ˈlevɪ/ *n.* an official demand and collection, esp. of a tax 征税

maga-girl *n.* a super model

Milan /mɪˈlæn, mɪˈlɑːn/ *n.* a city in Italy 米兰

obscurity /əbˈskjʊərətɪ/ *n.* one that is unknown 不知名的人

one-off /ˈwʌnɔːf, -ɒf/ *adj.* sth that is not repeated or reproduced

outfit /ˈaʊtfɪt/ *n. infml* a group of people working together

pluck /plʌk/ *v.* to pull (esp. sth unwanted) out sharply 猛拉，猛扯

pool /puːl/ *n.* a group of people who are available to work or do an activity when they are needed （一批）备用或可用人员

recrimination /rɪˌkrɪmɪˈneɪʃn/ *n.* (*usu. pl.*) an act of quarrelling and blaming one another 吵架

runway /ˈrʌnweɪ/ *n.* a narrow walkway extending from a stage into an auditorium 延伸台道；从舞台通向观众席中的窄的走道

sack /sæk/ *v. infml* to dismiss from a job

scout /skaʊt/ *v.* to go looking for sth

scrimp /skrɪmp/ *v.* to save money slowly and with difficulty, esp. by living less well than usual

sideline /ˈsaɪdlaɪn/ *n.* an activity pursued in addition to one's regular occupation 副业

skimpy /ˈskɪmpɪ/ *adj.* a skimpy dress is very short and does not cover very much of a woman's body 太短太小或暴露的服装

skinny /ˈskɪnɪ/ *adj. infml* very thin, esp. in a way that is unattractive 消瘦的，皮包骨的

Slav /slɑːv/ *adj.* 斯拉夫人的

star /stɑː(r)/ *v.* to have as a main performer 以……为主角，主演

stardom /ˈstɑːdəm/ *n.* the status of a performer or an entertainer acknowledged as a star

stereotype /ˈsterɪətaɪp/ *n.* a fixed general image or set of characteristics that a lot of people believe represent a particular type of person or thing 模式化的陈规老套

tangle /ˈtæŋgl/ *v.* to (cause to) become a confused mass of disordered and twisted threads

teeter /ˈtiːtə(r)/ *v.* to stand or move unsteadily, as if about to fall 站立不稳，跟跟跄跄地走；本文中指模特走猫步

upstart /ˈʌpstɑːt/ *n. derog* someone who has risen suddenly or unexpectedly to a high position and takes advantage of the power they have gained 暴发户，新贵

vertiginous /vɜːˈtɪdʒɪnəs/ *adj. fml* causing or suffering from vertigo (a feeling of great unsteadiness), esp. by being at great height above the ground（尤指因处于高处令人）眩晕的，感到眩晕的

wrap /ræp/ *v.* to cover sth in a material folded around 包，裹

yesteryear /ˈjestəjɪə/ *n.* the year before the present year 去年，当年之前的一年

Zeitgeist /ˈzaɪtɡaɪst/ *n. Ger.* the general spirit of a period in history, as shown in people's ideas and beliefs 时代精神，时代思潮

Notes

1. London's spring fashion week — London's fashion week is one of the big four fashion weeks in the world, held in the four fashion capitals: New York City, London, Milan, and Paris. It is an apparel trade show held in London twice each year, in February and September.

2. doughnut-dodgers — people who avoid eating sweet food like doughnut, here refers to those young girls who go on diet to become slim.

3. Kate Moss — (1974—) an English model who rose to fame in the early 1990s as part of the Heroin chic（海洛因时尚）model movement, best known for her waifish（瘦骨嶙峋的）figure, and her role in size zero fashion.

4. *Zoolander* — a 2001 American comedy film directed by and starring Ben Stiller. The film features a dimwitted（愚蠢的）male model named Derek Zoolander (a play on the names of Dutch model Mark Vanderloo and American model Johnny Zander), played by Stiller. 电影《超级名模》

5. But such stereotypes are **so last year**. — so outdated, outmoded, or out of fashion (不如此理解，"are"就该是"were")

6. Chanel — a Parisian fashion house created by Coco Chanel, specializing in luxury goods 香奈儿

7. Hermès — a French manufacturer of quality goods established in 1837 爱马仕
8. Courtauld Institute — commonly referred to as The Courtauld, a self-governing college of the University of London specialising in the study of the history of art 英国考陶德艺术学院
9. Burberry — a British luxury fashion house, distributing clothing and fashion accessories and licensing fragrances 巴宝莉
10. Vivienne Westwood — (1941—) an English fashion designer and businesswoman, largely responsible for bringing modern punk（朋克）and new wave fashions into the mainstream 维维安·韦斯特伍德
11. The best-known models of yesteryear often led rags-to-riches lives, courtesy of the rag trade. — The most famous models in the past years often led from-poverty-to-wealth lives, owing to the garment industry.

    a. rags-to-riches — usu. from rags to riches: becoming very rich after starting your life very poor

    b. rag trade — the garment industry

    c. courtesy of sb or sth — by the permission or generosity of 由于……的恩惠,承蒙……的允许
12. They were figures whose glossy confidence mirrored America's. — They were people whose attractive confidence reflected the confidence of America.
13. They were cultural icons…who became his wife. — 他们还是文化偶像,在歌词中受到赞美,如比利·乔尔的《上城女孩》。这首歌的 MV 由克里斯蒂·布林克利主演,后来她嫁给了乔尔。

    a. Billy Joel — (1949—) an American pianist, singer-songwriter, and composer. Since releasing his first hit song, "Piano Man," in 1973, Joel has become the sixth-best-selling recording artist and the fourth-best-selling solo artist in the United States, according to the RIAA(美国唱片业协会). He is also a six-time Grammy Award（格莱美奖）winner, a 23-time Grammy nominee and has sold over 150 million records worldwide.

    b. Christie Brinkley — (1954—) an American supermodel and actress.
14. Procter & Gamble's campaign…by 40%. — 据说,吉赛尔·邦辰的代言广告令宝洁公司的潘婷洗发水在巴西的销售量增长了 40%。

a. Procter & Gamble — The Procter & Gamble Company（宝洁公司）, also known as P&G, is an American multinational consumer goods company headquartered in downtown Cincinnati, Ohio, USA.

b. Gisele Bündchen — (1980—) a Brazilian fashion model and occasional film actress and producer. She is the goodwill ambassador for the United Nations Environment Programme（联合国环境规划署亲善大使）. In the late 1990s, Bündchen became the first in a wave of Brazilian models to find international success.

15. Heidi Klum, a German model … a televised fashion-talent contest. — 德国模特海蒂·克鲁姆在时尚达人电视比赛《超级名模时尚大比拼》中担任评委,该赛为电视淘汰赛。

Project Runway — an American reality television series on Lifetime Television, previously on the Bravo network, created by Eli Holzman which focuses on fashion design and is hosted by model Heidi Klum. The contestants compete with each other to create the best clothes and are restricted in time, materials and theme. Their designs are judged, and one or more designers are eliminated each week.

16. emerging economies — nations with social or business activity in the process of rapid growth and industrialization. The economies of China and India are considered to be the largest.

17. the economics of modelling — the way in which wealth is produced and used in the field of modelling

18. Tivo — a digital video recorder (DVR) developed and marketed by TiVo, Inc. and introduced in 1999

19. Model Alliance — (MA) a growing network of models and industry leaders dedicated to improving working conditions in the American fashion industry. Models have an industry voice through the MA. It seeks to improve the American modeling industry by empowering the models themselves.

20. The juiciest prize is to become the face of a luxury brand such as Dior or Burberry. — If a model becomes a spokesperson for a luxury brand such as Dior or Burberry, she can get the biggest reward.

Dior — (Christian Dior S. A.) a French luxury brand owned by

LVMH Moët Hennessy-Louis Vuitton(酩悦·轩尼诗-路易·威登集团), the world's largest luxury group. 迪奥

21. To have any chance… even for a cover-shoot. — 要想获得这种机会，模特首先要有为设计师拍摄杂志照片的经历。这让时尚杂志花很少的钱就能请模特拍照，甚至是拍封面照。

    a. have/get sth under one's belt — to have achieved or experienced sth useful or important（获得某经历或某事）

    b. peanut — a very small amount of money; a trifling sum

    c. cover-shoot — 封面照片

22. Viva London — the sister agency to the well established VIVA Paris and shares the majority of its board

23. DNA — a modeling agency in New York City, established in 1996 by Jerome and David Bonnouvrier, and one of the top-three agencies in the world

24. The giant Elite Model Management agency lost an American antitrust case on price-fixing in 2004 — 行业巨头名模管理公司2004年在美国的一场操纵定价的反垄断诉讼中输掉了官司

25. Doutzen Kroes —（1985— ）a Dutch model and actress 杜晨·科洛斯

26. Karl Lagerfeld —（1933— ）a German fashion designer, artist and photographer based in Paris 卡尔·拉斐格

27. Size 0 — a women's clothing size in the US catalog sizes system. Size 0 and 00 were invented due to the changing of clothing sizes over time, referred to as vanity sizing（虚荣尺码）or size inflation（尺码膨胀）, which has caused the adoption of lower numbers. Modern size 0 clothing, depending on brand and style, fits measurements of chest-stomach-hips from 30—22—32 inches（76—56—81 cm）to 33—25—35 inches（84—64—89 cm）. Size 00 can be anywhere from 0.5 to 2 inches（1 to 5 cm）smaller than size 0. "Size zero" often refers to extremely thin individuals（esp. women）, or trends associated with them.

28. Adele —（1988— ）an English singer-songwriter, musician and multi instrumentalist

29. Gucci — an Italian fashion and leather goods brand 古驰

30. throw one's weight around/about — to use one's position of authority to tell people what to do in an unpleasant and

unreasonable way; to give orders to others, because one thinks one is important 指手画脚，作威作福，耀武扬威

31. Marc Jacobs —（1963— ） an American fashion designer. He is the head designer for Marc Jacobs, as well as Marc by Marc Jacobs, a diffusion line, with more than 200 retail stores in 80 countries 马克·雅各布斯

32. Premier Model Management — one of the world's leading model agencies, based in London, founded in 1981 by former model Carole White and her brother Chris Owen

Questions

1. What are the changes in the modelling business?
2. What kind of model is preferred now by fashion houses?
3. Why do models make less money?
4. What are the reasons for skinny models to be preferred by designers?
5. Who have more say in fashion business, supermodels or super-brands?

新闻写作

报刊常用套语

为了表明"客观公正"，美英报刊记者以不肯定的第三者口气论述，如用"有人""人们"等；有的用"据称""据闻""据估计"等不确定的字眼及"事实不容否认""可以认为""根据"等较确定的套语。有的为省时，常用固定写法用语（set expressions）；还有以不确定的口气或审慎的态度报道，是怕事主找上门来纠缠。例如2003年美国女特工身份泄露案（Valerie Plame Leak case）就涉及退休记者 Robert Novok，《纽约时报》记者 Judith Miller 和《时代》周刊记者 Matt Cooper，特别检察官以国家安全及保密法为由逼迫他们出庭作证。有的用"事实不容否认""可以认为"等，以证明所言非虚假新闻，有事实依据或目击证人等。这也是报刊常用被动语态的一个重要原因。我们不如读读安徽大学马祖毅先生写的《英译汉技巧浅谈》一书中关于这类常见写法。如：

It affords no small surprise to find that… 对于……令人惊讶不已
It can be safely said that… 我们有把握讲……
It cannot be denied that… 无可否认……

It has been calculated that… 据估计……
It has recently been brought home to us that… 我们最近痛切感到……
It is alleged that… 据称……
It is arranged that… 已经商定……, ……已做准备
It is asserted that… 有人主张……
It is claimed that… 据称……, 有人宣称……
It is demonstrated that… 据证实……, 已经证明……
It is enumerated that… 列举出……
It is established that… 可以认定……
It is generally recognized that… 一般认为……, 普遍认为……
It is hypothesized that… 假设……
It is incontestable that… 无可置辩的是……
It is preferred that… 有人偏向于……
It is reputed that… 人们认为……, 可以认为……
It is striking to note that… 特别令人注意的是……
It is taken that… 人们认为……, 有人以为……
It is undeniable that… 事实不容否认……
It is universally accepted that… 普遍认为……, ……是普遍接受的
It may be argued that… 也许有人主张……
It was described that… 据介绍……, 有人描述说……
It was first intended that… 最初就有这样的想法……
It was noted above that… 前面已经指出……, 等等。

不过, 据本人纵览近几年报道性文章, 上述这类套语用得越来越少。(欲知更多套语, 见《导读》四章七节。)

Lesson 21

> 课 文 导 读

　　癌症在全世界的发病率呈逐年上升趋势，甚至成为威胁人类生命和健康的首要敌人。全球每年肿瘤新发病人数超过 1000 万人，年死亡人数超过 700 万。著名医学杂志《柳叶刀》预测假如现在的趋势持续而未得到控制的话，那么到 2030 年，全球癌症的发病人数将从 2008 年的 1270 万升至 2200 万，上升约 75%，男性增长高于女性，分别为 81% 和 69%。

　　人类对癌症的研究和治疗已经长达 200 年的时间，发展至今治疗手段包括手术治疗、放射治疗、化疗和靶向治疗等。过去几年，癌症免疫领域的快速发展产生了几种治疗癌症的新方法，通过增强免疫系统中某些成分的活性或者解除癌症细胞对免疫系统的抑制来发挥作用。癌症治疗以往的策略都是专注于直接攻击肿瘤细胞，而免疫治疗旨在通过人体免疫系统达到攻击肿瘤目的。本文中介绍的约翰·霍普金斯大学研究的基因疗法十分令人振奋，令我们看到了人类攻克癌症的新希望。

Pre-reading Questions

1. What do you know about cancer? How do you know that?
2. Do you know any treatment for cancer? What are the benefits and risks of each of the treatment?

Text

"This Is Not the End": Experimental Therapy That Targets Genes Gives Cancer Patients Hope

By Laurie McGinley

Stefanie Joho was 22 when she was diagnosed with colon cancer. She has been in remission for more than a year thanks to an imunotherapy treatment aimed at a genetic glitch, rather than aiming at the disease itself like chemotherapy does. (Michelle Gustafson/For The Washington Post)

1   The oncologist was blunt: Stefanie Joho's colon cancer was raging out of control and there was nothing more she could do. Flanked by her parents and sister, the 23-year-old felt something wet on her shoulder. She looked up to see her father weeping.

2   "I felt dead inside, utterly demoralized, ready to be done," Joho remembers.

3   But her younger sister couldn't accept that. When the family got back to Joho's apartment in New York's Flatiron district[1], Jess opened her laptop and began searching frantically for clinical trials, using medical words she'd heard but not fully understood. An hour later, she came into her sister's room and showed her what she'd found. "I'm not

letting you give up," she told Stefanie. "This is not the end."

4 That search led to a contact at Johns Hopkins University[2], and a few days later, Joho got a call from a cancer geneticist co-leading a study there. "Get down here as fast as you can!" Luis Diaz said. "We are having tremendous success with patients like you."

5 What followed is an illuminating tale of how one woman's intersection with experimental research helped open a new frontier in cancer treatment — with approval of a drug that, for the first time, targets a genetic feature in a tumor rather than the disease's location in the body.

6 The breakthrough, made official last week by the Food and Drug Administration[3], immediately could benefit some patients with certain kinds of advanced cancer[4] that aren't responding to chemotherapy. Each should be tested for that genetic signature, scientists stress.

7 "These are people facing death sentences," said Hopkins geneticist Bert Vogelstein. "This treatment might keep some of them in remission for a long time."

8 In August 2014, Joho stumbled into Hopkins for her first infusion of the immunotherapy drug Keytruda. She was in agony from a malignant mass in her midsection, and even with the copious amounts of OxyContin she was swallowing, she needed a new fentanyl patch on her arm every 48 hours.[5] Yet within just days, the excruciating back pain had eased. Then an unfamiliar sensation — hunger — returned. She burst into tears when she realized what it was.

9 As months went by, her tumor shrank and ultimately disappeared. She stopped treatment this past August, free from all signs of disease.

10 The small trial in Baltimore[6] was pivotal, and not only for the young marketing professional. It showed that immunotherapy could attack colon and other cancers thought to be unstoppable. The key was their tumors' genetic defect, known as mismatch repair (MMR) deficiency[7] — akin to a missing spell-check on their DNA. As the DNA copies itself, the abnormality prevents any errors from being fixed. In the cancer cells, that means huge numbers of mutations that are good targets for immunotherapy.

11 The treatment approach isn't a panacea, however. The glitch under scrutiny — which can arise spontaneously or be inherited — is

found in just 4 percent of cancers overall. But bore in on a few specific types, and the scenario changes dramatically. The problem occurs in up to 20 percent of colon cancers and about 40 percent of endometrial malignancies — cancer in the lining of the uterus.

12   In the United States, researchers estimate that initially about 15,000 people with this defect may be helped by this immunotherapy. That number is likely to rise sharply as doctors begin using it earlier on eligible patients.

13   Joho was among the first.

14   Even before Joho got sick, cancer had cast a long shadow on her family. Her mother has Lynch syndrome[8], a hereditary disorder that sharply raises the risk of certain cancers, and since 2003, Priscilla Joho has suffered colon cancer, uterine cancer and squamous cell carcinoma of the skin.

15   Stefanie's older sister, Vanessa, had already tested positive for Lynch syndrome, and Stefanie planned to get tested when she turned 25. But at 22, several months after she graduated from New York University, she began feeling unusually tired. She blamed the fatigue on her demanding job. Her primary-care physician[9], aware of her mother's medical history, ordered a colonoscopy.

16   When Joho woke up from the procedure, the gastroenterologist looked "like a ghost," she said. A subsequent CT scan revealed a very large tumor in her colon. She'd definitely inherited Lynch syndrome.

17   She underwent surgery in January 2013 at Philadelphia's Fox Chase Cancer Center[10], where her mother had been treated. The news was good: The cancer didn't appear to have spread, so she could skip chemotherapy and follow up with scans every three months.

18   By August of that year, though, Joho started having relentless back pain. Tests detected the invasive tumor in her abdomen. Another operation, and now she started chemo. Once again, in spring 2014, the cancer roared back. Her doctors in New York, where she now was living, switched to a more aggressive chemo regimen.

19   "This thing is going to kill me," Joho remembered thinking. "It was eating me alive."

20   She made it to Jess's college graduation in Vermont that May. Midsummer, her oncologist confessed he was out of options. As he left

the examining room, he mentioned offhandedly that some interesting work was going on in immunotherapy. But when Joho met with a hospital immunologist, that doctor told her no suitable trials were available.

21   Her younger sister wasn't ready for her to give up. Jess searched for clinical trials, typing in "immunotherapy" and other terms she'd heard the doctors use. Up popped a trial at Hopkins[11], where doctors were testing a drug called pembrolizumab.

22   "Pembro" is part of a class of new medications called checkpoint inhibitors[12] that disable the brakes that keep the immune system from attacking tumors. In September 2014, the treatment was approved by the FDA for advanced melanoma and marketed as Keytruda. The medication made headlines in 2015 when it helped treat former president Jimmy Carter for melanoma that had spread to his brain and liver[13]. It later was cleared for several other malignancies.

23   Yet researchers still don't know why immunotherapy, once hailed as a game changer[14], works in only a minority of patients. Figuring that out is important for clinical as well as financial reasons. Keytruda, for example, costs about $150,000 a year.

24   By the time Joho arrived at Hopkins, the trial had been underway for a year. While an earlier study had shown a similar immunotherapy drug to be effective for a significant proportion of patients with advanced melanoma or lung or kidney cancer, checkpoint inhibitors weren't making headway with colon cancer. A single patient out of 20 had responded in a couple of trials.

25   Why did some tumors shrink and others didn't? What was different about the single colon cancer patient who benefited? Drew Pardoll, director of the Bloomberg-Kimmel Institute for Cancer Immunotherapy at Hopkins, and top researcher Suzanne L. Topalian took the unusual step of consulting with the cancer geneticists who worked one floor up.

26   "This was the first date in what became the marriage of cancer genetics and cancer immunology[15]," Pardoll said.

27   In a brainstorming session, the geneticists were quick to offer their theories. They suggested that the melanoma and lung cancer patients had done best because those cancers have lots of mutations, a consequence of exposure to sunlight and cigarette smoke. The mutations

produce proteins recognized by the immune system as foreign and ripe for attack, and the drug boosts the system's response. [16]

28   And that one colon — cancer patient? As Vogelstein recalls, "We all said in unison, 'He must have MMR deficiency!'" — because such a genetic glitch would spawn even more mutations. The abnormality was a familiar subject to Vogelstein, who in the 1990s had co-discovered its role in the development of colon cancer. But the immunologists hadn't thought of it.

29   When the patient's tumor tissue was tested, it was indeed positive for the defect.

30   The researchers decided to run a small trial, led by Hopkins immunologist Dung Le and geneticist Diaz, to determine whether the defect could predict a patient's response to immunotherapy. The pharmaceutical company Merck[17] provided its still—experimental drug pembrolizumab. Three groups of volunteers were recruited: 10 colon cancer patients whose tumors had the genetic problem; 18 colon cancer patients without it; and 7 patients with other malignancies with the defect.

31   The first results, published in 2015 in the New England Journal of Medicine[18], were striking. Four out of the 10 colon cancer patients with the defect and 5 out of the other 7 cancer patients with the abnormality responded to the drug. In the remaining group, nothing. Since then, updated numbers have reinforced that a high proportion of patients with the genetic feature benefit from the drug, often for a lengthy period. Other trials by pharmaceutical companies have shown similar results.

32   The Hopkins investigators found that tumors with the defect had, on average, 1,700 mutations, compared with only 70 for tumors without the problem. That confirmed the theory that high numbers of mutations make it more likely the immune system will recognize and attack cancer — if it gets assistance from immunotherapy.

33   The studies were the foundation of the FDA's decision on Tuesday to green—light Keytruda to treat cancers such as Joho's, meaning malignancies with certain molecular characteristics. This first-ever "site-agnostic" approval by the agency signals an emerging field of "precision immunotherapy,[19]" Pardoll said, one in which genetic details are used to anticipate who will respond to treatments.

34   For Joho, now 27 and living in suburban Philadelphia, the hard

lesson from the past few years is clear: The cancer field is changing so rapidly that patients can't rely on their doctors to find them the best treatments. "Oncologists can barely keep up," she said. "My sister found a trial I was a perfect candidate for, and my doctors didn't even know it existed." (From *The Washington Post*, May 28, 2017)

New Words

agnostic /æɡˈnɒstɪk/ *adj.* uncertain of all claims to knowledge 不可知论者的

akin /əˈkɪn/ *adj.* similar

blunt /blʌnt/ *adj.* saying exactly what one thinks without trying to be polite 直言不讳的

carcinoma /ˌkɑːsɪˈnəʊmə/ *n.* a type of cancer 恶性上皮肿瘤

chemotherapy /ˌkiːməʊˈθerəpi/ *n.* (*abbr.* chemo) the treatment of disease using chemicals 化学疗法

colon /ˈkəʊlən/ *n.* 结肠

colonoscopy /ˌkəʊləˈnɒskəpi/ *n.* 结肠镜检查

copious /ˈkəʊpiəs/ *adj.* plentiful; abundant

demoralized /dɪˈmɒrəlaɪzd/ *adj.* 士气低落的,意志消沉的

endometrial /ˌendəʊˈmetriəl/ *adj.* 子宫内膜的

excruciating /ɪkˈskruːʃieɪtɪŋ/ *adj.* extremely painful

fentanyl /ˈfentænɪl/ *n.* a narcotic drug used in medicine to relieve pain 芬太尼;止痛剂

flank /flæŋk/ *v.* to have sth on both sides 位于两侧

frontier /ˈfrʌntɪə(r)/ *n.* border between what is known and what is unknown 尚待开发的领域;(知识的)前沿

gastroenterologist /ˌɡæstrəʊˌentəˈrɒlədʒɪst/ *n.* 胃肠病学家

geneticist /dʒəˈnetɪsɪst/ *n.* a person who studies or specializes in genetics 遗传学家

glitch /ɡlɪtʃ/ *n.* a problem that stops sth from working properly or being successful 小故障;失灵

immunology /ˌɪmjʊˈnɒlədʒi/ *n.* 免疫学

immunotherapy /ˌɪmjʊəʊˈθerəpi/ *n.* the treatment of disease by stimulating the body's production of antibodies 免疫疗法

infusion /ɪnˈfjuːʒn/ *n.* the act of adding one thing to another in order to make it better or stronger 输入;输液

intersection /ˌɪntəˈsekʃən/ *n.* a place where roads or other lines meet or cross 交点, 交叉

lining /ˈlaɪnɪŋ/ *n.* a layer of tissue on the inside of the stomach or other organ (胃等器官内部的) 保护层, 膜

malignant /məˈlɪgnənt/ *adj.* (of a tumor or disease) out of control and likely to cause death 恶性的

malignancy /məˈlɪgnənsi/ *n.* 恶性 (肿瘤等)

melanoma /ˌmeləˈnəʊmə/ *n.* 黑色素瘤

midsection /ˈmɪdˌsekʃ(ə)n/ *n.* 上腹部

mutation /mjuːˈteɪʃn/ *n.* [生物学] the changing of the structure of a gene, resulting in a variant form which may be transmitted to subsequent generations (基因结构的) 突变; 变种

offhandedly /ˌɒfˈhændɪdli/ *adv.* 即席地; 立即地

oncologist /ɒŋˈkɒlədʒɪst/ *n.* 肿瘤学家, 肿瘤医生

OxyContin /ˌɒksɪˈkɒntɪn/ *n.* 奥施康定 (镇痛药)

pivotal /ˈpɪvətl/ *adj.* of main importance or influence; crucial

panacea /ˌpænəˈsiːə/ *n.* sth that will solve all the problems 灵丹妙药; 万能药

pembrolizumab /pembrəʊˈlaɪzəˌmæb/ *n.* a humanized antibody used in cancer immunotherapy (trade name Keytruda) 派姆单抗 (抗癌药)

pharmaceutical /ˌfɑːməˈsuːtɪkl/ *adj.* relating to the production of drugs and medicines 制药 (学) 的

regimen /ˈredʒɪmən/ *n.* 养生法; (治疗) 方案

remission /rɪˈmɪʃn/ *n.* a period when an illness is less severe for a time (疾病的) 减轻; 缓解 (期)

scenario /səˈnɑːriəʊ/ *n.* the way in which a situation may develop 可能的情况; 设想

scrutiny /ˈskruːtəni/ *n.* the act of examining sth. closely (as for mistakes)

spawn /spɔːn/ *v.* to cause sth to happen or to be created 引发

squamous /ˈskweɪməs/ *adj.* 鳞状的

syndrome /ˈsɪndrəʊm/ *n.* a medical condition that is characterized by a particular group of signs and symptoms 综合征

unison /ˈjuːnɪsn/ *n.* (in ~) together at the same time 一起; 和谐; 齐唱

uterine /ˈjuːtəraɪn/ *adj.* 子宫的

uterus /ˈjuːtərəs/ *n.* womb [解剖学] 子宫

utterly /ˈʌtəli/ *adv.* completely (used esp. to emphasize that sth is very bad)

Notes

1. New York's Flatiron district — a neighborhood in the New York City borough of Manhattan, named after the Flatiron Building at 23rd Street, Broadway and Fifth Avenue. The Flatiron District encompasses within its boundaries the Ladies' Mile Historic District (仕女购物街区)and the birthplace of Theodore Roosevelt, a National Historic Site. 熨斗区,得名于1902年修建完工的熨斗大厦。
2. Johns Hopkins University — (commonly referred to as Johns Hopkins, JHU, or simply Hopkins) an American private research university in Baltimore, Maryland. Founded in 1876, the university was named for its first benefactor, the American entrepreneur, abolitionist(废奴主义者), and philanthropist Johns Hopkins. Johns Hopkins is now organized into 10 divisions on campuses in Maryland and Washington, D. C. with international centers in Italy, China, and Singapore. The University was ranked 10th among undergraduate programs at national universities, and 11th among global universities by U. S. News & World Report in its 2017 rankings. 约翰·霍普金斯大学
3. the Food and Drug Administration — (*abbr.* FDA or USFDA) a federal agency of the U. S. Department of Health and Human Services. The FDA is responsible for protecting and promoting public health through the control and supervision of food safety, tobacco products, dietary supplements, prescription and over-the-counter pharmaceutical drugs (medications), vaccines, biopharmaceuticals (生物制药), blood transfusions, medical devices, electromagnetic radiation emitting devices (ERED), cosmetics, animal foods & feed and veterinary(兽医的) products. The FDA has its headquarters in White Oak, Maryland. The agency also has 223 field offices and 13 laboratories located throughout the 50 states, the U. S. Virgin Islands, and Puerto Rico. In 2008, the FDA began to post employees to foreign countries, including China, India, Costa Rica, Chile, Belgium, and the UK. 美国食品药品管理局
4. advanced cancer — cancer at the late stage of development
5. She was in agony…every 48 hours. — 她因为腹部的恶性肿瘤包块而

痛苦万分，甚至在每天吞服大量的奥施康定镇痛药之外，还需要每48小时在手臂上使用芬太尼强镇痛贴剂。

6. Baltimore — a city on the East Coast of the U. S., in the state of Maryland. Here it refers to Johns Hopkins University which is located in Baltimore.

7. mismatch repair (MMR) deficiency — 错配修复功能缺陷（DNA mismatch repair is a system for recognizing and repairing erroneous insertion, deletion, and mis-incorporation of bases that can arise during DNA replication and recombination, as well as repairing some forms of DNA damage. With MMR deficiency, MMR proteins would fail to work coordinately in sequential steps to initiate repair of DNA mismatches.）

8. Lynch syndrome — often called hereditary nonpolyposis（非息肉病性）colorectal cancer (HNPCC), an inherited disorder that increases the risk of many types of cancer, particularly cancers of the colon (large intestine)（大肠）and rectum（直肠）, which are collectively referred to as colorectal cancer. People with Lynch syndrome also have an increased risk of cancers of the stomach, small intestine, liver, gallbladder ducts（胆囊管）, upper urinary tract, brain, and skin. 林奇综合征，即遗传性非息肉病性大肠癌。

9. primary-care physician — a doctor who provides basic medical treatment（基础护理医师）

10. Fox Chase Cancer Center — a NCIC National Cancer Institute-designated Comprehensive Cancer Center research facility and hospital located in the Fox Chase section of Philadelphia, Pennsylvania, U. S. The center is part of the Temple University Health System (TUHS) and specializes in the treatment and prevention of cancer. 福克斯切斯癌症中心，是美国天普大学医学院附属医院，国家癌症研究所下属癌症中心。

11. up popped a trial at Hopkins — A clinical trial at Johns Hopkins University was found unexpectedly during her searching.

    pop up — appear in a place or situation unexpectedly

12. checkpoint inhibitors — 免疫检查点抑制剂

13. The medication made headlines in… that had spread to his brain and liver. — As this drug helped treat former President Jimmy Carter for his melanoma that spread to his brain and liver, a lot of media

covered treatments with the drug and made it known.

  a. make /grab (the) headlines — to be reported in many newspapers and on radio and television

  b. Jimmy Carter — (1924 —) an American politician who served as the 39th President of the U. S. from 1977 to 1981. Carter has remained active in public life during his post-presidency, and in 2002 he was awarded the Nobel Peace Prize for his work with the Carter Center which was set up for advancing human rights. On January 20, 2017, at age 92, Carter became the oldest president to attend a presidential inauguration. 美国第39任总统吉米·卡特

14. once hailed as a game changer — once welcomed and cheered by people as the drug that can completely change the situation of cancer treatment

15. This was the first date … cancer immunology — Scientists later combined genetics with immunology to treat cancer and this was the first step of that bond.

16. The mutations produce proteins … boosts the system's response. — 基因变异所产生的蛋白质被免疫系统识别为异体并准备好攻击，而这种药物促进了系统的反应。

17. Merck — Merck & Co., Inc. doing business as Merck Sharp & Dohme (MSD) outside the U. S. and Canada, is an American pharmaceutical company and one of the largest pharmaceutical companies in the world. The company was established in 1891 as the U. S. subsidiary of the German company Merck, which was founded in 1668 by the Merck family. Merck & Co. was nationalized by the U. S. government during World War I and subsequently established as an independent American company in 1917. Merck & Co. is a leading pharmaceutical company by market capitalization and revenue. Its headquarters is located in Kenilworth, New Jersey. 默克集团是美国知名的制药公司，也是世界最大的制药公司之一，在美国与加拿大之外的地区称为默沙东公司。

18. the New England Journal of Medicine — (NEJM) a weekly medical journal published by the Massachusetts Medical Society. It is among the most prestigious peer-reviewed medical journals as well as the oldest continuously published one. The journal usually has

the highest impact factor of the journals of internal medicine.《新英格兰医学杂志》由美国麻州医学会出版,是一份全科医学周刊,其影响因子居全球医学期刊之首。
19. This first-ever "site-agnostic" approval … "precision immunotherapy," — The drug was approved for tumors with certain genetic qualities without regard to the location of the tumor, the first for the FDA. This indicates that a new research field of "precision immunotherapy" has emerged.

Questions

1. Why did Stefanie Joho's father weep on her shoulder?
2. According to geneticist in Johns Hopkins University, what is different in their new research on cancer treatment?
3. What is the response of Joho after her infusion of immunotherapy drug Keytruda?
4. Can immunotherapy help all cancer patients?
5. According to geneticists, why had melanoma and lung cancer patients done best in immunotherapy?

语言解说

借喻词和提喻词(Ⅱ)

以下是主编经年累月在读报和编书过程中积累的两种喻词,这对初读报者扩大知识面和词汇量是极其有益的。

Word	Meaning	Metonymical/Synecdochical Meaning
Broadway	百老汇大街(纽约一街名)	纽约戏剧业,美国戏剧业
The capitol	美国州议会或政府大厦	美国州议会,州政府
The Capitol	美国国会大厦,州议会大厦	美国国会,州议会
Capitol Hill	国会山(国会大厦所在地)	美国国会
Donkey	驴	美国民主党
Elephant	象	美国共和党
ends of Pennsylvania Street	宾夕法尼亚大街(首都华盛顿一街名)两端	美国国会和行政当局,白宫和国会大厦,美国行政和立法部门

续表

Word	Meaning	Metonymical/Synecdochical Meaning
green berets	绿色贝雷帽	（美国）特种部队
The Hill	= Capitol Hill	美国国会
Hollywood	好莱坞（洛杉矶一地名）	美国电影业、电影界或娱乐业
John	约翰（美国人一常用名）	美国人
J Street	华盛顿一街名	美国特工处
K Street	华盛顿一街名	美国游说界
Langley	兰利（弗吉尼亚州一地名）	中央情报局
Madison Avenue	麦迪逊大街（纽约一街名）	美国广告业
Oval Office	椭圆形办公室	美国总统办公室；总统（职务）
Pentagon	五角大楼	美国国防部
Silicon Valley	硅谷（美国加州一地名）	美国高科技集中地
1600 Pennsylvania Street	宾夕法尼亚大街（华盛顿一街名）1600号	（美国）白宫，总统府
Uncle Sam	山姆大叔	美国政府；美国人
Wall Street	华尔街（纽约一街名）	美国金融界
White House	白宫	总统府，行政部门
Buckingham Palace	（英国）白金汉宫	英国王宫
The City (of London)	伦敦城	英国金融界；英国商业界
Downing Street	唐宁街（伦敦一街名）	英国首相府或首相；英国政府或内阁
Fleet Street	舰队街（伦敦一街名）	英国新闻界或报业
Lion	狮	英国
London	伦敦	英国或政府
New Scotland Yard	新苏格兰场（伦敦一地名）	伦敦警察局，该局刑事调查（侦缉）处
Ulster	阿尔斯特（在爱尔岛北部）	北爱尔兰
Westminster	威斯敏斯特（伦敦西部一住宅区）	英国议会或政府

续表

Word	Meaning	Metonymical/Synecdochical Meaning
Windsor	温莎（英格兰东南部一城市）	英国王室
Whitehall	白厅（伦敦一街名）	英国政府
Brussels	布鲁塞尔（比利时首都）	欧洲联盟；北大西洋公约组织
blue helmet	蓝盔	联合国维和人员
blue helmets	蓝盔帽	蓝盔部队，联合国维和部队
Horn of Africa	非洲之角	索马里和埃塞俄比亚
Elysée Palace	爱丽舍宫	法国总统府；法国总统职位
Quai d'Orsay	凯道赛（巴黎一码头名）	法国外交部
Kremlin	克里姆林宫	苏联；苏联政府；俄罗斯；俄罗斯政府
Moscow	莫斯科	苏联；俄罗斯；俄罗斯政府
Evan	伊凡（苏联和俄罗斯人常用名）	苏联人；俄罗斯人
Beijing	北京	中国；中国政府

Lesson 22

课文导读

学外语是一门苦差事,需要的是笨功夫。只要你足够勤奋使自己双语在握,就等于掌握了一把开启新世界大门的钥匙,自然会受益匪浅,好处多多。此外,学习外语还可以提高你的认知能力,让你更聪明。研究表明,学习一门新语言可以提高智力,降低认知偏差,改善你的注意力,降低注意力的分散,甚至能够延缓阿尔茨海默病的发病。2012 年 3 月 18 日,《纽约时报》刊载了《科学》杂志撰稿人 Yudhijit Bhattacharjee 的署名文章 "Why Bilinguals Are Smarter",对双语如何影响人们的认知能力和解决问题的能力,甚至会影响人们的情感做了介绍。作者通过列举一系列权威的实验和研究,形象直观地描述掌握双语带给人们的好处。

Pre-reading Questions

1. What practical benefits have you got when you take English as your second language?
2. If you married someone from a different culture, what language would you like to teach your baby in the future?

Text

Why Bilinguals Are Smarter
By Yudhijit Bhattacharjee

1 Speaking two languages rather than just one has obvious practical benefits in an increasingly globalized world. But in recent years, scientists have begun to show that the advantages of bilingualism are even more fundamental than being able to converse with a wider range of people. Being bilingual, it turns out, makes you smarter. It can have a profound effect on your brain, improving cognitive skills[1] not related to language and even shielding against dementia in old age.

2   This view of bilingualism is remarkably different from the understanding of bilingualism through much of the 20th century. Researchers, educators and policy makers long considered a second language to be an interference, cognitively speaking, that hindered a child's academic and intellectual development.

3   They were not wrong about the interference: there is ample evidence that in a bilingual's brain both language systems are active even when he is using only one language, thus creating situations in which one system obstructs the other. But this interference, researchers are finding out, isn't so much a handicap as a blessing in disguise[2]. It forces the brain to resolve internal conflict, giving the mind a workout that strengthens its cognitive muscles[3].

4   Bilinguals, for instance, seem to be more adept than monolinguals at solving certain kinds of mental puzzles. In a 2004 study by the psychologists Ellen Bialystok and Michelle Martin-Rhee, bilingual and monolingual preschoolers were asked to sort blue circles and red squares presented on a computer screen into two digital bins — one marked with a blue square and the other marked with a red circle[4].

5   In the first task, the children had to sort the shapes by color, placing blue circles in the bin marked with the blue square and red squares in the bin marked with the red circle. Both groups did this with comparable ease. Next, the children were asked to sort by shape, which was more challenging because it required placing the images in a bin

marked with a conflicting color. The bilinguals were quicker at performing this task.

6   The collective evidence from a number of such studies suggests that the bilingual experience improves the brain's so-called executive function — a command system that directs the attention processes that we use for planning, solving problems and performing various other mentally demanding tasks. These processes include ignoring distractions to stay focused, switching attention willfully from one thing to another and holding information in mind — like remembering a sequence of directions while driving.

7   Why does the tussle between two simultaneously active language systems improve these aspects of cognition? Until recently, researchers thought the bilingual advantage stemmed primarily from the ability for inhibition that was honed by the exercise of suppressing one language system; this suppression, it was thought, would help train the bilingual mind to ignore distractions in other contexts. But that explanation increasingly appears to be inadequate, since studies have shown that bilinguals perform better than monolinguals even at tasks that do not require inhibition, like threading a line through an ascending series of numbers scattered randomly on a page.

8   The key difference between bilinguals and monolinguals may be more basic: a heightened ability to monitor the environment. "Bilinguals have to switch languages quite often — you may talk to your father in one language and to your mother in another language," says Albert Costa, a researcher at the University of Pompeu Fabra[5] in Spain. "It requires keeping track of changes around you in the same way that we monitor our surroundings when driving." In a study comparing German-Italian bilinguals with Italian monolinguals on monitoring tasks, Mr. Costa and his colleagues found that the bilingual subjects not only performed better, but they also did so with less activity in parts of the brain involved in monitoring, indicating that they were more efficient at it.

9   The bilingual experience appears to influence the brain from infancy to old age (and there is reason to believe that it may also apply to those who learn a second language later in life).

10   In a 2009 study led by Agnes Kovacs of the International School for Advanced Studies[6] in Trieste, Italy, 7-month-old babies exposed to two

languages from birth were compared with peers raised with one language. In an initial set of trials, the infants were presented with an audio cue and then shown a puppet on one side of a screen. Both infant groups learned to look at that side of the screen in anticipation of the puppet. But in a later set of trials, when the puppet began appearing on the opposite side of the screen, the babies exposed to a bilingual environment quickly learned to switch their anticipatory gaze in the new direction while the other babies did not.

11 Bilingualism's effects also extend into the twilight years. In a recent study of 44 elderly Spanish-English bilinguals, scientists led by the neuropsychologist Tamar Gollan of the University of California, San Diego[7], found that individuals with a higher degree of bilingualism — measured through a comparative evaluation of proficiency in each language — were more resistant than others to the onset of dementia and other symptoms of Alzheimer's disease[8]: the higher the degree of bilingualism, the later the age of onset.

12 Nobody ever doubted the power of language. But who would have imagined that the words we hear and the sentences we speak might be leaving such a deep imprint? (From *The New York Times*, Mar 18, 2012)

New Words

anticipate /æn'tɪsɪpeɪt/ *v.* to expect sth 预料；预期
adept /ə'dept/ *adj.* good at sth that needs care and skill 内行的；熟练的
ample /'æmpl/ *adj.* enough or more than enough 足够的；丰裕的
ascending /ə'sendɪŋ/ *adj.* (次序)渐进的；上升的
bilingual /ˌbaɪ'lɪŋgwəl/ *adj.* involving or using two languages 双语的；*n.* 会用两种语言的人
converse /kən'vɜːs/ *v.* to talk informally with another or others; exchange views, opinions, etc. by talking 交谈
cognitive /'kɒgnətɪv/ *adj.* relating to the mental process involved in knowing, learning, and understanding things 认知的；认识过程的
cue /kjuː/ *n.* a signal for sth else to happen 暗示，提示
dementia /dɪ'menʃə/ *n.* a state of mental disorder 痴呆
distraction /dɪ'strækʃn/ *n.* sth that stops you paying attention to what you are doing 使人分心的事
handicap /'hændɪkæp/ *n.* a permanent or mental condition that makes it

difficult or impossible to use a particular part of your body or mind 生理缺陷；智力低下；残疾

inhibition /ˌɪnhɪˈbɪʃn/ *n.* when sth is restricted or prevented from happening or developing 压制，抑制（作用）

interference /ˌɪntəˈfɪərəns/ *n.* an act of deliberately getting involved in a situation where you are wanted or needed 介入，干预，干涉

monolingual /ˌmɒnəˈlɪŋgwəl/ *adj.* knowing or able to use only one language 单语的；*n.* 只用一种语言的人

neuropsychologist /ˌnjʊərəʊsaɪˈkɒlədʒɪst/ *n.* 精神心理学家

obstruct /əbˈstrʌkt/ *v.* to block a road, an entrance, a passage, etc. so that sb or sth can't get through 阻碍

random /ˈrændəm/ *adj.* done or chosen, etc. without sb deciding in advance what is going to happen 随机的，随意的

scatter /ˈskætə(r)/ *v.* to move or to make people or animals move in every direction 散开，使分散

sequence /ˈsiːkwəns/ *n.* the following of one thing after another; succession 次序，顺序

shield /ʃiːld/ *v.* to serve as a protection for 保护

simultaneous /ˌsɪmlˈteɪniəs/ *adj.* existing, occurring, or operating at the same time; concurrent 同时发生的

suppress /səˈpres/ *v.* to put an end, often by force, to a group or an activity that is believed to threaten authority 镇压，平定

tussle /ˈtʌsl/ *n.* a rough physical contest or struggle 扭打，争斗

twilight /ˈtwaɪlaɪt/ *n.* the period just before the end of the most active part of sb's life 暮年

willfully /ˈwɪlfəli/ *adv.* deliberately, voluntarily, or intentionally 故意地

workout /ˈwɜːkaʊt/ *n.* a period of exercise

Notes

1. cognitive skills — also known as cognitive ability or cognitive functioning. It is a set of abilities, skills or processes that are part of nearly every human action. Cognitive abilities are the brain-based skills we need to carry out any task from the simplest to the most complex. 认知技能

2. a blessing in disguise — a common expression for a seeming misfortune that turns out to be for the best 因祸得福

3. cognitive muscles — cognitive abilities 认知能力

4. sort blue circles and red squares ... and the other marked with a red

circle. — 将电脑屏幕上的蓝色圆圈和红色方块分别放进两个标记蓝色方块和红色圆圈的电子收纳箱中。[The test by the psychologists is an application of Stroop Test（斯特鲁测验）, a popular psychological test that is widely used in clinical practice and investigation. It is a demonstration of interference in the reaction time of a task. When the name of a color (e. g., "blue," "green," or "red") is printed in a color not denoted by the name (e. g., the word "red" printed in blue ink instead of red ink), naming the color of the word takes longer and is more prone（倾向于）to errors than when the color of the ink matches the name of the color. 斯特鲁测验又称Stroop Color-Word Test，是公认的衡量行为控制系统能力最好办法之一。该测试向受测者展示不同颜色的单词，要求受测者说出字体颜色。难点在于，这些单词是一些颜色的名称。"蓝色"一词可能是用红色墨水书写的，而你必须说红色。但是，"蓝色"一词却非常突出地一直闪现在你的大脑中，你很想说蓝色。这时你就需要一种抑制该想法的系统，才能说出红色。]

    sort sth into sth — to put things in a particular order or arrange them in groups according to size, type, etc.

5. the University of Pompeu Fabra — a university in Barcelona, Spain, founded in 1990（西班牙）庞培法布拉大学
6. the International School for Advanced Studies — (*abbr.* SISSA) an international, state supported, post graduate teaching and research institute with a special statute, located in Trieste（迪里亚斯特）, Italy. Instituted in 1978, SISSA's aim is to promote science and knowledge, particularly in the areas of Mathematics, Physics and Neuroscience（神经系统科学）. 意大利国际高等研究院
7. the University of California, San Diego — UC San Diego or UCSD, public, located in California, established in 1960, one of the ten University of California campuses 加州大学圣地亚哥分校
8. Alzheimer's disease — also Alzheimer disease, the most common form of dementia. There is no cure for the disease, which worsens as it progresses, and eventually leads to death 阿尔茨海默病，俗称老年痴呆症

Questions

1. What practical benefits can you get by being bilingual besides conversing with various people?

2. Some researchers claim that bilingualism can be interference, but in what way does the interference influence our brain system?
3. According to a study in 2004, bilingual experience improves the brain's executive function that directs the attention processes we can use for arduous tasks. What do the processes refer to?
4. What is the major difference between bilinguals and monolinguals?
5. How bilingualism affect people in their old age?

广告与漫画

内容和语言特色

1. 广告(advertisement)在美英报刊尤其是报纸中,约占篇幅的一半以上。西方广告内容广泛,千奇百怪。除了新产品、新技术、求职、招聘、娱乐、旅行、烟酒、购车置业等外,甚至还有色情和出租丈夫的广告。有些广告有助于我们了解这些国家的社会生活,甚至政治、经济、科技等动态。广告使用的照片和文字必须要有针对性,能打动和招徕看客,激起欲望。因此文字必须简明、生动、形象,经常运用比喻、双关、夸张、对仗、拟人化等修辞手段。下面举一幅为例:

2004年大选时,小布什(George W. Bush)和切尼(Dick Cheney)针对民主党候选人John Kerry,用奔袭的狼群作比喻,作竞选广告:

狼群下面的说明文字:PAID FOR BY BUSH-CHENEY 04 AND THE REPUBLICAN NATIONAL COMMITTEE AND APPROVED BY PRESIDENT BUSH

主题是:Primal Fear:Bush said Kerry's weakness would draw predators.

首要恐惧:布什说克里的软弱会招来食肉动物,"软弱招人欺"。他鼓吹"弱肉强食"的森林法则,显然是玩弄竞选伎俩。

2. 漫画(cartoon)有别广告,画家从新闻取材,通过夸张、比喻、象征、寓意等手法,借幽默、诙谐的画面,针砭时弊。漫画犹如社论,立场鲜明,内行一看,就知奥妙。有些漫画十分含蓄,如果读者缺乏背景知识和想象力,便会一头雾水。有时一画或一言寓两事。语言简洁,常用时髦词、委婉语和名言。如:"The Bug Stop here.(我来拍板,责无旁贷。)"稍不注意,易欣赏或理解有误。下面举一幅为例:

次贷危机后,开放信贷又遭讽:Finally! Credit Markets Are Thawing!("信贷市场终于解冻了!")救生圈上字:The Economy(经济[有救了])

北极熊代表失业者:Yipee(哎呀!)(对 Thawing 表示惊恐)Thawing 是双关语,冰融化了,北极熊也像次贷危机(subprime mortage crisis)时的房贷者一样要被淹死了。(2009/4/2 *Time*)

(详见《导读》三章一、二节)

Unit Eight
Entertainment

Lesson 23

课 文 导 读

在经历几次诺贝尔文学奖的提名之后,鲍勃·迪伦终于被瑞典文学院授予2016年诺贝尔文学奖。年届75岁的迪伦成为自1901年诺贝尔文学奖创立以来首位获得该殊荣的音乐人。瑞典文学院在迪伦的获奖词中说:迪伦将他的诗歌通过歌曲的形式展现出来,这与古希腊的诗人荷马和萨福通过音乐表达的经典作品别无二致。鲍勃·迪伦的作品虽然是让人"听"的,但完全可以把它们当做诗歌来"读"。

即便如此,诺贝尔文学奖该不该颁给歌手仍旧成为广泛热议的话题,有媒体认为,迪伦获奖是诺贝尔文学奖历史上最具争议的结果。甚至连迪伦本人在颁奖典礼上由他人代为朗读的演讲中也提到:我不止一次地问自己,我的歌曲创作是文学吗?

此文并未直接探讨这种争议,而是回顾了迪伦作为音乐人和诗人的创作经历,介绍了他的作品和影响力,从侧面进行了回应。

不过迪伦获奖至少让我们意识到文学的界限变宽了,正如《纽约时报》评论的那样:"瑞典文学院选择一位流行音乐人授予世界文学界最高的荣誉戏剧化地重新定义了文学的边界,引发了对歌词是否与诗歌具有同等艺术价值的讨论……迪伦获奖被认为是弥合了高雅文学和更具商业气息作品之间的鸿沟。"

Pre-reading Questions

1. Who is Bob Dylan? What do you know about him and his music?
2. Do you think Bob Dylan is worthy of the Nobel Prize of Literature?

Text

Bob Dylan[1] : "The Homer[2] of Our Time"

By Randy Lewis

1　　Bob Dylan opened the doors of what was possible in popular music with his 1965 single "Like a Rolling Stone," a 6-minute epic built on four poetically surrealistic verses linked by the emotionally liberating "How does it feel?" chorus.

2　　Then he blew those doors off the hinges[3] the following year with his "Blonde on Blonde" album, which took his literate lyrics into the realm of the epic poets of ancient times.

3　　In announcing Dylan as the 2016 recipient of the Nobel Prize for literature, the Swedish Academy's[4] permanent secretary, Sara Danius, said the selection honors Dylan "for having created new poetic expressions within the American song tradition." Then she suggested that an interviewer start with his "Blonde on Blonde" to find out what all the fuss was about.

4　　So expansive was what Dylan had to say at this creative peak of the mid-1960s that in "Blonde on Blonde," he released the first double album by a major pop figure. Album-closer[5] "Sad Eyed Lady of the Lowlands[6]" is an 11-minute, 19-second Hellenic rock music volley that has launched at least a thousand interpretations over the last 50 years.

5　　"With your mercury mouth in the missionary times/And your eyes like smoke and your prayers like rhymes/And your silver cross, and your voice like chimes/Oh, who among them do they think could bury you?" Dylan sings.

6　　That's just the opening. It continues to overflow with evocative allusions, revealing adjectives and imaginative metaphors, each setting the stage for[7] another question posed to the song's unidentified subject, often presumed to be Dylan's first wife, Sara Lownds[8].

7　　As Bruce Springsteen[9] put it when inducting Dylan into the Rock and Roll Hall of Fame[10] in 1988, "Dylan was a revolutionary. The way Elvis[11] freed your body, Bob freed your mind."

8　　When Dylan made the pilgrimage from his home in Hibbing, Minn., to the vibrant folk music revival scene anchored in New York City's Greenwich Village[12] in the late 1950s, he came armed with a trove of songs by Woody Guthrie[13], Lead Belly[14], Robert Johnson[15] and other folk and blues musicians.

9　　Initially, he was but one of hundreds of aspiring folkies performing songs written by others. Quickly discovering that folk music kingpin Ramblin' Jack Elliott[16] also was touting Guthrie's music to younger audiences in New York, Dylan began to put more effort into writing his own songs.

10　　His 1962 debut, "Bob Dylan," showed a young artist strongly out of the traditional folk realm, singing versions of folk, country and blues standards such as "House of the Risin' Sun," "Man of Constant Sorrow," "Pretty Peggy-O" and "Baby, Let Me Follow You Down."

11　　He quickly shot to the top of the folk music heap with his next album, "The Freewheelin' Bob Dylan," which contained several soon-to-be classic songs — "Blowin' in the Wind," "A Hard Rain's a-Gonna Fall," "Don't Think Twice, It's All Right" and "Masters of War."

12　　Other musicians quickly took notice of the budding musical poet. Folk trio Peter, Paul & Mary[17] latched onto[18] "Blowin' in the Wind," L. A. rock group the Turtles turned "It Ain't Me, Babe" into a pop hit, Cher[19] did the same for "All I Really Want to Do," and the Byrds[20] helped forge a new hybrid of folk and rock with electrified versions of Dylan songs such as "Mr. Tambourine Man" and "My Back Pages."

13　　His impact wasn't limited to a single continent. Emerging at roughly the same time as Beatlemania[21] was igniting in the U. K., Dylan's music inspired the Fab Four[22] to think beyond the theme of love that dominated their early pop songs.

14　　Where the Beatles' earliest hits were built around simply stated sentiments such as "I want to hold your hand," Dylan was writing about love with richly observed sophistication: "I'm a-thinkin' and a-wonderin' all the way down the road/I once loved a woman, a child I'm told/I give her my heart but she wanted my soul," he sang in "Don't Think Twice, It's All Right."

15　　In particular, Beatle John Lennon[23], who had grown up reading the great poets and often entertained himself scribbling fanciful wordplay in the vein of[24] Lewis Carroll[25], took notes of Dylan's songwriting and soon moved it into more self-reflective material such as "Help!" and "Girl."

16   Dylan's songs were so plentiful and consistently original that they seemed to pour down through him from the heavens.

17   Of "Like a Rolling Stone," Dylan told The Times' then-pop music critic Robert Hilburn in 2004 that songwriting was often a mysterious process. "It's like a ghost is writing a song like that," Dylan said. "It gives you the song and it goes away, it goes away. You don't know what it means. Except the ghost picked me to write the song…

18   "I wrote 'Blowin' in the Wind' in 10 minutes, just put words to an old spiritual, probably something I learned from Carter Family[26] records. That's the folk music tradition. You use what's been handed down. 'The Times They Are A-Changin'' is probably from an old Scottish folk song."

19   For all the profound influence his 1960s songs exerted, that impact continued in the next decade, when he returned to touring in 1974 after a long hiatus with the album "Planet Waves," which included another of dozens of his songs recorded multiple times by other artists, "Forever Young."

20   He offered up what sounded like a blessing to a generation that had gone to hell and back[27] during the turbulent 1960s with all the turmoil created by the Vietnam War, the civil rights movement, the emergence of women's liberation and other social and political concerns: "May you grow up to be righteous/May you grow up to be true/May you always know the truth/And see the lights surrounding you."

21   His next album, "Blood on the Tracks" in 1975, was considered a full-blown return to form and triggered *Rolling Stone* magazine[28] to devote thousands of words of commentary from multiple writers exploring the meaning of songs such as "Tangled Up in Blue," "Idiot Wind," "Simple Twist of Fate" and "Lily, Rosemary and the Jack of Hearts[29]."

22   "Tangled Up in Blue" opened the album with another expansive tale, a careening literal and metaphorical road trip[30]. And again, Dylan offered a nod[31] to the power of poetry in one verse: "Then she opened up a book of poems/And handed it to me/Written by an Italian poet/From the thirteenth century/And every one of them words rang true[32]/And glowed like burnin' coal."

23   Dylan's foundational place in pop music also gave rise to a music

industry phrase that has functioned over time either as a badge of honor or a kiss of death to those tagged as "the new Dylan,"[33] a club that included Springsteen, John Prine, Loudon Wainwright III and Steve Forbert.[34]

24 "There is no way to accurately or adequately laud Bob Dylan," producer, songwriter and musician T Bone Burnett once said. "He is the Homer of our time. The next Bob Dylan will not come around for another millennium or two, making it highly unlikely that it will happen at all." (From *Los Angeles Times*, October 13, 2016)

New Words

anchor /'æŋkə(r)/ *v.* to connect sth to a solid base; to hold sth firmly in place

allusion /ə'luːʒn/ *n.* sth said or written that mentions a subject, person etc indirectly 隐喻，典故

blues /bluːz/ *n.* a slow sad style of music that came from the southern US 布鲁斯，蓝调音乐

budding /'bʌdɪŋ/ *adj.* beginning to develop or become successful

careen /kə'riːn/ *v.* to move forwards quickly without control, making sudden sideways movements

chime /tʃaɪm/ *n.* (*usu. pl.*) the sound of a set of bells

chorus /'kɔːrəs/ *n.* the part of a song that is repeated after each verse 副歌

debut /'deɪbjuː/ *n.* the first time an actor, musician, athlete, etc., does sth in public or for the public

evocative /ɪ'vɒkətɪv/ *adj.* making people remember sth by producing a feeling or memory in them

expansive /ɪk'spænsɪv/ *adj.* wide, extensive

freewheeling /ˌfriː'wiːlɪŋ/ *adj.* not worried about rules or what will happen in the future 无拘无束的，随心所欲的

full-blown /ˌfʊl 'bləʊn/ *adj.* having all the qualities of sth that is at its most complete or advanced stage

Hellenic /he'lenɪk/ *adj.* of or relating to the ancient or modern Greeks or their language （古）希腊的

hiatus /haɪ'eɪtəs/ *n.* a break in an activity, or a time during which sth does not happen or exist

induct /ɪnˈdʌkt/ *n*. to officially give sb a job or position of authority, esp. at a special ceremony
kingpin /ˈkɪŋpɪn/ *n*. (esp. in news reports) the person or thing in a group that is the most important or that has the most power（组织或活动中的）主要人物，领袖
laud /lɔːd/ *v*. to praise sb or sth
literate /ˈlɪtərət/ *adj*. lucid, polished; clear to the understanding
mercury /ˈmɜːkjəri/ *n*. a bearer of messages or news 信使
Minn. *abbr*. Minnesota 明尼苏达州（美国中北部州）
missionary /ˈmɪʃənri/ *adj*. relating to efforts to gain new religious followers or to people sent to spread a religion 传教的，教会的
pilgrimage /ˈpɪlɡrɪmɪdʒ/ *n*. a journey to a holy place or a place connected with sb or sth famous 朝圣之行；漫游
rambling /ˈræmblɪŋ/ *adj*. (of speech or writing) lacking a coherent plan; diffuse and disconnected 杂乱无章的，漫无边际的
rosemary /ˈrəʊzməri/ *n*. an herb that has a sweet smell and that is used in cooking and perfumes 迷迭香
scribble /ˈskrɪbl/ *v*. to write sth quickly or carelessly
sophistication /səˌfɪstɪˈkeɪʃn/ *n*. the quality of being more advanced or complex than others 复杂巧妙，世故
spiritual /ˈspɪrɪtʃuəl/ *n*. a religious song of the type sung originally by African-Americans（尤指美国南部黑人的）圣歌
surrealistic /səˌriːəˈlɪstɪk/ *adj*. of or concerned with surrealism (a modern type of art and literature in which the painter, writer etc, connects unrelated images and objects in a strange dreamlike way) 超现实主义的
tambourine /ˌtæmbəˈriːn/ *n*. a small drum, esp. a shallow one-headed drum with loose metallic disks at the sides played by shaking or striking with the hand 铃鼓，小手鼓
tangled /ˈtæŋɡld/ *adj*. complicated or not easy to understand
tout /taʊt/ *v*. to try to persuade people to buy goods or services you are offering
trio /ˈtriːəʊ/ *n*. a group of three people or things
trove /trəʊv/ *n*. a valuable collection; treasure
turbulent //*adj*. causing unrest, violence, or disturbance
turmoil /ˈtɜːmɔɪl/ *n*. a state of confusion, excitement, or anxiety

vibrant /ˈvaɪbrənt/ *adj.* full of activity or energy in a way that is exciting and attractive

volley /ˈvɒli/ *n.* a lot of questions, insults, attacks etc. that are all said or made at the same time

Notes

1. Bob Dylan — Robert Allen Zimmerman (1941—), an American songwriter, singer, artist, and writer. He has been influential in popular music and culture for more than five decades. Much of his most celebrated work dates from the 1960s, when his songs chronicled (记载) social unrest. Early songs such as "Blowin' in the Wind" and "The Times They Are A-Changin'" became anthems for the American civil rights and anti-war movements. As a musician, Dylan has sold more than 100 million records, making him one of the best-selling artists of all time. He has also received numerous awards including eleven Grammy Awards, a Golden Globe Award, and an Academy Award. The Pulitzer Prize jury in 2008 awarded him a special citation for "his profound impact on popular music and American culture, marked by lyrical compositions of extraordinary poetic power." In May 2012, Dylan received the Presidential Medal of Freedom from President Barack Obama. In 2016, he received the Nobel Prize in Literature "for having created new poetic expressions within the great American song tradition."

2. Homer — ancient Greek poet to whom are attributed *The Iliad* and *The Odyssey*, two epic poems which are the central works of Greek literature. Almost nothing is known of him, but it is thought that he was probably born on the island of Chios and was blind. 古希腊游吟诗人荷马(约公元前9世纪 — 前8世纪)，著有史诗《伊利亚特》和《奥德赛》。

3. blew those doors off the hinges — utterly surpassed the record made by the first album

   blow the doors off — to speed past another car; to be considerably better or more successful than

4. the Swedish Academy — Founded in 1786 by King Gustav III, it is one of the Royal Academies of Sweden. It is known for making the annual decision on who will be the laureate for the Nobel Prize in Literature, awarded in memory of the donor Alfred Nobel. 瑞典学院

5. album closer — the last song in the album
6. the Lowerlands — the central part of Scotland which is lower than the land surrounding it 英国的苏格兰低地
7. setting the stage for — preparing for sth or making sth possible
8. Sara Lownds — the first wife of Bob Dylan. Sara married Bob Dylan during a secret ceremony in November 1965, and the couple had four children together. Their marriage is often cited by music writers as the inspiration for many of Dylan's songs created throughout the 1960s and '70s, including "Sad Eyed Lady of the Lowlands," "Love Minus Zero/No Limit," and "Sara." The pair finally divorced in June 1977.
9. Bruce Springsteen — (1949 —   ) an American singer-songwriter. He is best known for his work with the E Street Band (东大街乐队). Nicknamed "The Boss," Springsteen is widely known for his brand of poetic lyrics. He has earned numerous awards for his work, including 20 Grammy Awards, two Golden Globes, and an Academy Award as well as being inducted into both the Songwriters Hall of Fame and the Rock and Roll Hall of Fame in 1999. In 2016, Springsteen was awarded the Presidential Medal of Freedom. 布鲁斯·斯普林斯汀
10. Rock and Roll Hall of Fame — The Rock and Roll Hall of Fame and Museum is located on the shore of Lake Erie in downtown Cleveland, Ohio, U. S. The Rock and Roll Hall of Fame Foundation was established on April 20, 1983, by Atlantic Records founder and chairman Ahmet Ertegun to recognize and archive the history of the best-known and most influential artists, producers, engineers, and other notable figures who have had some major influence on the development of rock and roll. "摇滚名人堂"是一个西方摇滚乐成就奖。这些入主的音乐人，首先他们被提名的时间必须距离首张专辑发行25年以上，此外要对推动摇滚乐发展做出了卓越的贡献，并且在摇滚史上具备不朽的地位。
11. Elvis — Elvis Aaron Presley (1935 — 1977) was an American singer and actor. Regarded as one of the most significant cultural icons of the 20th century, he is often referred to as the "King of Rock and Roll," or simply "the King." 埃尔维斯·普雷斯利是美国摇滚和流行歌手，绰号"猫王"，代表歌曲有《伤心旅店》《温柔的爱我》。因为太知名以致部分人只知道他叫"Elvis"。
12. Greenwich Village — a neighborhood on the west side of Lower

Manhattan, New York City. It has been known for being the home of many artists, especially those who are young and who do not want to live according to the accepted standards of society. It is also known as a fashionable place where many homosexuals live. 格林威治村,也称"西村",在 19 世纪后期和 20 世纪上半叶以波希米亚主义首都和垮掉的一代诞生地著称。格林威治村是在 1910 年前后在美国形成的,那里聚集着各种各样的艺术工作者、理想主义者甚至工联分子,他们大都行为乖张,和世俗格格不入,在战后成为了美国现代思想的重要发源地。

13. Woody Guthrie — (1912 — 1967) an American singer-songwriter and musician whose musical legacy includes hundreds of political, traditional, and children's songs, along with ballads and improvised works. 伍迪·格斯里,美国唱作人与民谣歌手,最为人熟知的歌曲是《这是你的土地》("This Land Is Your Land")。

14. Lead Belly — Huddie William Ledbetter(1889 — 1949),best known as Lead Belly(铅肚), was an American folk and blues musician notable for his strong vocals, virtuosity(精湛技艺)on the twelve-string guitar, and the folk standards he introduced. 莱德·贝特,美国黑人民谣歌手,以演唱布鲁斯歌曲闻名。

15. Robert Johnson —(1911 — 1938) an American blues singer-songwriter and musician. His landmark recordings in 1936 and 1937 display a combination of singing, guitar skills, and songwriting talent that has influenced later generations of musicians. 鲁伯特·约翰逊一生只录制了 29 首歌曲,但仍旧是布鲁斯历史上最值得纪念的人物之一。他的吉他演奏技巧对后来众多吉他手有着重要影响。

16. Ramblin' Jack Elliott — (1931 —) an American folk singer and performer. Elliott's nickname comes not from his traveling habits, but rather the countless stories he relates before answering the simplest of questions. He is the winner of Grammy Award and the National Medal of Arts. Elliott's guitar had a big impact on Bob Dylan. 杰克·艾略特,美国民谣歌手,伍迪·格斯里的学生。

17. Peter, Paul & Mary — an American folk group formed in New York City in 1961, during the American folk music revival phenomenon. The trio was composed of songwriter Peter Yarrow, Paul Stookey and Mary Travers. Peter, Paul & Mary 是 20 世纪 60 年代最受欢迎的三重唱组合,这个三人组合在他们的传奇生涯中共

获得了 5 个格莱美奖。
18. latch onto sth — to become very interested in sth
    latch — to fasten a door, gate, or window with a latch（门栓）
19. Cher —（1946 — ）born Cherilyn Sarkisian, an American singer and actress. Commonly referred to as the Goddess of Pop, she is described as embodying female autonomy in a male-dominated industry. She is known for her distinctive contralto（女低音）singing voice and for having worked in numerous areas of entertainment, as well as adopting a variety of styles and appearances during her five-decade-long career. 雪儿，美国女演员及歌手，其在音乐上的成绩主要是在 20 世纪六七十年代。
20. the Byrds — an American rock band, formed in Los Angeles, California in 1964. Although they only managed to attain the huge commercial success of contemporaries for a short period in late 1965, the Byrds are today considered by critics to be one of the most influential bands of the 1960s. 飞鸟乐队，由五人组成，将乡村摇滚成功带入流行音乐。
21. Beatlemania — a term that originated and was coined during the early 1960s to describe the intense fan frenzy directed towards the English rock band the Beatles（披头士/甲壳虫乐队）. The phenomenon began in 1963 and continued past the group's break-up in 1970, despite the band ceasing public performances in 1966. After the Beatles, the term mania was used to describe the popularity of later acts, as well as popularity of public figures and trends outside the music industry. 披头士狂
22. Fab Four — the nickname for the Beatles
23. John Lennon —1940 — 1980, an English singer and songwriter who co-founded the Beatles. He and fellow member Paul McCartney formed a celebrated songwriting partnership. Born and raised in Liverpool, Lennon became involved in the skiffle（早期爵士乐）craze as a teenager; his first band, the Quarrymen, evolved into the Beatles in 1960. When the group disbanded in 1970, Lennon embarked on a sporadic solo career that produced albums including John Lennon/Plastic Ono Band and Imagine. After his marriage to Yoko Ono(小野洋子) in 1969, he added "Ono" as one of his middle names. Lennon disengaged himself from the music business in 1975 to raise

his infant son Sean, but re-emerged with Ono in 1980 with the new album *Double Fantasy*. He was murdered three weeks after its release. He was posthumously（去世后）inducted into the Songwriters Hall of Fame in 1987, and into the Rock and Roll Hall of Fame twice, in 1988 as a member of the Beatles and in 1994 as a solo artist.

24. in the vein of — in a particular style of speaking or writing about sth

25. Lewis Carroll — Charles Lutwidge Dodgson (1832 — 1898), better known by his pen name Lewis Carroll, was an English writer, mathematician, logician, Anglican deacon, and photographer. His most famous writings are *Alice's Adventures in Wonderland*. He is noted for his facility at word play, logic and fantasy. 刘易斯·卡罗尔，英国儿童作家、数学家，其作品《爱丽丝漫游奇境记》闻名全球。

26. Carter Family — a traditional American folk music group that recorded between 1927 and 1956. Their music had a profound impact on bluegrass（兰草音乐）, country, Southern Gospel（福音音乐）, pop and rock musicians as well as on the U.S. folk revival of the 1960s. They were the first vocal group to become country music stars. 卡特家族是第一个成为乡村音乐明星的声乐组合，是第一个入选乡村音乐名人堂的乐队。

27. go to hell and back — to go through a very difficult situation

28. *Rolling Stone* magazine — an American biweekly magazine that focuses on pop culture. It was founded in San Francisco in 1967 by Jann Wenner, who is still the magazine's publisher, and the music critic Ralph J. Gleason. It was first known for its musical coverage and for political reporting by Hunter S. Thompson. In the 1990s, the magazine shifted focus to a younger readership interested in youth-oriented television shows, film actors, and pop music. In recent years, it has resumed its traditional mix of content.

29. the Jack of Hearts — a playing card. Jack is a card that has a man's picture on it and is worth less than a queen and more than a ten. Hearts is a heart shape printed in red on a playing card. 红桃杰克

30. "Tangled Up in Blue" opened the album … metaphorical road trip — 《愁肠难解》以另一个宏大的故事开启了这部专辑，它仿佛是文字世界的公路旅行，时而平实，时而隐晦，随心所欲。

31. offer a nod to the power of poetry — to acknowledge the power

of poetry

　　　　give / offer sb a nod — to give permission to do sth
32. rang true — sounded to be true
33. Dylan's foundational place in pop music … those tagged as "the new Dylan,"— 迪伦在流行音乐界奠基者地位开创了音乐产业时代,这对于那些被贴上"新迪伦"标签的音乐人来说,随着时间的推移,要么是荣誉勋章,要么是死亡之吻。

　　　　a. badge of honor — sth that shows that you have a particular quality 荣誉勋章

　　　　b. the kiss of death — sth that spoils or ruins a plan, activity etc
34. a club that included Springsteen, John Prine, Loudon Wainwright III and Steve Forbert — The "club" mentioned here is not a real organization but the sort of singers who had been considered as of the Dylan style. All these people are American pop or folk singers and song writers who had been active in the 1970s.

Questions

1. For what did Bob Dylan win the 2016 Nobel Prize for Literature?
2. Why did Sara Danius suggest that interviewers start with Bob Dylan's "Blonde on Blonde"?
3. What made Bob Dylan put more effort into writing his own songs?
4. How did the music of Bob Dylan influence The Beatles in the UK?
5. How did Bob Dylan describe his songwriting in his interview?
6. According to the author, how do Bob Dylan and his music influence the society?

语 言 解 说

时髦词 Mogul, Mentor 和 Guru

　　报刊语言追求新和奇,时髦词语自然常见诸报端,英文谓之 buzzword,兼指重要但又难懂的专门术语,有时带贬义。《纽约时报》专栏作家 William Safire 在政治词典里给的词义是:小部分行话或含糊其辞的时髦词("a snippet of jargon, or a vague vogue word")。1974 年出版的 Buzzwords 一书作者 Robert Mueller 将此词界定为小集团内切口或行话、俚语、头面人物爱用的词语等。时髦词语里有新词,但绝大部分是旧词新义,不常看报者望文生义,往往出错。

2016年特朗普当选美国总统,合众国际社(UPI)网站发表的一篇报道中说特朗普"... going from business mogul and tabloid sensation to a reality television star — and now the 45th president of the United States."(从商界大佬变成小报上轰动一时的人物,之后又变成电视真人秀明星,现在又成了美国第45任总统。)"mogul"原指曾经征服印度的蒙古统治者,现指"有权势的显要人物(an important, powerful, or influential person)"。再例如:

It was the ultimate battle of the tech kings: Steve Jobs vs. Microsoft mogul Bill Gates. (*The Daily Beat*, Aug. 16, 2013)

"mentor"的意思是"a wise and trusted counselor or teacher"或"an influential senior sponsor or supporter",即"有智慧且可以信赖的导师"或"有影响的资深赞助者或支持者"。例如:

By reaching out to a local high school or non-profit to become a mentor for a high achieving, low-income student. (*The Daily Beat*, Dec. 9, 2014)

"mentor"用于政治领域常指总统等高官身边的"受信赖的顾问",如候选人的竞选顾问,总统的政治、法律、经济顾问等。作时髦词的用法,已逐渐被"guru"代替。有时为避免重复,这两个词也可交替使用。

"guru"的原意指印度教或锡克教的宗教领袖或宗教教师,后转喻到政治领域,指"有权势或影响的政治保护人或支持者",后来词义进一步变化,用来指"任一领域所公认的领军人物(a recognized leader in a field)"或"受人信赖的顾问或导师(a trusted counselor and adviser; a mentor)"。例如:

a. The elder senator was her political guru.

b. the city's cultural gurus

本书第四版曾有一篇选自 *The Sunday Times* 的关于沃伦·巴菲特(Warren Buffett)的特写,文中写到他来到哥伦比亚商学院后,"he feel under the spell of Benjiamin Graham, an investment guru..."而巴菲特毕业后"worked for his mentor"。这里称他的导师(his mentor)为"投资大师"(investment guru)。

应该说明,报刊为赶时髦和创新,有时时髦词用得并不完全符合词义。(见《导读》二版"常见时髦词")

Lesson 24

课文导读

好莱坞硬汉、动作影星阿诺德·施瓦辛格在一系列电影中所扮演的"终结者"(Terminator)形象,早已经深入人心。那句经典台词"I'll be back!"总会让观众对他的下一个形象充满期待。2011年1月3日,63岁的施瓦辛格结束了长达7年的州长政治生涯。此后,人们不由自主地在猜想,施瓦辛格的下一个人生目标是什么?演电影,当教授,建智库……似乎,仅仅给他再加上学者、商人两个新头衔还远远不够。2012年9月,他又手持自传,全面回顾了他那令人难以置信的真实生活,再次引起世人的注目。

自传描写他从童年到成年的种种经历,既有传奇人生,也有失败和与常人不同之处。难怪书名叫"Total Recall"。青年读者应该学习他做事情的自信心和坚忍不拔、敢于闯荡、勇于创新的精神,但不要崇尚他那放荡不羁的性格和生活。

Pre-reading Questions

1. Have you ever seen any of the films starring Mr Arnold Schwarzenegger?
2. What is your impression of Mr Schwarzenegger?

Text

He's Back All Right, Now with a Memoir
"Total Recall," by Arnold Schwarzenegger with Peter Petre[1]
By Janet Maslin

1   When Arnold Schwarzenegger was governor of California, a reporter asked about the Cohiba[2] label on the cigar Mr. Schwarzenegger was smoking. "That's a Cuban cigar," the reporter said. "You're the governor. How can you flout the law?[3]"

2   The answer was as good a one-sentence encapsulation of the

bodybuilder/entrepreneur/movie star/politician/braggart's philosophy as all of "Total Recall," his 646-page memoir, provides. "I smoke it because it's a great cigar," he said.

3 This is only one of countless ways Mr. Schwarzenegger has prized self-interest throughout his long, glory-stalking and (as he loves pointing out) extremely lucrative career. "Total Recall" contains nonstop illustrations of how he aims high, tramples on competitors, breaks barriers and savors every victory, be it large or small. Those who mistake "Total Recall" for a salacious tell-all may not 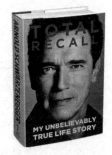 be that interested in how many Mr. Olympia[4] contests he won (seven) or who he beat for a Golden Globe[5] in 1977 (Truman Capote[6] and the kid who played Damien in "The Omen"[7]). Let's get the scandalous stuff out of the way, because Mr. Schwarzenegger certainly wants to.

4 About the son he conceived with the family housekeeper, Mildred Baena, in 1996, he says only this: that he had always promised himself not to fool around with the help[8]. That once, "all of a sudden," he and Ms. Baena "were alone in the guesthouse." And immediately after that: "When Mildred gave birth the following August…"

5 What "Total Recall" actually turns out to be is a puffy portrait of the author as master conniver. Nothing in his upward progress seems to have happened in an innocent way.

6 The book begins with the obligatory description of his Austrian childhood and says that he and his brother were forced to do situps to earn their breakfast. He also explains how the bodybuilder photos he pinned up in his room made his mother seek a doctor's advice. The doctor assured her that these were surrogate father figures, so there was nothing "wrong" with her red-blooded, heterosexual boy.

7 The book moves on to describe a hair-raising stint in an Austrian Army tank unit, where antics included driving one tank into water and trying to drag-race with another. This earned him an early release from service. He went on to win bodybuilding titles in Europe, move to America, garner the attention of the filmmakers who would feature him in "Pumping Iron"[9] and land the Hollywood acting role he coveted in "Stay Hungry."[10]

8   When told by an acting coach to summon a sense memory of victory, he says, "I had to explain that actually I was not especially exhilarated when I won, because to me, winning was a given."

9   And so it goes, through progress from pedestal to pedestal, until "Conan the Barbarian"[11] makes him an action star. Mr. Schwarzenegger and his co-writer, Peter Petre, had to brush up on[12] the details of his acting career by reading biographies and movie journals; his memory for slights, triumphs and salaries seems more reliable than his memory for work. But one way or another we learn how raw meat was sewn into his Conan costume for a scene in which he is attacked by wolves. (Sadly, the audio version of "Total Recall" is not fully read by him. You would have to rewatch the film to hear him say: "Hither came I, Conan, a thief, a reaver, a slayer, to tread jeweled thrones of the earth beneath my feet." But it might be worth it.[13])

10   In 1977 he met Maria Shriver[14], who would become his wife and enthusiastic helpmate until the matter of Ms. Baena and her son came to light. Although Mr. Schwarzenegger says that others wrongly imagined that to "marry a Kennedy"[15] was one of his goals, he too speaks of their union as an accomplishment. Among many noxious references to his wife are a buddy's pre-wedding quip ("Oh boy, wait until she hits menopause") and his way of commissioning an Andy Warhol[16] portrait of her. "You know how you always do the paintings of stars?" he says he asked Mr. Warhol. "Well, when Maria marries me, she will be a star!" He does not appear to be joking.

11   When Mr. Schwarzenegger was at the height of his movie career, he thought of quip making as one of his strong suits[17]. (In "Commando,"[18] about a man whose neck he has just broken: "Don't disturb my friend, he's dead tired.") But he was personable enough to cultivate his Democratic Kennedy in-laws and also grow close to the Republican circle of President George H. W. Bush[19]. He claims to have been included in a decision-making meeting about the initial gulf war invasion of Iraq[20].

12   His account of his own political career is, of course, careful to accentuate the positive. He ran for governor of California in 2003's recall election[21] even after Karl Rove[22] told him that Condoleezza Rice[23] was being groomed as a future candidate of choice. He emphasizes his

centrist credentials as a Republican favoring a social safety net, solar energy and stem cell[24] research but also facing down his state's three most powerful public-employee unions[25]. He claims to have done his best to grapple with the state's dire budget woes. But he atypically keeps the crowing minimal: "I do not deny that being governor was more complex and challenging than I had imagined."

13　　This book ends with a not-great list of "Arnold's Rules." They are basic ("Reps, reps, reps"), boorish ("No matter what you do in life, selling is part of it"), big on denial[26] ("When someone tells you no, you should hear yes") and only borderline helpful[27]. When he met Pope John Paul II[28] in 1983, they talked about workouts. The pope rose daily at 5 a.m. in order to stick to his regimen. If he could do it, this book says, you can do it, too. (From *The New York Times*, September 30, 2012)

New Words

accentuate /əkˈsentʃʊeɪt/ v. to stress or emphasize

antics /ˈæntɪks/ n. (pl.) behavior that seems strange, funny, silly or annoying 古怪可笑的举动

atypically /eɪˈtɪpɪkəl/ adv. not typically, different from what is usual 非典型地,非同寻常地

boorish /ˈbʊərɪʃ/ adj. rude 粗鲁的;粗鄙的

braggart /ˈbræɡət/ n. one given to loud, empty boasting; a bragger 自夸者,大言不惭的人

California /ˌkælɪˈfɔːnjə, -ˈfɔːniːə/ n. a state in the western US on the Pacific Ocean

centrist /ˈsentrɪst/ n. a person who supports the centre in politics; a moderate 中立派;温和派; adj. marked by or adhering to a moderate political view 温和派的

conceive /kənˈsiːv/ v. to become pregnant with (offspring) (使)怀孕

conniver /kəˈnaɪvə/ n. one who works (together with sb) secretly to achieve sth, esp. sth wrong 阴谋家,串谋者

covet /ˈkʌvət/ v. to desire eagerly (esp. sth belonging to another person) 贪求;觊觎

credentials /krəˈdenʃlz/ n. pl. anything that proves a person's abilities, qualities, or suitability (任何证明人的能力、资格等的)证明;资格

crow /krəʊ/ v. to express pride openly, esp. when taking pleasure from

someone else's misfortune 洋洋得意,幸灾乐祸
Cuban /ˈkjuːbən/ *adj.* 古巴的;古巴人
drag-race *v. AmE* to have a car race that is won by the car that can increase its speed fastest over a very short distance 参加短程汽车加速赛
encapsulation /ɪnˌkæpsjʊˈleɪʃən/ *n.* expression in a brief summary 概括
exhilarated /ɪɡˈzɪləˌreɪtɪd/ *adj.* feeling extremely excited and happy 异常兴奋的
feature /ˈfiːtʃə(r)/ *v.* to include as a leading performer 由……主演
flout /flaʊt/ *v.* to show contempt for; scorn 轻视,蔑视
garner /ˈɡɑːnə(r)/ *v.* to acquire, to get by one's own efforts 取得,获得
given /ˈɡɪvn/ *n.* sth taken for granted 理所当然的
glory-stalking *adj.* 风光无限的,伴随荣耀的
grapple /ˈɡræpl/ *v.* (with) to work hard to deal with sth difficult 努力设法解决
groom /ɡruːm/ *v.* to prepare (someone) as for a specific position or purpose 培养(某人),使做好准备
hair-raising /ˈheəˌreɪzɪŋ/ *adj.* causing excitement, terror, or thrills 令人兴奋、恐惧或刺激的
heterosexual /ˌhetərəˈsekʃʊəl/ *adj.* sexually oriented to persons of the opposite sex 异性恋的,异性性取向的
hither /ˈhɪðə(r)/ *adv.* here; to this place
in-laws /ˈɪnlɔːz/ *n.* one's relative by marriage, esp. the father and mother of one's husband and wife 姻亲,亲家
lucrative /ˈluːkrətɪv/ *adj.* producing wealth; profitable 可赚大钱的,利润丰厚的,能获利的
memoir /ˈmemwɑː(r)/ *n.* an account of the personal experiences of an author 自传,回忆录
menopause /ˈmenəpɔːz/ *n.* [医]停经,更年期,绝经期
noxious /ˈnɒkʃəs/ *adj.* harmful or poisonous 有害的,有毒的
obligatory /əˈblɪɡətrɪ/ *adj.* sth must be done because of a rule or a law 必须做的
pedestal /ˈpedɪstl/ *n.* a base on which a pillar or statue stands (柱子或雕像的)基座,基础
personable /ˈpɜːsənəbəl/ *adj.* pleasing in personality or appearance; attractive 风度翩翩的;招人喜爱的
puffy /ˈpʌfɪ/ *adj.* 爱炫耀的,自夸的
quip /kwɪp/ *n.* a clever amusing remark made without planning it in

advance（即兴的）俏皮话，嘲讽，妙语
reaver *n.* one who robs 抢劫者
recall /rɪˈkɔːl/ *n.* the procedure by which a public official may be removed from office by popular vote 罢免
regimen /ˈredʒɪmən/ *n.* a regulated system, as of diet, therapy, or exercise, intended to promote health or achieve another beneficial effect 养生法
reps /reps/ *n.* = repeats 重复
salacious /səˈleɪʃəs/ *adj. fml* expressing or causing strong sexual feelings, usu. in an unpleasant or shocking way 好色的，淫秽的
scandalous /ˈskændələs/ *adj.* containing material damaging to reputation; defamatory 诽谤的，丑闻的
situp /sɪtˈʌp/ *n.* an exercise in which you sit up from a lying position while keeping your legs straight on the floor 仰卧起坐
slayer /ˈsleɪə/ *n.* killer, murderer
slight /slaɪt/ *n.* the act or an instance of slighting, insult 冷落，轻蔑，怠慢
stalk /stɔːk/ *v.* to walk in a proud or angry way, with long steps
stint /stɪnt/ *n.* a limited or fixed period of work or effort 规定期限，任期
surrogate /ˈsʌrəgət/ *adj.* substitute 替代的，作为代用品的
trample /ˈtræmpl/ *v.* to deliberately ignore 践踏；无视（*cf.* tread)
tread /tred/ *v.* to press beneath the feet; trample 践踏，踩（*cf.* trample)
woe /wəʊ/ *n.* a cause of trouble; problem
workout /ˈwɜːkaʊt/ *n.* a period of physical exercise（尤指体育的）训练，赛前集训

Notes

1. "Total Recall," by Arnold Schwarzenegger with Peter Petre — the book is written by the two.

   a. Total Recall — "Total Recall: My Unbelievably True Life Story"（《全面回忆：我那难以置信的真实生活》），Arnold Schwarzenegger's memoir, a New York Times bestseller published in October 2012, by Arnold Schwarzenegger and his co-writer Peter Petre. The name of the memoir is borrowed from a 1990 American dystopian（反乌托邦的）science fiction action film directed by Paul Verhoeven and starring Arnold Schwarzenegger, which is referred to as the audio version of "Total Recall" in Para 9.

  b. Arnold Schwarzenegger — (1947—) an Austrian and American former professional bodybuilder, actor, businessman, investor, and Governor of California (2003—2011).

  c. Peter Petre — an American writer

2. Cohiba — a brand for two kinds of cigar, one produced in Cuba for Habanos S. A., the Cuban state-owned tobacco company, and the other produced in the Dominican Republic for US-based General Cigar Company. 高希霸
3. "That's a Cuban cigar… How can you flout the law?" — Following the Cuban Revolution of 1959, Cuba-US relations deteriorated substantially and have been marked by tension and confrontation since. The US does not have formal diplomatic relations with Cuba and has maintained an embargo (禁运) which makes it illegal for U. S. corporations to do business with Cuba.
4. Mr. Olympia — the title awarded to the winner of the professional men's bodybuilding contest held annually by the International Federation of BodyBuilding & Fitness (IFBB). The first Mr. Olympia was held on September 18, 1965 at the Brooklyn Academy of Music, New York City. There is also a female bodybuilder crowned, the Ms. Olympia, as are winners of Fitness Olympia and Figure Olympia for fitness and figure competitors. 奥林匹亚先生：奥林匹亚健美大赛男子专业健美最终冠军的荣誉称号。
5. Golden Globe — The Golden Globe Award is an honor bestowed by the 93 members of the Hollywood Foreign Press Association (HFPA) recognizing excellence in film and television, both domestic and foreign. The annual formal ceremony and dinner at which the awards are presented is a major part of the film industry's awards season. The 1st Golden Globe Awards were held in January 1944 at the 20th Century-Fox studios in Los Angeles. 美国影视金球奖
6. Truman Capote — (1924 — 1984) an American author, many of whose short stories, novels, plays, and nonfiction are recognized literary classics, including the novella *Breakfast at Tiffany's*《蒂凡尼早餐》(1958) and the true crime novel *In Cold Blood*《冷血》(1966), which he labeled a "nonfiction novel." At least 20 films and television dramas have been produced from Capote novels, stories

and screenplays. 杜鲁门·卡波特,美国著名作家、编剧,1977年因出演电影《怪宴》(*Murder by Death*)获金球奖最佳新人奖(Best Acting Debut in a Motion Picture-Male)提名。

7. "The Omen" — a 1976 American/British suspense horror film directed by Richard Donner. The film received numerous accolades (奖励)for its acting, writing, music and technical achievements.《凶兆》。1977年,该剧中饰演小男孩达米恩(Damien)的演员哈维·史蒂芬斯(Harvey Stephens)获金球奖最佳新人奖提名。

8. to fool around with the help — to involve in a sexual relationship with the house servant (口) 与佣人搞不正当的男女关系

        fool around — to spend time idly or aimlessly

9. "Pumping Iron" — a 1977 docudrama(文献纪录片) about the world of bodybuilding, focusing on the 1975 International Federation of Bodybuilding (IFBB) Mr. Universe and Mr. Olympia competitions. Inspired by a book of the same name by Charles Gaines and George Butler, the film nominally focuses on the competition between Arnold Schwarzenegger and one of his primary competitors for the title of Mr. Olympia, Lou Ferrigno. The film helped launch the acting careers of Arnold Schwarzenegger. 电影纪录片《健美之路》,另译为《铁金刚》或《泵铁》。

10. "Stay Hungry" — an American dramatic comedy film in 1976, for which Arnold Schwarzenegger was awarded a Golden Globe for New Male Star of the Year.《饥饿生存》,施瓦辛格凭借该片中的出色表现荣获1977年金球奖"最佳新人奖"。

11. "Conan the Barbarian" — a 1982 American sword and sorcery(魔法)/adventure film directed and co-written by John Milius. It is about the adventures of the eponymous character in a fictional prehistoric world of dark magic and savagery. The film stars Arnold Schwarzenegger and James Earl Jones, and tells the story of a young barbarian (Schwarzenegger) who seeks vengeance for the death of his parents at the hands of Thulsa Doom (Jones), the leader of a snake cult. This was Schwarzenegger's breakthrough film, which was a box-office hit (十分卖座的电影)。《野蛮人柯南》,又译《王者之剑》,乃施瓦辛格在银幕上名副其实的成名之作。

12. brush up on — to refresh one's memory of; review one's knowledge of

13. But it might be worth it — But it might be worth rewatching the film to hear what he says.
14. Maria Shriver —（1955— ）an American journalist and author of six best-selling books. She has received a Peabody Award, and was co-anchor（共同主持）for NBC's Emmy-winning coverage of the 1988 Summer Olympics. She was formerly First Lady of California as the wife of Arnold Schwarzenegger, from whom she is now separated. She is a member of the Kennedy family (her mother, Eunice Kennedy Shriver was a sister of John F. Kennedy, Robert F. Kennedy, and Edward Kennedy).
15. marry a Kennedy—On April 26, 1986, Schwarzenegger married Maria Shriver, who is the niece of the former President John F. Kennedy. On May 9, 2011, Shriver and Schwarzenegger separated after 25 years of marriage. 肯尼迪家族是美国的名门望族，无论是在金钱财富上，还是在政治权力上，都曾经达到登峰造极的程度。所以，与肯尼迪家族联姻，即意味着高攀。本句中的 a Kennedy 指肯尼迪家族的一员。
16. Andy Warhol —（1928 — 1987）an American artist who was a leading figure in the visual art movement known as pop art. 安迪·沃霍尔，美国艺术家、印刷家、电影摄影师，是视觉艺术运动波普艺术最有名的开创者之一。
17. he thought of quip making as one of his strong suits — he thought of telling witticism as one of what he is good at

    one's strong(est) suit — one's best quality or what one is good at
18. "Commando" — a 1985 American action-comedy film starred by Arnold Schwarzenegger. The film was a commercial success. It was also the 7th top-grossing film of 1985 worldwide. 《魔鬼司令》，又译《独闯龙潭》，是施瓦辛格第一次以现代战士角色出镜，并且奠定了他的这一现实人物形象，是他的代表作之一。commando 本义为"突击队员"。
19. George H. W. Bush —（1924— ）the 41st President（1989 — 1993）of the U. S. He is often referred to as "George H. W. Bush," "Bush 41," "Bush the Elder," and "George Bush, Sr." to distinguish him from his son, 43rd President George W. Bush. 乔治·赫伯特·沃克·布什，第 41 任总统。常被称为"老布什"，以区别于其长子、担任过 43 任总统的乔治·沃克·布什。

20. gulf war invasion of Iraq — a war waged in 1990 by a UN-authorized coalition force from 34 nations led by the US, against Iraq in response to Iraq's invasion and annexation（吞并）of Kuwait. 指的是第一次海湾战争或伊拉克战争。

21. recall election — a procedure by which voters can remove an elected official from office through a direct vote before his or her term has ended. The 2003 California gubernatorial recall election（州长罢免选举）was a special election permitted under California state law. Governor Gray Davis of California was recalled over the state budget. The voters replaced incumbent（在职的）Democratic Governor Gray Davis with Republican Arnold Schwarzenegger. 罢免选举

22. Karl Rove — (1950—) American Republican political consultant and policy advisor. He was Senior Advisor and Deputy Chief of Staff（白宫办公厅副主任）during the George W. Bush administration until Rove's resignation on August 31, 2007. 卡尔·罗夫是小布什的恩师，助选高手。

23. Condoleezza Rice — (1954—) an American political scientist and diplomat, Secretary of State (2005 — 2009), and the first female African-American secretary of state, as well as the second African American (after Colin Powell), and the second woman (after Madeleine Albright). Rice was President Bush's National Security Advisor during his first term, making her the first woman to serve in that position. 康多莉扎·赖斯，曾任国务卿，是小布什的亲信。

24. stem cell — Stem cells are biological cells found in all multicellular organisms（多细胞生物），that can divide through mitosis（细胞有丝分裂）and differentiate into diverse specialized cell types and can self-renew to produce more stem cells. Adult stem cell treatments have been successfully used for many years to treat leukemia（白血病）and related bone/blood cancers through bone marrow transplants. 干细胞

25. facing down his state's three most powerful public-employee unions — defeating and showing confidence before the three most powerful public-employee unions in California

  face down — to appear strong and confident when someone is

threatening or criticizing you 压倒,降服

three most powerful public-employee unions — probably refers to the three National trade union organizations: American Federation of Labor and Congress of Industrial Organizations (AFL-CIO 美国劳工联合会－产业工会联合会), Change to Win Federation (CtW 改变以获胜联盟), Industrial Workers of the World (IWW,世界产业工人联盟)

26. be big on sth — to like sth very much; be enthusiastic about sth
27. and only borderline helpful — and almost helpful but not enough

borderline — *adj.* almost reaching a particular level 勉强可以的,刚刚够格的
30. Pope John Paul II — (1920 — 2005) born in Poland, reigned as Pope of the Catholic Church from 1978 until his death in 2005. He was the second-longest serving Pope in history and the first non-Italian since 1523. 约翰·保罗二世,罗马天主教第 264 任教皇,梵蒂冈国国家元首。

Questions

1. What is "Total Recall"?
2. What does "Total Recall" contain?
3. What happened to Mr Schwarzenegger with his housekeeper Mildred Baena?
4. What information can you get from the book about Arnold Schwarzenegger's childhood?
5. Can you name some films starring Arnold Schwarzenegger?
6. How did Mr Schwarzenegger start his political career?
7. What is Peter Petre's attitude towards Schwarzenegger and his book?

学 习 方 法

名师指点词语记忆法

对未入门者而言,报刊里陌生词语随处可见,是一大拦路虎。如何记忆词汇? 英语界前辈李赋宁先生在《英语学习经验谈》一书里作了指导:"语法知识固然重要,但是词汇知识也同样重要,因为思想和概念首

先要通过词来表达。……首先要弄清楚词义,同学们查英汉字典时,往往发现一个词有好几个解释,有时多到十几个解释。如何选择一条最恰当的解释,就是我们在阅读中首先要解决的问题。我们一定要开动脑筋,紧密地结合上下文的意思来寻找一条最合适的解释,这样才能真正培养我们的阅读能力,这样才能把生词透彻理解,牢固地记住。词汇表对初学外语的人是有帮助的,但是我们不应依赖词汇表,我们应该尽早地多利用字典,尽早地结合上下文来寻找词的恰当的意思和正确的解释,也就是说我们应该尽早地培养我们的独立阅读能力。

"同学们还应该学会逐渐使用以英语解释词义的英语字典。为什么?因为阅读科学文献一定要概念明确。英汉字典往往只给一个汉语译名,这个汉语译名本身的含义可能并不完全相当于原来那个英语单词的词义。因此有时查了英汉字典,仍然感到理解得模模糊糊。至于以英语解释词义的英语字典,所用的方法是给每个词都下一个明确的定义,所以查了这种字典往往理解得更加清楚。

"在查字典时,除了要寻找合适的解释外,还应该注意一下所查的那个词的词源意义。例如,向日葵在英语中俗名是 sunflower(太阳花),但学名是 heliotrope,为希腊文 helios(太阳)+希腊文 tropos(转动)所组成。经常注意词源意义就会增加、扩大我们对于构词法的知识,培养我们分析词义的能力。

"除了词源意义外,在查字典时,我们还应该注意词的搭配,尤其要注意动词和名词的搭配、形容词和名词的搭配、动词和副词的搭配等。例如, meet requirements(满足需要), close attention(密切的注意), talk freely(信口开河)。在阅读时还应该把表示相同的或类似的概念的词和短语都搜集在一起,加以比较,又把表示相反的概念的词和短语搜集在一起,加以对照。这样来理解内容,这样来记生词,效果一定更好。例如,以前学的'The Story of Fire'课文中第一句: Fire could be harnessed and made to work for man. 在这里,动词 harnessed 和短语 made to work 就是表示相同或类似概念的同义词或同义现象,应该搜集在一起,加以比较。同一课也有不少表示相反概念的词和短语:combustible 和 incombustible, materials which burn 和 materials which will not burn 等都应联系起来记。用这样的方法来记单词,才记得多,记得牢。我不赞成同学们把单词抄在生字本或卡片上,孤立地、机械地死背硬记,而是应该把几个词联系起来记。当然在开始的阶段,记单词必须花很大的劳力。每课书上词汇表中有用的词都应有意识地记住。要做到眼到、口到、手到、心到。那就是说把每一个要记住的单词看上几遍,念上几遍,写上几遍,记上几遍。这样机械的死功夫在初学阶段十分必要,到了一年以后就用不着费这样大的气力来死记了。就应该用我上面说的那些办法来更有效地扩大词汇，培养独立阅读的能力。但是即使达到比较熟练的阶段也不能放弃某些较费力的活动，以便达到进一步的准确和熟练程度。例如每日清晨朗读半小时，每日抄写半页课文或资料，每日记住一两个写得好的句子。基本功要经常地练，不断地练，才能保证外语学得又快又好。"

Lesson 25

课文导读

　　电视真人秀节目已经风靡世界,是最具竞争优势的收视率争夺者。因为节目和观众互动广泛,极大地满足了观众多方面的心理需求,在电视产业链运营方面具有独特的优势,其社会影响力前所未有。节目的参与者们就像昔日的电影明星一样,为人所崇拜、迷恋和追捧。真人秀所产生的偶像及其迷恋者甚至已经形成了一个个社会交际网。电视真人秀节目的创新引领着电视业的新潮流,改变了电视行业的运作模式。

　　英国是传统媒体业的鼻祖,其纸介媒体逐步形成了对新闻产业模式的影响并延续至今。今天,它在影视产业新经济中再次抢得先机,世界上许多广受欢迎的电视真人秀节目大多首创于英国。自从1998年英国提出"创意产业"的概念以来,该产业已经逐渐超过其老牌的金融业,跃升为一个有强劲上升趋势的新型经济增长点。在100多个国家的电视台以各种形式演绎创自英国的各类"达人秀"之际,英国正在有步骤、有计划地展开在电视娱乐业称雄世界的宏图。虽然它遇到各国同行的竞争,但是有英国政府支持,而且强调创新,优势还是明显的。

Pre-reading Questions

1. What is the reality TV?
2. What kind of reality TV programs do you like best?

Text

The Reality-television Business: Entertainers to the World
Many of the world's most popular television shows were invented in Britain. But competition is growing.

1　　NOT many Britons watch "Who Wants to be a Millionaire?"[1] these days. The quiz show, which routinely drew more than 15m viewers in the late 1990s, now attracts fewer than 5m. While "Millionaire" is

fading in the country that invented it, though, it is thriving elsewhere. This week Sushil Kumar[2] won the top prize on the Indian version of the programme. Côte d'Ivoire[3] is to make a series. Afghanistan is getting a second one. In all, 84 different versions of the show have been made, shown in 117 countries.

2   Hollywood may create the world's best TV dramas, but Britain dominates the global trade in unscripted programmes — quiz shows, singing competitions and other forms of reality television. "Britain's Got Talent"[4], a format created in 2006, has mutated into 44 national versions, including "China's Got Talent" and "Das Supertalent"[5]. There are 22 different versions of "Wife Swap"[6] and 32 of "Masterchef"[7]. In the first half of this year, Britain supplied 43% of global entertainment formats — more than any other country (see chart).

3   London crawls with programme scouts.[8] If a show is a hit in Britain — or even if it performs unusually well in its time slot — phones start ringing in production companies' offices. Foreign broadcasters, hungry for proven fare, may hire the producers of a British show to make a version for them. Or they may buy a "bible" that tells them how to clone it for themselves.

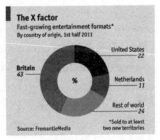

The X factor
Fast-growing entertainment formats*
By country of origin, 1st half 2011

Britain 43
United States 22
Netherlands 11
Rest of world 24

*Sold to at least two new territories
Source: FremantleMedia

"The risk of putting prime-time entertainment on your schedule has been outsourced to the UK,"[9] says Tony Cohen, chief executive of FremantleMedia[10], which makes "Got Talent," "Idol" and "X Factor."[11]

4   Like financial services, television production took off in London as a result of government action. In the early 1990s broadcasters were told to commission at least one-quarter of their programmes from independent producers. In 2004 trade regulations ensured that most rights to television shows are retained by those who make them, not those who broadcast them. Production companies began aggressively

hawking their wares overseas.

5   They are becoming more aggressive, in part because British broadcasters are becoming stingier. PACT[12], a producers' group, and Oliver & Ohlbaum[13], a consultancy, estimate that domestic broadcasters spent £1.51 billion ($2.4 billion) on shows from independent outfits in 2008, but only £1.36 billion in 2010. International revenues have soared from £342m to £590m in the same period. Claire Hungate, chief executive of Shed Media[14], says that 70%—80% of that company's profits now come from intellectual property — that is, selling formats and tapes of shows that have already been broadcast, mostly to other countries.

6   Alex Mahon, president of Shine Group[15], points to another reason for British creativity. Many domestic television executives do not prize commercial success. The BBC is funded almost entirely by a licence fee on television-owning households. Channel 4 is funded by advertising but is publicly owned. At such outfits, success is measured largely in terms of creativity and innovation — putting on the show that everyone talks about. In practice, that means they favour short series. British television churns out[16] a lot of ideas.

7   Yet the country's status as the world's pre-eminent inventor of unscripted entertainment is not assured. Other countries have learned how to create reality television formats and are selling them hard. In early October programme buyers at MIPCOM[17], a huge television convention held in France, crowded into a theatre to watch clips of dozens of reality programmes. A Norwegian show followed urban single women as they toured rural villages in search of love. From India came "Crunch," a show in which the walls of a house gradually closed in on contestants.[18]

8   Ever-shrinking commissioning budgets at home are a problem, too. The BBC, which provides a showcase for independent productions as well as creating many of its own, will trim its overall budget by 16% in real terms[19] over the next few years. The rather tacky BBC3[20] will be pruned hard — not a great loss to national culture, maybe, but a problem for producers, since many shows are launched on the channel. Perhaps most dangerously for the independents, ITV[21], Britain's biggest free-to-air commercial broadcaster, aims to produce more of its own programming.

9   Meanwhile commissioners' tastes are changing. Programmes like "Wife Swap," which involve putting people in contrived situations (and are fairly easy to clone), are falling from favour. The vogue is for gritty, fly-on-the-wall documentaries like "One Born Every Minute" and "24 Hours in A&E."[22] There is a countervailing trend towards what are known as "soft-scripted" shows, which mix acting with real behaviour.[23] "Made in Chelsea" and "The Only Way is Essex" blaze that peculiar trail.[24]

10   These trends do not greatly threaten the largest production companies. Although they are based in London, their operations are increasingly global. Several have been acquired by media conglomerates like Sony[25] and Time Warner[26], making them even more so. Producers with operations in many countries have more opportunities to test new shows and refine old ones. FremantleMedia's new talent show, "Hidden Stars"[27], was created by the firm's Danish production arm. Britain is still the most-watched market — the crucible of reality formats. But preliminary tests may take place elsewhere.

11   There is, in any case, a way round the problem of British commissioners leaning against conventional reality shows.[28] Producers are turning documentaries and soft-scripted shows into formats, and exporting them. Shine Group's "One Born Every Minute," which began in 2010 as a documentary about a labour ward in Southampton, has already been sold as a format to America, France, Spain and Sweden. In such cases the producers are selling sophisticated technical and editing skills rather than a brand and a formula. With soft-scripted shows, the trick is in casting.

12   The companies that produce and export television formats are scattered around London, in odd places like King's Cross[29] and Primrose Hill[30]. They are less rich than financial-services firms and less appealing to politicians than technology companies. But they have a huge influence on how the world entertains itself. And, in a slow-moving economy, Britain will take all the national champions it can get. (From *The Economist*, November 5, 2011)

New Words

acquire /əˈkwaɪə(r)/ v. to get sth by buying it

casting /ˈkɑːstɪŋ/ n. the selection of actors or performers for the parts of a presentation 角色分配

clip /klɪp/ n. a short piece of film, TV, or reality TV program 剪辑

commission /kəˈmɪʃn/ v. to ask sb to write an official report, produce a work of art for 委托撰写或制作 (cf. commissioner)

conglomerate /kənˈɡlɒmərət/ n. a large firm consisting of several different companies 联合大公司;企业集团

contestant /kənˈtestənt/ n. a person who takes part in a competition or a quiz

contrived /kənˈtraɪvd/ adj. false and deliberate, rather than natural 做作的,不自然的

countervailing /ˈkaʊntəveɪlɪŋ/ adj. having equal power, force or effect

crucible /ˈkruːsɪbl/ n. a melting pot 熔炉

crunch /krʌntʃ/ n. a critical situation that arises because of a shortage of time or money or resources 危急关头

fare /feə(r)/ n. the intellectual food that are regularly consumed, esp. in entertainment 精神食粮

free-to-air /friː tuː eə(r)/ adj. (电视节目和频道)免费接收的

fly-on-the-wall /flaɪ ɒn ðə wɔːl/ adj. (纪录片)纪实性的,写实的

gritty /ˈɡrɪti/ adj. describing a tough or unpleasant situation in a very realistic way 逼真的,真实的,活生生的

hawk /hɔːk/ v. to sell or offer for sale from place to place 叫卖,兜售

hit /hɪt/ n. sth such as a CD, film, or play that is very popular and successful

labour /ˈleɪbə(r)/ n. the process of giving birth to a baby

mutate /mjuːˈteɪt/ v. to develop into different styles as the result of a change 衍生

Norwegian /nɔːˈwiːdʒən/ adj. belonging or relating to Norway, or to its people, language, or culture 挪威的,挪威人(的)

outsource /ˈaʊtsɔːs/ v. to obtain goods or services from an outside supplier 将……外包;外购

pre-eminent /priˈemɪnənt, prɪˈemənənt/ adj. more important, powerful or capable than other people or things 卓越的,杰出的,超凡的

prune /pruːn/ v. to cut out unwanted or unnecessary things 精简或除去不需要的部分

retain /rɪˈteɪn/ v. to continue to have 保持,持有

scout /skaʊt/ *n.* a person employed to seek new players 星探
stingy /ˈstɪndʒɪ/ *adj.* not generous, being unwilling to spend money 吝啬的，小气的
tacky /ˈtækɪ/ *adj.* tastelessly showy 低劣的；乏味的
trim /trɪm/ *v.* to cut down on; make a reduction in 削减
unscripted /ʌnˈskrɪptɪd/ *adj.* not finished with or using a script 无脚本的 *cf.* **script** *n.* & *v.*
vogue /vəʊɡ/ *n.* the popular taste at a given time 流行，时髦

Notes

1. Who Wants to be a Millionaire? — the most internationally popular television franchise of British origin, created in 1998, having aired in more than 100 countries worldwide. In its format, large cash prizes are offered for correctly answering a series of multiple-choice questions of increasing difficulty. The maximum cash prize (in the original British version) is one million pounds. Most international versions offer a top prize of one million units of the local currency; the actual value of the prize obviously varies widely, depending on the value of the currency. 《谁想成为百万富翁？》
2. Sushil Kumar — an Indian name 苏希尔·库马尔
3. Côte d'Ivoire — or Ivory Coast, officially the Republic of Côte d'Ivoire, a country in West Africa. 科特迪瓦，旧称"象牙海岸"。
4. Britain's Got Talent — 英国达人秀
5. Das Supertalent —（德语）德国达人秀
6. Wife Swap — a British reality television programme, first broadcast in 2003, the final episode was broadcast in December 2009. In the programme, two families, usually from different social classes and lifestyles, swap wives/mothers — and sometimes husbands — for two weeks. In fact, the programme will usually deliberately swap wives with dramatically different lifestyles, such as a messy (邋遢的) wife swapping with a fastidiously (挑剔地) neat one. Despite using a phrase from the swinging (性滥交，交换配偶的) lifestyle, couples participating in the show do not share a bed with the "swapped" spouse while "swapping" homes. 《换妻生活》
7. Masterchef — a television cooking game 《谁是厨神》
8. London crawls with programme scouts. — There are many people

who are employed by reality television programme producers in London to search for new players.

crawl with — to be full of

9. The risk of putting prime-time ... outsourced to the UK. — Foreign broadcasters have outsourced the risk of failure in prime-time entertainment to the UK. 国外的电视台把黄金时段娱乐节目的失败风险转包给了英国。(指上文中说的一档新节目首先在英国的电视节目里上演，成功后其他国家的电视台才开始仿制。)

10. FremantleMedia — FremantleMedia, Ltd. is an international television content and production subsidiary（子公司）of Bertelsmann's RTL Group（贝塔斯曼旗下的 RTL 集团），Europe's largest TV, radio, and production company. Its world headquarters are located in London.

11. "Got Talent," "Idol" and "X Factor" —《达人秀》《偶像》和《X 音素》
    "X Factor" — a television music competition originated in the U.K., where it was devised（设计）as a replacement for *Pop Idol*. It is now held in various countries. The contestants are aspiring（有志向的）pop singers drawn from public competitive auditions（试听）. The "X Factor" of the title refers to the undefinable（不确定的）"something" that makes for star quality. The prize is usually a recording contract, in addition to the publicity（报道；宣传；推广）that appearance in the later stages of the show itself generates, not only for the winner but also for other highly ranked contestants.

12. PACT — *abbr.* Producers Alliance for Cinema and Television 英国影视制作公司联盟

13. Oliver & Ohlbaum — 奥利弗和欧哈巴姆联合咨询公司

14. Shed Media — Shed Media Group, a British creator and distributor of television content.

15. Shine Group — a company that includes production companies of scripted and non-scripted television

16. churn out — to produce large quantities of sth very quickly

17. MIPCOM — a TV and entertainment market which is held in the town of Cannes（戛纳）once every year, normally in October 世界视听内容交易会

18. From India came "Crunch" ... on contestants. — 印度制作的《危机关头》，真人秀表演者在房子里，里面的墙壁却在移动着，越来越紧地逐渐挤向表演者。

19. in real terms — accurate, true, by taking account of related price changes 扣除物价因素，按实值计算
20. BBC3 — BBC 3 频道
21. ITV — Independent Television（英国）独立电视集团
22. The vogue is for gritty, fly-on-the-wall documentaries like "One Born Every Minute" and "24 Hours in A&E." — 流行的是直面现实、拍摄手法逼真的纪实影片，比如《忙碌的产房》和《急诊室的 24 小时》。

    a. fly-on-the-wall documentaries — documentaries made by filming people as they do the things they normally do, rather than by interviewing them or asking them to talk directly to the camera

    b. "One Born Every Minute" — a British observational documentary series which shows the day to day activity of a labour ward（产房）.

    c. "24 Hours in A&E" — a British medical documentary set in King's College Hospital. 91 cameras filmed for 28 days, 24 hours a day in A&E (Accident and Emergency Room). it offers unprecedented access to one of Britain's busiest A&E departments.
23. There is a countervailing trend … real behaviour. — 现在，所谓的"软脚本"（即将表演形式和真实行为糅为一体）节目大有与此势均力敌的趋势。
24. "Made in Chelsea" and "The Only Way is Essex" blaze that peculiar trail. —《切尔西制造》和《埃塞克斯是唯一的生活方式》即此类真人秀的开路先锋。

    Made in Chelsea — a British BAFTA（英国电影和电视艺术学院）award-winning reality television show, a soap set in the wealthy Chelsea district of London

    The Only Way is Essex — a British BAFTA award-winning reality television show based in Essex, England

    blaze a trail — to be the first to do or to discover sth that others follow 作开路先锋；领先
25. Sony — Sony Corporation 索尼公司并购了好莱坞原八大电影公司中的三家（哥伦比亚、米高梅和联艺），因此也成为全世界最大的电影公司。
26. Time Warner —（美国）时代华纳公司
27. "Hidden Stars" — one of the new entertainment formats brought to

MIPCOM 2011 by FremantleMedia. It is a fresh format that sees friends and family submit performances from singers who would never normally enter a talent show. Celebrity mentors（名人导师） assess the entries（参赛者）before making secret surprise visits to the unsuspecting singers, who are then invited to audition live on the spot. Each mentor, a star of today, chooses the contestant they think is a star of tomorrow.《挖掘新星》

28. There is … against conventional reality shows. — Some commissioners have their own ideas and do not agree with conventional reality shows, but British producers know how to tackle with the problem. 一些喜欢求新的制作人反对老生常谈的真人秀节目,而英国的节目制作人自有办法对付。

29. King's Cross — an area of central London. The area formerly had a reputation for being a red light district. 国王十字区

30. Primrose Hill — a hill of 256 feet located in London, and also the name given to the surrounding district. The hill has a clear view of central London. 樱草山

Questions

1. Why does Tony Cohen say "The risk of putting prime-time entertainment on your schedule has been outsourced to the UK"?
2. What are the effects when broadcasters were told to commission at least one-quarter of their programmes from independent producers?
3. What are the reasons for creativity in British programmes?
4. What happened at MIPCOM held in France in early October, 2011?
5. What kind of challenges does Britain face?

学习方法

词根的重要性

要多快好省学习生词,学了一定数量的词汇后,就应该学点构词法。这里有个公式：Modern English＝Old English＋Middle French,英语与低地德语同属西日耳曼语支,基本词汇相似之处甚多。初学英语时大都比较熟悉,讲法语的诺曼人征服英国并统治约百年（Norman Conquest）,

英语报刊里大约 70% 以上词汇都是希腊、拉丁词根加词缀构成的,一度通过法语大量引进,学了构词法可以成百上千记忆和猜词,一本万利。这类构词专著出了一大批,不妨翻翻复旦大学陆国强先生在《现代英语表达与理解》一书中对词根以图表形式作的如下有益的研究:

"英语中不少词是由词根加词缀构成的。词根是词中表示主要意义的成分,而词缀则是表示附加意义或语法意义的成分。如 unacceptable 这一词,其词根是 accept,而 un-和-able 是词缀。英语中词根有不同形式,有的是完整的词,在句中可作为一个独立的单位使用,如 working 中的 work。有的并不是完整的词,而与其他构词成分结合起来构成一个词,如 audience 中 audi 是词根,表示'听'的意思,-ence是名词性词缀。通过语源分析,掌握词根的意义对整个词的理解具有决定性作用。"见其所列图表:

词根	意义	实例	
agr	farm	agronomy	(农艺学)
aqua	water	aquarium	(水族馆)
anthrop	man	anthropology	(人类学)
astron	star	astronomy	(天文学)
bio	life	biology	(生物学)
capit	head	capitation	(人头税)
celer	speed	celerity	(迅速)
chrome	color	chromosome	(染色体)
chron	time	chronology	(年代学)
crat	rule	autocrat	(专制君主)
dent	tooth	dentist	(牙科医生)
dict	say	diction	(措词)
eu	well, happy	eugenics	(优生学)
frac	break	fracture	(骨折)
gamos	marriage	monogamous	(一夫一妻制的)
ge	earth	geology	(地质学)
greg	group	gregarious	(好群居的)
gress	move forward	progress	(进展)
gyn	women	gynecologist	(妇科医生)
homo	same	homogeneous	(同类的)
hydr	water	dehydrate	(脱水)
ject	throw	eject	(逐出)
junct	join	conjunction	(连接)

loq	speak	loquacious	(饶舌的)
mar	sea	maritime	(海上的)
med	middle	intermediary	(中间的)
meter	measure	thermometer	(温度表)
mit	send	remit	(汇寄)
mono	one	monotony	(单调)
pater	father	paternal	(父方的)
pathos	feeling	pathology	(病理学)
ped	foot	pedal	(踏板)
phobia	fear	hydrophobia	(恐水病)
phone	sound	telephone	(电话)
port	carry	portable	(手提的)
pseudo	false	pseudonym	(假名)
psych	mind	psychic	(心理的)
rect	rule	direct	(指导)
scope	see	telescope	(望远镜)
scrib	write	inscribe	(刻写)
sec	cut	dissect	(解剖)
sequ	follow	sequence	(连续)
spect	look	inspect	(检查)
spir	breathe	respiration	(呼吸)
tact	touch	tactile	(触觉的)
term	end	terminal	(终点)
vid	see	video	(电视的)
voc	call	convocation	(召开)

　　理解词根的含义固然十分重要,但对词缀的意义也不能忽视,特别是一些衍生出新义的词缀必须注意。如 anticulture 反正统或传统文化的/ antihero 反对以传统手法塑造主角的。